That's How the Light Gets In

That's How the Light Gets In

A Credo of Friendship

by

Donald B. Harris

Williamsburg, Virginia
1994

Credo Institute, P.O. Box 2105, Williamsburg, VA 23187-2105.

© 1994 by Donald B Harris. All Rights Reserved.

Printed in the United States of America.

Cover art by Ann Murphy

Design by Mary Ann F. Williamson

Typesetting by ES Corp, Williamsburg, VA

ISBN 0-9643691-0-9

Library of Congress Catalog Card Number: 94-092445

*For Ruth
and our beloved family.*

That's how the light shines in.

Thank You

How can I begin to list the names of the scores of my brothers and sisters who have given me their love and helped me to grow in the Spirit? For together we form the Credo family—each unique, all of equal value. However, the writing of *That's How the Light Gets In* has been a four-year labor of love, and the encouragement I received from the following people, who took the time to read various drafts, gave me light along the way.

Will Armstrong; Peter Chase; Martha Hamilton-Phillips; Jonathan, Ruth, Tim, and Amy Harris; David Holmes; Jim Johnson; Gary Moon; Alan Jones; Irving Stubbs; Anne Turner; Peter Valerio; and Ricks and Marion Wilson. I will always remember David's unwavering commitment to thoughtful editing.

Anthem

The birds they sang at the break of day.
Start again, I heard them say.
Don't dwell on what has passed away,
Or what is yet to be ...

The wars they will be fought again.
The holy dove will be caught again
bought and sold and bought again
the dove is never free ...

You can add up the parts,
but you won't have the sum.
You can strike up the march,
there is no drum.
Every heart to love will come
But like a refugee.

Ring the bells that still can ring.
Forget your perfect offering.
There is a crack in everything.
That's how the light gets in.

—Leonard Cohen

Table of Contents

Thank You vii
Table of Contents xi
Prologue xvii
    Love And Fear xviii
    An Invitation xxiv

Part I

Hospitality 1

Chapter 1
Icons Of Hospitality 3
    Icon I: The Accepting Family 8
    Icon II: The Accidental Community 17
    Icon III: A Generous Spirit 22
    Icon IV: Inclusive Love 26

Part II

My Credo Pilgrimage 29

Chapter 2
The Keel Is Laid, 1967-1970 31

San Francisco: The Hunger For Spirituality 31
Heroes In The Seaweed 40
The Age Of Aquarius 44
De Colores 46
Thorns Among The Flowers 47
Let Go, Let God 49

Chapter 3
The Launching Of Credo, 1971-1974 55

Release Your Song 59
Getting Underway 61
The Christening 63
Setting The Course 66
Charlie Bamforth: "My Credo Experience" 68
Brad Hall: "My Wilderness Journey" 72
Running On Empty 77
A Wolf In Sheep's Clothing? 81
The Healing Community 82
Credo House: A Safe Harbor 85
Certainly An Ember 87

Chapter 4
Sea Trials, 1974-1979 91

The Dark Night Of The Soul 91
Love Comes Like A Refugee 103
Esperanza House 104
Bulldozing Hope 107

Chapter 5
Pilgrim Credo: The Voyage, 1976-1982 113

A Port In The Storm 122
Life Together 125
The Demonic 128
Confronting Fear In A Friendly Port 132

Chapter 6
Adrift On An Indifferent Sea, 1982-1989 141

Inclusion And Integrity 142
The Spirituality Of Friendship 147
Gratitude 151

Chapter 7
The Hungry Sheep, 1989-1994 153

Governors Island, New York City 155
The Hungry Sheep 158
The Shepherd 160
The Drowning Can See 170

Chapter 8
Home Port: Credo Institute 181

The Campus 182
The Marginal And Homeless 184
Wage Earners 185
Counselors 187
In-Patient Substance Abuse Wards 189

Part III

The Credo Weekend 191

Chapter 9
The Setting: The World Within Our Selves 193

Resetting The Bones 193
Trying To Be Free 196
Estrangement 197
Excluding Love 199
Sterile Consolation 202
A Third In Our Midst 204
Finding A Way In, Not Out 210
The Power Of Love 211

Chapter 10
Friendship, The Medicine Of Life 213

Chapter 11
The Structure 223
The Pain of the Human Condition 224
Attempts At Resolution: Personal Assessment 226
Reconciliation:
    Resolution Through Loving Support 227

Chapter 12
The Credo Weekend 229
Day One: Friday Night 230
Day Two: Saturday 238
Day Three: Sunday 249
A New Way Of Life 259

Chapter 13
Companion And Leader 261
Building Community 267
Right or Wrong 268
Subjective Leadership 269
The Passion 274

Chapter 14
The Partnership Of Credo 277
Twelve Step Fellowships 278
Group Psychotherapy 282
Religious Retreats 283

Part IV

The Need For Credo:
Love Is The Only Engine Of Survival 287

Chapter 15
A Famine Of The Spirit 289

Chapter 16
The Cradle Of The Best And The Worst 297

Alice In Wonderland 299
Control From Without... 302
Our Addictive Society 305

Chapter 17
The Breaking Of The Ancient Western Code.......... 309

Our View Of Nature 310
Our Use Of Technology 313
Our Source of Hope 316
Our Convulsive Society 317
A Machine Running Without Oil 318
The Fearful Fall 321
There's A Crack In Everything 325

Works Cited 327

Publications 327
Songs 329

Prologue

That's How the Light Gets In is a book about love, in the most profound sense of the word. This is a book which talks of the experience of love on virtually every page, for nothing is more important in our lives than love. I can think of no prominent spiritual leader of any culture, in the East or the West, who does not grant that love is the essence of our being. We need love under all conditions. It is the oxygen we breath, the marrow in our bones, the water that moistens our parched lips. We cannot receive or give too much love. But love does not stand alone.

> *A man is to be compared to a beast*
> *if he has no one to rejoice with him, no one to unburden his mind.*
> *Scarcely any happiness can exist without friendship.*
> —Aelred of Rievaulx

I hope that this book rekindles in you a desire for deep friendship: an ability to lessen defenses and accept the compassion extended from another person who enters into your life and accepts you, just as you are.

Love And Fear

Serenity is when you can accept others loving you.

We are often trapped within ourselves because of our fear of others. We fear that we will be found unacceptable if we are truly known. We fear that others will take advantage of us if we allow them to enter our hearts. *Where fear has replaced love, we find death.* We see it among former friends and families who now hunt each other down in the Balkans or Rwanda. We see it among husbands and wives who destroy their children on a domestic battleground.

This struggle between love and fear is part of the fabric of all of our lives. *That's How the Light Gets In* is the story of that struggle not only in my own life, but also in the lives of those whom I have touched, and in the society within which we encounter each other. In my experience, this struggle for love to conquer fear is a continuing cycle, a part of being human.

In western culture, the central parable is the conflict between love and fear which plays out in the life of Jesus. His life is an universal metaphor, a paradigm, whether we personally accept the story of his life as symbolic, or historical fact. Perfect love came into the world in the person of Jesus. He taught, he healed, he loved—and he required nothing in return. But the people he touched, even those closest to him, could not fully comprehend such a gift.

*He was in the world; but the world,
though it owed its being to him, did not recognize him.
He entered his own realm, and his own would not receive him.*
—John 1:10-11

Many who encountered Jesus sought to discern what his ulterior motives might be, so that they could erect defenses against him. Yet, try as they might, people could discover no evidence that he was truly a threat to them. Watching him as he healed, they saw only compassion, and no desire for recognition. Hearing him teach, they heard the same holy writ they accepted. With constancy he offered them his friendship.

Suspicion and fear persisted in the hearts of many to whom Jesus offered his love. When they saw him casting out demons out of the goodness of his heart, they interpreted this as proof that he was in league with Evil. When love stared them in the face, they were afraid. Purity of love was too good to believe, and so they chose not to believe. "He must be crazy," said some. "He is trying to undermine the faith of the Chosen People," said others. "He is planning an uprising against the State," said still others. In sum, the lover from Nazareth was considered dangerous.

*This man of love, choosing never to return evil for evil, never to exchange love for fear, was finally betrayed by a kiss:
And he came up ... and said, "Hail Master!" And ... kissed him.
Jesus said ... , "Friend, why are you here?"
Then they came up and laid hands on him, and seized Jesus.*
—Matt 26:30

The friend, Judas, using a sign of love, betrayed love, and set in motion the execution of Jesus. Whether or not we are believers, we know that the life of Jesus was not extinguished by his death. The love he embodied is still with us now.

What we as humans do with regard to love today is not any different than what was done then. My perception of the cycle of life is this: Love is offered, but, through the distortion of human fear, love is tainted. But light shines through those human hearts that authentic love touches. Love always conquers fear: life always conquers death; it transcends any stain with which we taint it.

> *Every heart to love will come*
> *But like a refugee.*
> *—Anthem*, Leonard Cohen

As you read these pages, and reflect on the stories of the struggle between love and fear among friends, and the organizations that we humans construct, I hope you will see that nothing human is alien to you. You are a part of that struggle which binds us together as human beings. Every person you meet in these pages, every event that unfolds could have involved you. We are in this life together: in the joy and in the sorrow of being human. If we are to be more than beasts, then we need to be friends. If we are to be friends, then we need to allow love to overcome fear, so that we may have compassion for one another in our fragile state.

> *Love is but a song we sing, fear the way we die...*
> *If you hear the song I sing, you will understand*

*You hold the key to love and fear, all in your trembling hand.
Just one key unlocks them both. It's there at your command.*
—Get Together, Chet Powers

Over twenty years ago, when I was a young man in the Navy, I established the community of Credo. It was a community in the sense that we were committed to a mutual effort to encourage our shipmates, our fellow pilgrims in the seagoing services to start on the road to greater compassion and friendship.

Ever since 1971, the people of the Credo communities live out in flesh and blood the thoughts and dreams of these pages. Because it is a reflection of humanity, the Credo community has experienced the cycle of love entering, fear corrupting, and love triumphing in the hearts of those who are touched by the extended Credo family.

The centerpiece of Credo is the Credo Weekend. It is a continuing effort of diverse men and women to offer their neighbors an experience of deep friendship: a Weekend retreat where men and women can pause on their life's journey long enough to be refreshed by the joy of love experienced without fear.

Is *That's How the Light Gets In* the account of a personal pilgrimage, or the history of an emerging spiritual movement? I have arranged and rearranged sections so as to form a clean separation between the two. Some readers of the manuscript even suggested that *Light* be split into two books. My conclusion is that I cannot separate the story of the Credo community from that of my life, because we are inextricably intertwined.

That is the case because Credo's origins come from my understanding of love, hope, and friendship which in turn are rooted in my life's experiences of love and fear. I founded Credo in order to offer to others a way to salvage love, hope, and friendship. As the Credo family has grown, so have I. Through the years many simple, suffering, valiant people have taught me more about compassion than I was ever able to extend to them. For Credo is a School of Love, you see, and I am as much a student as a teacher. *That's How the Light Gets In* is the account of my personal pursuit of intimacy which bore fruit in my founding Credo and its unique weekend retreat.

First, I describe my personal pilgrimage that was the seed bed of the concepts that are at the root of Credo. I then recount the life of Credo, which began in San Diego and is now world wide. *That's How the Light Gets In* tells what Credo is and how it has evolved. At the request of many Credo family members, I next discuss the details of the Credo process. Finally, I present my understanding of the state of affairs that makes Credo necessary.

The concept behind the Weekend is disarmingly simple: Love is life. Love is reciprocal. Love brings hope. What is unique about the Weekend is that there are no lessons taught, no information sheets distributed, only the songs of scores of artists. It is for this reason you will find lyrics of Credo songs liberally scattered throughout the text. I want you to grasp what music can say and do when taken seriously.

> Music can free people to let go of their hidden fears, which are usually quite irrational, so they can then open up all of their senses to others whom they once counted as threatening. It's that quality which makes music such a universal lingo that may transform the conscience of human beings.
>
> —Carlos Santana

The Weekend provides an environment where people feel safe enough to reach out to one another in order to experience a sense of friendship and community. The goal of the Weekend is to help neighbors not only to rediscover that love, but also to build upon it in friendship. Credo encourages human intimacy so that we may immerse ourselves in the love which makes each one of us whole.

In ordinary circumstances people are distracted by the events around them that spell danger. They are like deer on the edge of the forest who, although hungry, are reluctant to accept the nourishment offered by a caring hand. The deer who gets nourished is the one who takes risks, who overcomes fear and gradually approaches the source of life. On the Credo Weekend we all stand at the edge of the forest, but we agree among ourselves that this is not the hunting season. Because of that safety, we can abandon unnecessary defenses in order to build trust.

And we have the advantage over the wild animal on the edge of the forest because we have the quality of empathy. We can talk to each other and walk in each other's shoes. We can achieve an understanding of one another's reluctance to take a risk. We can talk through our sources of pain. We can understand and care for another. Out of this comes hope, freed by compassion, bringing us a sense of wholeness and a desire to heal the fearful nature of others. On the Credo Weekend we seek to embrace this life-giving spirit of love.

Today Credo is flourishing in the Navy around the world. Many chaplains from varied traditions have made their own contributions to the Credo family, greatly enriching the Community's response. Over the years Credo in the Navy has introduced marriage-enrichment retreats, pre-deployment Weekends for families about to be separated because of a scheduled cruise, Weekends for teen-age dependents, and a deeper consideration of spirituality in Credo II. Credo has addressed the special issues of women in the Navy, what it is to be a man, the bereavement of a crew when there have been fatalities on board ship, support for those who have been abused, and even the needs of those in military prison, or the brig.

Chaplains based at Credo/Naples have become circuit riders bringing Credo Weekends to personnel throughout Europe, the United Kingdom, the Mediterranean, the Persian Gulf, and even to the base in Spain where Credo/Esperanza once flourished. Credo/Okinawa serves the Pacific Rim, including mainland Japan and Korea. There are Credo centers in Norfolk, Mayport, San Diego, and Honolulu in addition to the ones in Naples and Okinawa. Its concepts are taught as part of the curriculum of the Advanced School of the Chaplain Corps. After years of struggle, Credo has been judged by its fruits and it prospers. The beauty of its prosperity is that it is in the hands of others, many of whom I will never know. Credo has taken on a life of its own, and others must provide the later history.

An Invitation

Credo is a subjective concept, one which does not lend itself to a practical application without a full understanding of its underpinnings. So often when those who have experienced the Weekend try to describe Credo to another person they are at a loss for words. They find it frustrating because they do not want the listener to place Credo within a common category: a self-help group, a religious retreat, or psycho-therapy. Although the Weekend has elements of each, Credo is unique. Thus any verbal comparisons are bound to miss the mark.

As you seek to understand Credo try to lay aside conventional categories. Try to remain open to an unconventional image, or to a paradigm shift,* in the way people achieve health, human wholeness and spiritual growth.

Many have asked how I conceived of the design of Credo. What books did I read? What doctrines of the savants of psychology did I embrace? What group processes did I incorporate? What other retreats served as a model? I cannot answer these questions, for Credo came not from books but from my experiences in life, including the loving hearts that touched mine.

I invite you to walk with me for a while. At the end of our time together you will be able to answer for yourself the question "What is Credo?" by assimilating my experiences within your own understanding of life. Ultimately your definition of Credo will be as personal and authentic for you as mine is for me. The truths of Credo are transcendent, not relative. They are internal and eternal, and they are experienced in a unique way by each person.

The journey has not ended for me with Credo, for the quest for love is constant in the story of human life. Join in the most important task of all: prepare to fully give and receive love.

---

* An example of what I mean by the term "paradigm shift" happened a few years ago. When Swiss watchmakers heard a reference to a time piece, they had a specific image, a paradigm, in mind. Automatically they would picture an instrument containing interlocking gears powered by a mainspring that moves hands on a dial. One year, at the annual Swiss watchmakers' exposition, a new time piece was displayed: the quartz watch. The Swiss craftsmen looked at it, saw that it had neither interlocking gears, nor a mainspring, and so they rejected it because it did not meet their definition of a watch. A visiting American from Texas Instruments had a broader concept of what made a watch. He accepted the new invention, and within a matter of a few years the quartz watch captured 80% of the market. Like that American, approach Credo with a mind unencumbered by preconceptions. You will be pleased with what you see and feel.

I

Hospitality

All You Need Is Love

Love, love, love
Love, love, love
Love, love, love

There's nothing you can do that can't be done.
Nothing you can sing that can't be sung.
Nothing you can say,
but you can learn how to play the game.
It's easy.

Nothing you can make that can't be made.
No one you can save that can't be saved.
Nothing you can do,
but you can learn how to be you in time.
It's easy:
All you need is love;
All you need is love;
All you need is love;
Love is all you need.

Nothing you can know that can't be known.
No one you can see that isn't be shown
Nowhere you can be
where it isn't meant for you to be
It's easy:
All you need is love;
All you need is love;
All you need is love;
Love is all you need.

—John Lennon

1

Icons Of Hospitality

Four images, or icons, of hospitality have molded my life; and it is the reflection of love expressed in hospitality which is the essence of the Credo experience. My four seminal encounters with loving hospitality are in the accepting Anker Family; the Accidental Community of shipboard life experienced as a shipmate; the generous spirit of Don Ignácio Milan; and the inclusive love of Aelred of Rievaulx.

How can I give love
when I don't know what love is?
How can I go forward
when I don't know which way I'm going?

—*How?*, John Lennon

Warmth and acceptance were scarce commodities in my life as a child; ours was a tumultuous and chaotic household with few boundaries. My parents parted ways when I was 7 years old and my brother 11. The rift caused a gaping wound for my mother and her two sons, manifested in feelings of anger and helplessness. Even to this day, fifty years later, I am still changing dressings as the wound slowly heals.

As a child I was unable to form deep friendships because of the trauma of my early years. Fear was at the core of the internal dynamics of our household. The divorce made permanent the wrenching disintegration of what family we had, and the ensuing years were lonely. I am grateful for one classmate, Donald Yaceshyn, a loyal and caring companion who valued me when I felt I had no value, and gave me much more than I was capable of returning. His family was a happy one and I remember it as a refuge. On occasion I would hang out at their home, talking to his kind mother while she was doing the family ironing.

One day, while sitting in my high school library waiting for the bell to ring, I picked up the catalogue of The College of William & Mary. I looked through the pictures and saw a warm and orderly campus: friendly students walking by stately brick buildings—not the least of which was the Christopher Wren Building, with its symmetry of form and inviting stability. On one page was a list of the priorities of the College—first co-educational college, first with an honor system, first with an elective system of studies, first Greek letter fraternity (Phi Beta Kappa) etc.

Because of my chaotic childhood I was looking for order combined with intellectual stimulation. The college seemed to have both. And my correspondence with the admissions office was personal and cordial. The catalogue and the administration conveyed the safe, nurturing environment I knew I needed to flourish. So, when I was 17, I left my home in Belmont, a suburb of Boston, to go far away to Virginia. It was the beginning of a long pilgrimage which reached its fruition in Credo. I felt that The College of William & Mary was a chance to be born again, leaving behind my old friendless self, much as a snake sheds its skin.

Even today I recall the feelings I had forty years ago when I left my shattered home to start a new life as a college student at William & Mary. It was not that easy, for I found that I was only able to form tentative friendships. Tentative, more because of my inability to accept them, than because of the way they were offered.

I remember those first nights in the dormitory in Williamsburg, lying in my steel framed bed, hearing the strange southern accents of my class mates echoing off the gray concrete floors. My room-mate, "Jimbo," contributed to my lonely days. He was an orphan from The Episcopal Boys' Home in Roanoke, Virginia, and would while away hours on the edge of his bed silently pitching playing cards into his empty hat while I would lie on the other bed gazing out the window. But, in a matter of weeks I did not have even his companionship. He was killed in an alcohol-related automobile accident.

Vowing to form the accepting relationships that I lacked as a child, I gave my classmates what they wanted. When they looked upon me favorably, I counted them as friends. I appeared to them to be happy and full of life and was fun to be around.

People came to me when they felt depressed. They told me that because of my warm and friendly demeanor I made them feel better. So, on one level I succeeded. My isolation apparently was diminished by friends who sought me. But inside I was consumed with doubts about my worth as a man and as a person. In reality, isolation increased within me—as I could never know whether my friends valued me for who I was, or how I appeared.

When my friends in one of the better fraternities liked me enough to want me to become a pledge, I became anxious. When they offered themselves to me in brotherhood, I reluctantly rejected them. When they realized my essential melancholy, my real self, I feared that they would regret accepting me as their fraternity brother. Hence seeking friendship through appearance and meeting other people's needs (but not my own), I assured that true friendship would never happen.

The paradox was bitter: even as I established my worth with others, my broken spirit sabotaged that very effort. In my decision not to trust an offer of love, I extended precisely the isolation I abhorred. Of course, I now know that the only way to end alienation is not by controlling the action of the giver, but by being open to the love of another. But in my student days that idea was beyond my comprehension.

This is not to say that my first days at William & Mary were desolate. I remember Biff Kirwan, a senior who lived a couple of doors down from me in the dorm. He intuitively sensed my situation and in many different ways was quietly by my side extending his hospitality to me. He understood, and in his gentle way extended to me a life-line. In the same way Dudley Jensen, the dorm resident assistant, responded by involving me in the swimming team, something I had never done before.

I also remember fondly the kindness of the Neiman family. Fraser was my English professor, and in his way would show concern. It got so I would enroll in his classes to order to enjoy his presence, even when the subject matter was too heady for my taste. His dear wife Stella gave me a warm and maternal welcome to their home, thereby extending my sense of belonging to the unique community that is Williamsburg.

As the college years unfolded, I enjoyed the kindness of Vince Malandra, a classmate from Elmira, New York, and a football player. He was a young man whose strength was in his faith as well as in his athletic prowess. It felt good to be around his spiritual and physical vitality. David Titus, another lonely classmate, and I would go out to dinner often, trying to be friends to each other.

An important young man was Charles Anker, who had returned to William & Mary after leaving to serve in Korea. We formed a close companionship, my first approximation of friendship. We were both outsiders, and much about our lives was left unsaid, but we enjoyed each other and were inseparable—together in our aloneness. After we graduated from William & Mary, Charlie and I went to the University of Iowa in the graduate English program.

There, in Iowa City, we lived in an apartment which was actually a garage renovated by an enterprising landlord. Money was scarce, the winter was long, and we felt lost in a school five times as large as our alma mater. After the spring semester we decided to transfer to a more hospitable climate. Charlie was admitted to the University of Southern California, and I to the intimate academic community of Claremont Graduate School.

The summer before our transfers, Charlie and I returned to our respective homes. In Boston, I occupied myself with odd jobs to earn money for school, delivering newspapers, and becoming a part of the cleanup crew at Fenway Park which enabled me to see the Red Sox, a treasured source of release when I was a kid.

But soon I became restless and had a yearning, almost a compulsion, to head for California. I had a premonition that there I would experience something transforming. I looked in the papers and contracted with an agency to drive a big Oldsmobile to Long Beach, California. The agency cautioned me not to replace any blown out tires with new ones, and to save the tire carcasses as proof of purchase. It was an odd request, I thought, from a strange man working out of a store-front office. But I wanted to get to California, and so I asked no questions.

I loaded all my belongings, and stopping only to fill up the gas tank, I drove alone for 48 hours from Boston to Southern California, without benefit of the Interstate Highway system. Driving non-stop was the way I could get there fastest with the least amount of expense, although my overloaded vehicle did experience a series of blowouts, two of them in the mountains of rural Arkansas. I arrived in Southern California with a back seat full of old tires, and turned the car over to the appropriate agency. In later years, when I called to drive another car out, I found that the owners of the agency were in prison for operating a stolen car ring.

Icon I: The Accepting Family

But my premonition about California was accurate. What I found there in Dairy Valley, near Long Beach in greater Los Angeles, was indeed transforming: Charles' family was my first experience of genuine inclusion and hospitality. Just as my relationship to Charles was my first tentative experience of friendship, so his home provided my first experience of being within an intact, loving family. The Ankers were hard-working Dutch milk-ers who owned a small family dairy farm. The sons rose with their father before dawn, to wash and milk their small herd. When they were done, they came into the kitchen for coffee and a good breakfast prepared by Bertha, their mother. There was always a quiet time when one of them, usually Bertha, read the day's scripture reflection from *Our Daily Bread,* a booklet designed to help people in their personal prayer life.

Bertha was an open, welcoming, jovial, and accepting mother, who made me feel welcome. Chris, the father, had an inquiring intellect that had never been formally trained in his youth in The Netherlands; but when he returned from his early morning chores I would enjoy sitting with him at the kitchen table and engaging in long discussions about the teachings of the Bible. As I settled into that warm and cohesive family, I experienced inclusion within a family bound together with bonds of love and faith.

For all of the Anker family's labors, operating a small dairy farm and selling the milk to the local cooperative meant considerable work for the amount of money earned. Despite the picturesque name, Dairy Valley was not a romantic, bucolic setting. To begin with, there was no valley—just a flat area of dirt where cows were penned in and fed bales of feed. And in one part of the town there was an ever-expanding mountain of manure. Several of the Anker's neighbors had sold their farms and taken the profit from their real estate transactions to move their herds to greener pastures hundreds of miles away from the city. But the Anker family was not in a position to do that, so they existed in an economically precarious situation. Yet the parents and their five sons and daughters had a coherence I had never known before.

A strong factor which nurtured their solidarity was their membership in a close-knit Dutch American community, whose life centered around their Reformed Church. I would go with the family to worship on Sunday and look around at the stalwart Dutch men and women singing hymns with gusto and conviction. There was such homogeneity and cohesion in their common life and faith. I can only remember having this profound experience of unity two other times, twelve years later at an African-American congregation in Waukegan, Illinois, and then another twelve years later at another enclave of Dutch people, this time potato farmers, in Manhattan, Montana.

Within the Anker family I also found their teen-aged son, Christian, who became for me the accepting brother I had always yearned for. Almost at first sight our hearts united one with the other, and I felt a warm unconditional acceptance from him which filled me with joy. On the surface we had little in common. I was a graduate student inclined toward intellectuality, whereas he was suspended from high school for dumping manure on the principal's front porch; I was the son of an MIT professor, he and his father milked cows.

But it made no difference. Christian and I would polish his metallic blue 1958 Chevy Impala, and then go down to the auto dealers to look at the new models. Still vivid in my memory are the astonishing 1959 Buicks with their preposterous gull wing fins.

Tragically, the experience was to be fleeting. Within a matter of weeks, my young surrogate brother Christian discovered he was suffering from bone cancer. In a little over a year, he was dead.

But those few months were precious. I remember one late afternoon sitting by my friend's bedside after his leg had been amputated. He was dying. Yet I was able to enjoy his warmth and hopefulness, his genuine charity. Christian never despaired, never showed any anger. I was with a young man whose faith appeared complete. He believed that he was in God's hands, and that if God willed for him to live only a few more months, that was something he could accept. He truly lived the words of Jesus, *"Not my will, but Thine be done."* His witness to me was neither a matter of words, nor of Bible proof-texts. I was confronted with the authenticity of his whole being, which was one of love and hope.

The power of his charisma would become the inspiration for the Credo approach some eleven years later: where, as with Christian, friendships are formed directly, with no artifice, no lectures, only the relationship of one true self to another. The love extended by that faithful, unpresuming young man and his family changed my life. As happens to some on a Credo Weekend, I had a glimpse of what the grace of love brings.

Recently my friend Charles, now an United Methodist minister at The Church of the Wayfarer in Carmel, California, wrote of Bertha, his mother, in *Waysign* the weekly church newsletter. He completes my understanding of what Bertha brought to me in my search:

My mother was the fourth of thirteen children, raised on a farm in Northwest Iowa. Having finished the eighth grade, she pleaded with her father to send her to the Academy (high school) so she could become a nurse. But girls were expendable on a farm that had ten of them, and despite a week long pleading and crying jag, she was farmed out to work in the houses of the local doctor and the minister.

She met my father through a pen pal column in a church magazine, he a dairyman living in California. He stopped by to visit her on his way to visit his relatives in the Netherlands and on his return they were married and drove to California where she knew no one. She helped my father by milking cows and cleaning up the milkhouse even after the first child arrived, only gradually quitting as the family swelled to seven plus three miscarriages.

Still the House was filled with her singing, all religious songs, and always a bit off key. We cruel children complained and asked her not to sing. It was a good thing she had a strong faith as her last child was a hydrocephalic who lived to eleven but had to be diapered and treated as a baby for all those years. She and my father had considered placing her in an institution, but when the doctor said that she wouldn't live long without love, they could not do it. Later my eighteen year old brother had a leg removed because of bone cancer and he died at the age of twenty. Once she told [my wife] Barbara that at times under these stresses, she would sit out on the lawn in the darkness and sob uncontrollably.

When I was growing up I thought that she was one of the most beautiful women in the world and nobody could cook like she could. Being away from home for long periods of time changes your perspective. She wasn't the most beautiful person in the world and her cooking was pretty limited. Truth is expensive and takes painful capital out of our memories. But I also thought of the dreams and the illusions with which she surrounded all of us and I wonder how hard our failures must have wounded her. Instead of her last years being happy, her confidence and ability were eroded by senile dementia driving her into an ever smaller world where, finally, even we no longer had names.

On Mother's Day I can again pay tribute to her spirit, her self-sacrificing love and her toughness which saw her through some terrible valleys of hurt. Although the memories remain mottled with pain, her faith was a brilliant light and perhaps her greatest gift to us.

It is within this same Dutch community that I found my dear and loyal wife, Ruth. In fact, she sang at Christian's funeral. The constancy of Ruth's love has been an anchor for my life. Our partnership, grounded in the solid, unadorned faith exemplified in that community, has been a source of strength for each other, for our sons, and for many to whom we extend the hospitality of our home. Ruth's faith is reflected in the words of her favorite hymn:

> *If thou but suffer God to guide thee,*
> *and hope in him through all thy ways,*
> *he'll give thee strength whate'er betide thee,*
> *and bear thee through the evil days.*
> *Who trusts in God's unchanging love*
> *builds on a rock that nought can move.*
>
> *Sing, pray, and keep his ways unswerving;*
> *so do thine own part faithfully,*
> *and trust his word, though undeserving;*
> *thou yet shall find it true for thee;*
> *God never yet forsook in need*
> *the soul that trusted him indeed.*

—Georg Neumark, transl. Catherine Winkworth

Because of my exposure to lives of genuine love and commitment, I could no longer be satisfied with the life of the intellect, alone. No longer did my goal of being a college professor teaching English seem satisfying. For this reason, I abandoned my pursuit of a doctorate in English and impulsively joined the Coast Guard. To this day, I have no idea why I felt compelled to join the Coast Guard. I had no interest in the military, nor did I know anything about the Guard. As I had taken seriously my call to California, so I responded to this leading, as well. In both cases, by following my intuition my life was permanently changed.

After attending Officer Candidate School in Yorktown, Virginia in the winter of 1960, I was stationed on the Coast Guard Cutter *Klamath*, a 255-foot long patrol gunboat whose home port was Seattle. It was there, as a young ensign, that I tried to live out my new understanding of life. I placed love as the top priority in all relationships, and because I did, I was able to enhance the lives of the crew.

I particularly cared for Bob, a hard working and responsible young man who served in my division with never a complaint. Although he was now in the Coast Guard, as the eldest son in an impoverished family of eight children he felt a responsibility for the rest of his brothers and sisters. He often acted as a buffer between them and their two alcoholic parents.

One day, while the ship was underway, as he was standing watch with me as a radarman, Bob let me in to his personal life. He told me he feared for the safety of his seven younger brothers and sisters because his pending transfer to another command would remove him from the area.

I raised the potential implications of Bob's transfer to the captain of our ship—a naive thing for a line officer to do, because the structure of the military hierarchy is maintained by avoiding intimate contact between officer and enlisted man. By providing the commanding officer with the information about Bob's family, I might have crossed the line of discretion. But it was something I had to do, now that, because of the quiet witness of my adoptive brother, Christian, I was able to make love my top priority. Predictably, the commanding officer rejected my concern out of hand saying, "We are not in the social work business."

Not long after, Bob was transferred from the ship. His father, drunk and violent within the home, bolted out into a cold winter night in Seattle. The next day his body was found naked and frozen, stripped of everything of value. At an officer's cocktail party a week or two later, the captain came over to me and said, "Well, Don, I guess you were right about the radarman's family. I'm truly sorry." Much as the commanding officer was affected by what happened, I realized that he could not cross an unspoken boundary: he and I were employed by the Coast Guard to drive ships, not to bring compassionate attention to the crew.

I loved the adventure and brotherhood of the sea-going life, but if I was to remain true to my developing priorities I could not go to sea as a deck officer. I was too aware not only of the powerlessness of the poor, but also the inability of the Coast Guard to fully respond to their need. My initial active duty tour was over in a year, and rather than seeking to extend it, I left active duty to find a service oriented career. After a month or two of wandering, I became a social case worker in Long Beach, California. I presumed that the agency would agree that my highest priority as a social worker would be to bring hospitality and concern to the forgotten in our society.

I particularly remember Elmer and his family—gaunt figures who could have stepped out of *Grapes of Wrath*. Because I understood the welfare system better than they, I was able to ensure that Elmer and his wife received daily insulin shots for their chronic diabetes. I scheduled an eye exam and obtained glasses for their son, so that he could see the blackboard and not continue to fail at school.

The county provided work for each head of the household in order to defray the welfare costs. Elmer worked for the county twice as much as he was required—so much that I was instructed by a supervisor to tell Elmer to stop working so much, since he was not being paid. When I relayed the message to him, Elmer paused for a few moments and said, "Mr. Harris, I like to get up and go to work. I feel like I am supporting my family. Besides, I am setting a good example for my son. If you don't mind, I think I will continue to work those hours."

Each time I met with Elmer, I felt fulfilled giving to him the acceptance and honor which had been extended to me by Christian and his family. I did not realize that at the same time the left hand was giving, the right hand was taking away. Another person in the same welfare office, a few desks away, was acting with equal diligence to prove Elmer and his family were non-residents of California and ineligible for the aid I was extending.

Eventually the State of California was able to accumulate enough documentation to suggest that Elmer's legal residence was at one time in Texas, and I was directed to place Elmer and his family on a train for Lubbock. Not only was I fully aware that their son would receive no more help for his vision, but also I knew the parents would receive no more insulin.

It was then that I realized that, as with the Coast Guard, I was not hired to bring hope to the poor. In this case I was hired to administer funds as directed by the legislature. Just as in my heart I was not a ship driver, so also in my heart I was not a welfare sleuth. Once more, I looked around for some way that I could make a living and live out my ideals.

So, in the fall of 1961, I left the agency and entered the Church Divinity School of the Pacific, the Episcopal seminary in Berkeley with the express purpose of preparing to return as a chaplain to the sea-going life ministering to the common man. I had chosen the Episcopal Church because of its liturgy and worship, and because it was inclusive of both my Catholic and Protestant sensibilities. I felt that as an Episcopal priest I could reach the breadth of the population of sailors from devout Irish Catholic to stalwart Calvinist. I was as much at home with a rosary as with a revival, for, in my mind, each of these expressions are from people yearning for the love of God. The Navy, I reasoned, would employ me to care. In this way I would have a chance to mirror the genuine inclusion and hospitality of the Anker family who, simply by being themselves, changed my life.

Icon II: The Accidental Community

For me, seminary was a preparation and a means of entry into a life of service to those who were alienated from the love of God. I never lost sight of my goal to live among my brothers in the naval services, sharing their pain, bringing them hope. In so many ways I felt like them, yet, by the grace of God, I was filled with unwavering compassion and a deep seated faith. If I could be used by God in any way to bring solace to those who were abused in so many ways, if their broken hearts could be mended so that they might receive love and, freed from fear, pass it on, then perhaps the cycle of alienation and abuse would be broken, and I would have a fruitful life.

I learned what I could, and I found a passion in worship that I had never known before. But that passion was not confined to the chapel setting. Each day, at the conclusion of seminary classes, I would drive to the Coast Guard Training Center in neighboring Alameda, and spend several hours with those recruits who, at the end of their emotionally rigorous day, needed a chaplain to talk to. I felt it was a chance to apply what I was reading in seminary to the world as it is. At the Protestant chaplain's invitation I also participated with him in leading Sunday worship.

Toward the beginning of my seminary experience I learned that the family of Bob, the Coast Guard radarman I mentioned before, disintegrated. Bob's 16-year-old brother, Roger, called to tell me that he was facing institutionalization because teen-age boys are not wanted by potential foster parents. Without hesitation I sent him a bus ticket and Roger joined me.

I had made a heartfelt and imprudent decision, and it was only through the dedicated help of the ethics professor, Greer Taylor, and the seminary community who rallied around Roger, that the boy received shelter from the storm. All the time I was at seminary I studied the gospel through the lens of the responsibility I felt toward Roger and the recruits whom I counseled.

Because of my care and the commitment of the seminary community, Roger completed high school—no mean accomplishment for such an emotionally damaged boy—and joined the Coast Guard. But the stress of recruit training was too great for Roger, particularly since he had to stand on his own without the immediate support of his seminary "family." He was given a medical discharge and returned to Seattle.

The lessons I learned would have to be taught again later. First, no matter how much I love a suffering person, that person needs to find the resources within himself to use that love for his spiritual health. Second, no matter how much I desire to lend a vulnerable person my strength, that strength is not something that comes from another, it must come from within the person, himself.

Upon receiving my commission as a Navy chaplain, I was stationed for seven months in Washington, D.C., where I was chaplain to the sailors of the Ceremonial Guard. We worked closely together as we buried the dead in Arlington National Cemetery. Selected for their size and appearance, the members of the Ceremonial Guard were an interesting group of young men. They were tall and handsome, presenting an image of the Navy at its best. But behind their facade were many troubled sailors. They were not quite the all-stars they appeared to be, or most of them would have been sent directly to advanced technical schools. Furthermore, with no emotional support, they had to deal with death and grief on a daily basis.

Many were as troubled as they were inarticulate. Some tried to say how they felt by referring to songs. I remember one sailor in particular, Ben Nelson, who found great value in the song *People*, sung by Barbra Streisand. He used that song as a vehicle for his exploration of himself with me, as the song articulated what he found hard to express. It drew us closer to each other, chaplain and sailor, by our sharing the content and the emotions the lyrics raised within each of us. This experience was a seed which would reach its maturity in the design of Credo.

But life would soon take another turn. Ruth and I were married the Saturday after Thanksgiving Day in 1964, and anticipated spending our first year together in the Washington, D.C. area. She had put together the wedding plans virtually by herself while teaching school full-time. However, the week before our marriage I was informed that I was to proceed to Norfolk, Virginia to replace an ill chaplain on a squadron of destroyers preparing to leave for a six-month deployment to the Mediterranean.

Now, after a brief respite in Washington, Ruth would have to fashion a life for herself among the packing boxes in an anonymous apartment in Norfolk, a city and area that was unfamiliar to her. In a matter of a few weeks I was at sea for six months. For both of us the adjustment was major.

On the one hand, Ruth became a permanent substitute school teacher, and sang in a Gilbert and Sullivan community group in a city, state, and Southern culture she had never known before. On the other hand, I became a circuit-riding chaplain with no permanent base, shifting from ship to ship by high-line (an evolution where two ships come alongside each other on the high seas and a person is strapped in a metal chair and hauled by block and tackle across the turbulent sea to the other vessel). Two new and challenging worlds.

The Profane Monastery

Another adjustment was equally challenging, but far more fulfilling. It was the experience of hospitality that came with my being arbitrarily placed within a community of strangers, many of whom felt as alone as I did. As I returned to the sea-going life I first learned to love in the Coast Guard, once again I experienced in the crew the comfort of an accidental community. The exposure was much more compelling now that I was their chaplain. Their response to me was quite unlike either the inclusive embrace that a warm God-fearing family extended to me, or the open heart of my new found brother, Christian. I experienced a similar depth of acceptance, but it was based on their needs, which were legion.

The community of strangers I am referring to, were the men who lived with me aboard ship, first in the Coast Guard, and then the Navy. Although it may sound strange, I think of a combat vessel at sea as a profane monastery: a band of men brought together into a shared life with a common mission. Their days and nights have the same unvarying cycle marked by bells: for the sailor the bells mark off each four hour watch, for the monks the bells mark the cycle of Benedictine prayer: None, Sext, Matins, Compline, etc.

I was surrounded by hundreds of shipmates and together we forged bonds of necessity as we experienced the separation and excitement of long deployments. Now that I was a chaplain, rather than a line officer, it was easier for me to be involved with the entire ship's company. In the case of the chaplain, the prohibition against officers "fraternizing" with enlisted men was relaxed.

The beauty of a shipboard community is that it is unrelentingly inclusive. You have no choice but to live beside your shipmate, who might be a thief or a scholar, perhaps a little of both. Within this inclusive environment you are afforded the opportunity to accept or reject the hospitality of your brother. Hospitality may sound like a pretentious word if you picture a drunken sailor coming back from liberty with his arm around his shipmate's shoulder, but it *is* hospitality. It is acceptance on the most basic of levels: being your brother's keeper. This is another key ingredient of the Credo experience.

Icon III: A Generous Spirit

Who would ever want to marry me? I give away all that I have.
—Don Ignácio Milan

The third icon of hospitality that has deeply affected me is the life of Don Ignácio Milan, whom I met in 1975. He was a frail ascetic Spanish nobleman born in the nineteenth century. It is hard to tell an exact age when looking into the face of one who had endured first the religious persecution of the Twenties; then the hunger and devastation of the Spanish Civil War, where over one third of the male population was slain, and finally the deprivation of World War II and its aftermath of political and economic isolation.

I first met Don Ignácio at his bedside in *Villa Ballena (The House of the Whale)*—an unpretentious but elegant retreat house located in Chipiona, along the Atlantic shore of Andalucía in southern Spain. The chill wind of winter whipped across the long deserted beach, where at the far end I could see a monastery. Before us the waves lapped around a pre-Christian lighthouse a few yards from Don Ignácio's dwelling. Near its base I could even see in the surf the remnants of Phoenician stone fish traps.

I was in my Navy blues with the bright gold braid on my arms. My good friend Pedro Díaz was by my side as we looked for a site to hold Credo Weekends in Spain. I had met Pedro as the professor of the Spanish class that I took when stationed in Rota. He was a warm and expansive man with a great love for Americans. In addition to teaching, Pedro was responsible for encouraging close social contact between the Spaniards and the U S Navy personnel on the base.

Pedro took me to see his family friend, Padre Bernardino, at the Franciscan monastery, *Santuario Nuestra Senora de Regla*, last renovated in the sixteenth century by Ponce de Leon, the discoverer of Florida. Pedro's friend was an aged Franciscan monk with failing eyesight who listened intently and directed us to *Villa Ballena*, and its owner, Don Ignácio.

Bundled up in the chilling wind, Pedro and I rapped on the glass pane of the front door of the villa. A widow from the fishing village dressed in traditional black came to the door and graciously led us to a bedroom which was at the end of a tiled corridor.

The frail figure of Don Ignácio, suffering from influenza, rose from his sick bed and bowed graciously. "You are especially welcome," he said humbly. "I will forever be grateful for the Americans who brought food to our little town of Chipiona when we were hungry." After we outlined the purpose of our quest, Don Ignácio offered us his house, *Villa Ballena*, as a site for Credo Weekends. As he bid us good-bye, he said, " I am honored to have an opportunity to give back what we have received."

The villa has an interesting history. As was the custom for all young men of means, Don Ignácio and his brother were privileged to attend the month-long *Ejercicio Espiritual (Spiritual Exercises)* of Ignácio de Loyola. Both brothers were so moved by the experience that they wanted to extend the blessing they had received to the less fortunate fishermen of their town, Chipiona. Normally the common man could not afford to participate in the spiritual training routinely provided for the noblemen.

At first, the two brothers provided funds to a local convent to accomplish their mission, but learned that the funds were misappropriated, leaving little for the benefit of the poor men on retreat. Not to be daunted, Don Ignácio joined with his brother, an architect, to build *Villa Ballena*, thereby ensuring that the *Spiritual Exercises* would be available to all men, rich and poor alike. The retreat house, resplendent with tile of Moorish design, was built to nourish the souls of Don Ignácio's humble neighbors, including their children who were welcome to enjoy the beach in the summer.

The structure was a haven for many spiritual seekers through the years, and a place of refuge for Christians persecuted by the anti-clerical regime that governed Spain in the Twenties. As he welcomed the American sailors, Marines, and members of their families into his home during the ensuing months, Don Ignácio could see his dream fulfilled in yet another way. Once more he was helping common people in their search for the love of God.

What was remarkable about Don Ignácio in his response, and Pedro, for that matter, was that he was able to transcend the limits erected by formal religion. After all, he was raised in one of the most staunch Roman Catholic cultures in history. Catholicism was the glue which bound his people together in their 800-year struggle to reclaim Spain for the Faith. Here was a traditional Jesuit-trained nineteenth-century nobleman who could see God at work in something very foreign to his institutional understanding, although, I might add, not contrary to the essence of his faith.

It would be difficult for such a religiously trained person to accept the proposition that an Anglican priest could convey with purity the message of God's love. But even if he could overcome that prodigious hurdle, it took a leap of faith for Don Ignácio to accept that the music of folk and rock musicians, which is the primary resource of a Credo Weekend, could be a means of grace. That gracious man was so filled with love and servanthood, that he showed no indication such concerns even crossed his mind.

He re-configured the nave of the baroque chapel he built within the retreat house so that it could be used as the meeting place for the Credo program. Together with two widows named Catalina and Rosario (who had beautifully weathered and lined faces), the frail man removed the pews from his chapel and lined the floor with mattresses so that those on the Credo Weekend could sit comfortably along the walls which were covered with folk frescoes of the life of Jesus.

Don Ignácio even offered me the use of his chapel's altar, complete with communion vessels, linens, and vestments. I was overwhelmed by his loving acceptance of me and expressed to him how grateful I was for his generosity, but explained to him (with the help of Pedro since Don Ignácio did not understand English) that our worship would be informal. On the chapel floor within our gathering, I explained to him, we would spread a cloth on which we would place the bread and wine, so as to minimize the anxiety of any one who was uncomfortable with ritual. With a quiet smile Don Ignácio bowed from the waist and said he understood.

He charged only $1 per person for the use of the facility for the Weekend. Rosario and Catalina prepared simple and hearty meals, and Don Ignácio, wearing vest and black bow tie typical of local waiters, served the sailors elegantly. Sometimes between meals, the aged gentle man would slip out to drive to Seville, seventy miles away, where he would visit the elderly folks who lived in another structure he and his brother had built to serve their less fortunate neighbors. Many of the residents were younger than he.

Don Ignácio insisted upon only one thing: each of his Navy guest's names would be entered in the ledger which listed all those who had made a retreat at *Villa Ballena* over the years. At the end of each retreat, after the American sailors and Marines would roll up their sleeping bags and prepare to return to the base, each would pause by a small table where frail Don Ignácio sat with his time-worn register. With a sense of deep satisfaction evident to all, the holy man would enter their names alongside the hundreds of Spaniards who had come before.

Once he told me how impressed he was that the American youth showed such seriousness during the retreat, wistfully observing that this was not always the case with modern Spanish youth. As we walked along the beach, one day, I asked Don Ignácio whether he had ever been married. He looked into my face with a twinkle in his kind eyes, and answered, "Who would ever want to marry me? I give away all that I have." Indeed, this was so, for as the years passed by, he even offered to give us *Villa Bellena* as a permanent residence for the Credo Community. Tempting as the offer was, I was not at a point in my journey where I could consider such a radical move.

Don Ignácio has since died, and his gracious structure has fallen to the wrecker's ball in order to make room for another anonymous beach-front condominium. I returned eighteen years later with my son Jonathan and could not find a trace.

Icon IV: Inclusive Love

Along the wilderness of the Scottish border of Britain some eight hundred years ago lived Aelred, a man of deep inclusive love. Maturing into manhood at the Scottish Court, he was an intimate friend of David, the young heir to the throne of Scotland. During this time, inspired by Bernard of Clairvaux, Benedictine reform was sweeping across the monastic communities of Western Europe. It brought a renewed emphasis to a spirituality based on simplicity, unencumbered by wealth and ornament.

The news of Bernard's teaching prompted long and impassioned conversations among Aelred, David and their friends in the court of Scotland. One day, Aelred quite precipitously walked out of that court of privilege to enter a newly formed community of Cistercian monks who were living a way of life modeled after the teachings of Bernard of Clairvaux.

Within a matter of months young Aelred had infused his brothers within the community with the grace of his ability to extend unconditional acceptance—Aelred held each one as sacred and precious. Aelred's love was contagious, and his community became legendary. Although very young, soon Aelred was elected abbot by his brothers. The doors of the monastery were open to all who would enter. Tradition asserts that not only was no one ever expelled, but also, over the years only one person out of the hundreds who sought brotherhood in the community chose to leave.

Aelred lived the message of hope and hospitality, and his love was contagious. He was extremely active, happily covering the countryside with new communities of love, until his latter years when he became crippled with arthritis. Yet even then, Aelred would not consider retiring to a solitary life, but rather he asked his brothers to build an alcove next to the community refectory so that he could be available to his friends and enjoy their company. For the rest of his life it was his custom to invite his brother monks to come to his bedside for familiar conversations. Walter Daniel in his book, *The Life of Aelred*, recounts:

> Every day they came to [the alcove] and sat in it, twenty or thirty at a time, to talk together of the spiri-

tual delights of the Scriptures. ... There was nobody to say to them 'Get out, go away, do not touch the abbot's bed;' they walked and lay around his bed and talked with him as a little child prattles to his mother. He would say to them, "My sons, say what you will; only let no vile word, no detraction of a brother, no blasphemy against God proceed out of your mouth."

Aelred died as he had lived, surrounded by a host of his brothers. Before his death, he completed *Spiritual Friendship*, a book that his friend Bernard of Clairvaux had urged him to write. When I read it for the first time in 1986, fifteen years after founding Credo, I discovered in it a mother lode for my understanding of life. *Spiritual Friendship* captured in words the spirit which led me to found Credo. For me, Aelred is an icon of inclusion and hospitality. He opened his heart, his monastic family, his life to all who shared life's journey with him.

These, then, are my four icons of hospitality: the warm acceptance of the Anker family; the unity of shipmates trying to make it through life together; the generous constancy of Don Ignácio, a nobleman who devoted his life to bringing the love of God to even the most humble; and the sublime metaphor of love and inclusiveness which was Aelred. My vision of Credo is that it can help prepare the hearts of many of us to live such lives of warmth and acceptance.

II

My Credo Pilgrimage

The Attics Of My Life

In the attics of my life,
full of cloudy dreams unreal.
Full of tastes no tongue can know,
and lights no eye can see.
When there was no ear to hear,
You sang to me.

I have spent my life
seeking all that's still unsung.
Bent my ear to hear the tune,
and closed my eyes to see.
When there were no strings to play,
You played to me.

In the book of love's own dreams,
where all the print is blood.
Where all the pages are my days,
and all my lies grow old.
When I had no wings to fly,
You flew to me,

In the secret space of dreams,
where I dreaming lay amazed.
When the secrets all are told,
and the petals all unfold.
When there was no dream of life,
You dreamed of me.

—Robert Horton and Jerry García

2

The Keel Is Laid, 1967-1970

San Francisco: The Hunger For Spirituality

In the San Francisco Bay area, the Sixties were a time of revolutionary ferment. I was stationed across the bay from San Francisco at the Coast Guard Training and Supply Center at Alameda. There, young men were prepared for service in the Coast Guard. Their duties would be largely concerned with assisting navigation as well as providing search and rescue operations, with the possibility of a few being sent to Vietnam to pilot river patrols.

Social and moral change was in the air, and for many the rupture of traditional values was ominous: the sexual and drug revolution rose from the embers of the assassinations of John F. Kennedy, Robert F. Kennedy, and Martin Luther King, and the disorder these events presaged. Timothy Leary was urging people to enter the realm of the spirit through LSD: "Turn on, tune in, drop out." The Beatles were entering their stage of experimentation with Eastern mysticism and hallucinogenic drugs, and the nation's apocalyptic Vietnam involvement was looming, fraught with impassioned protests from the idealistic.

Not only was it a time of sexual revolution, but the whole country was being shaken to its roots in other areas. Conventional institutions such as the churches and law enforcement agencies were not automatically viewed as benevolent, as they had been by the middle class in the past. In fact, with the advent of the wide-spread usage of marijuana among the "normal" youth, the police had shifted from being protectors to being adversaries. A full-blown war in Vietnam was looming: our culture was becoming chaotic, born of failed authority and disintegrating boundaries. The myths of America (as best typified by the stability and sentimental warmth expressed in the art of Norman Rockwell) were being challenged, and the nation, we can see now in retrospect, was in danger of moral anarchy.

One Sunday night in 1963 at the boot camp, I began a class for recruits who were preparing for baptism. I expected a handful to attend, but instead each Sunday night found my spacious office filled with recruits, who even sat on the floor. There was no question that many of the young men sincerely sought to become Christians, for while I was there I must have baptized over one hundred young men. But, I sensed that this response was part of a broader trend taking shape: a rebirth of mysticism, an interest in the transcendent. Whether or not they thought of themselves as believers, young man after young man expressed a yearning to enter the realm of the spirit in order to discover the meaning of life and his place within it.

It was an exhilarating time. I was thankful that the national crisis of the sexual revolution and Vietnam was forcing people to look at their root beliefs. Although I was very concerned for the youths who were consuming mind-altering drugs, I was heartened both by their hunger for spirituality and by their disillusionment with materialism. Of course a person is naive to believe that a milligram of any chemical could provide a short cut on the journey into one's soul. Nevertheless, at least there were people who wanted to make the journey. I could see that young people were flirting with the essence of life: love, inclusion, community. Whether or not their means were misbegotten, their hearts were in the right place. I began to consider a constructive way to help them experience this love they sought.

The "Summer of Love" of 1966 was a unique happening in the Haight Ashbury area of San Francisco, one that made the Bay Area giddy. From across the nation young people gathered in this fabled neighborhood to create an alternative to the gathering storm of Vietnam. Their guiding ideals were: Make love, not war. Live together in harmony. Share clothes, food, lodging with your neighbor. Work together for the common good. None too different than what the early church professed in the first century, AD.

Unfortunately, because of the link to the new freedom of The Pill (which allowed sexual intercourse with no fear of the implications of pregnancy), love became confused with recreational sex. That which was meant for mutual giving became a source of individual gratification. In addition, because the quest for spirituality became identified with a skewed understanding of Eastern religion, it led to spiritual narcissism. The consumption of mind-altering drugs, often in conjunction with the Eastern search, amplified the trend toward individualism, a potential foe of community.

Along with my understanding of the emerging interest in mysticism, I saw in each individual a microcosm of the social ferment that was unfolding: the hunger for love and inclusion. The line outside my office at the boot camp kept growing longer. I knew that I could not see them all. I accepted that I was incapable of ministering to all of the recruits who sought my counsel; and that there was no reason for me to attempt to assume all their burdens. If these young men, who lived in such physical and emotional proximity in the barracks, could realize that they shared essentially the same struggles and desires, they could accept the responsibility of supporting one another.

My chapel services were filled to overflowing. Certainly the stress of boot camp contributes to chapel attendance, but in checking the records I saw that the recruit attendance was more than double the norm for the Training Center. I was under no illusion that their response was solely due to whatever gifts I had to offer as a young chaplain. There was something more going on. For those who wanted to listen, it could be heard in the cry from the popular music which was beginning to dominate the consciousness of this generation.

The rock music was held in such high regard by the young men, that, in order to reach the recruits in a compelling way, I turned for my sermon texts to these lyrics, rather than biblical texts to which the young men had little exposure. An example would be from Leonard Cohen's "Suzanne":

And Jesus was a sailor, when he walked upon the water
And he watched the world go by from his lonely wooden Tower.
And when he knew for certain only drowning men could see him
He said, "All men will be sailors then, until the sea shall free them."
Yet he himself was broken, long before the sky would open
forsaken, almost human, he sunk before your wisdom like a stone.

In this way I was able to convey the spiritual content of Scripture in a language that would be palatable to those to whom I was speaking. I found it fascinating that the words of Leonard Cohen, a secular Jewish poet from Montreal, could so compellingly address the content of the New Testament.

But Leonard Cohen was not the only secular artist who struck a Christian chord. I remember many years later, I was involved in a Credo Weekend with the homeless in Salt Lake City with my co-leader Peter Chase, an Episcopal priest. After Peter listened to the song "Good Shepherd" by the Jefferson Airplane, he gave a wry smile to the other participants, and remarked, "I never thought I would get good sermon material from an acid rock group":

If you want to get to heaven, over on the other side
Stay out of the way of the blood-stained bandit
O Good Shepherd, feed my sheep.
One for Paul, one for Simon, one for to lay my heart with joy
Can't you hear my lambs a-calling
O Good Shepherd, feed my sheep.

I needed to get to the root of what I saw happening within the consciousness of those recruits I had come to know, and the only way was to take a broad look at those whom I was serving in the recruit training center. My random exposure to those recruits who were experiencing difficulties in boot camp would give me a skewed picture had I not included some time spent with recruits who were handling the twelve weeks of training well. Many of these I would meet during the Sunday services, of course, and I would invite them to come to my office when they had some spare time. In this way, I met several young men who had a more balanced view of life than their troubled shipmates.

Later, when I toured the lighthouses along the northern California coast I would be able to renew these friendships first made in recruit training. Some I still keep in touch with almost thirty years later. It is interesting to see how individually our lives have unfolded.

Perhaps I spent my most satisfying time with a teenage recruit named Jeff Bridges. He came by after hours, talked of his dreams, and played me his songs on the guitar I always had leaning against a chair in the office. Our paths were to cross several times in the years ahead.

To be sure that my impressions were accurate, I needed the permission of my commanding officer to poll a prepresentative sample of the recruit population. Because I was trusted by both Captain Curwen and the recruits, I was able to administer, with the assistance of my brother chaplain, Conall Coughlin, an extensive survey to the total recruit population.

The questionnaire asked them about their family life, their sexual activity, and their use of illegal drugs, as well as tobacco, and alcohol. Over an eighteen month period Conall Coughlin and I administered the survey three times, six months apart. As the information was processed by painstaking manual analysis, it was confirmed that drug abuse was growing and had roots in a spiritual problem.*

I also worked with a young Coast Guardsman, Peter Valerio, who was leading a group for faltering recruits to help them get a hold on their lives so that they could successfully complete training. Peter used music as a way to prompt frank discussions among the young men, many of whom had experimented with drugs,

---

* The results of the survey are still in my possession. At the time, a psychiatrist at the Naval Hospital tried to use the computing facilities of Stanford University to analyze the data, but was not able to secure enough computer time.

and he confirmed what I had suspected, that a feeling of lostness and spiritual death was the paramount concern of the recruits in the group. He describes his work in this way:

> I was assigned as clinical director for the Coast Guard Drug Rehabilitation Center. Here were young men, some of our country's finest, who were busily involved in destroying their lives with drugs. The idea was that in exchange for "confessing" drug abuse, the Coast Guard would grant an amnesty. The Coast Guardsman would be assigned to drug rehabilitation with the eventual goal of returning him to duty. This was a problem for some.
>
> Distrust of the system ran high. Many of the Coast Guardsmen were unwilling to talk about anything. In desperation, I decided to play different sets of music and have them talk about their thoughts and feelings. This was a back door to getting people to talk, but it worked.

At the U. S. Public Health Service in San Francisco, Dr. Merrill I. Berman was the psychiatrist for the Coast Guard. He is one of the most sensitive and astute men I have ever known, and was deeply concerned with the lives of the recruits. Together Peter, Conall, Merrill and I started working with these troubled Coast Guardsmen.

Chaplain Richard Hutcheson, the captain in charge of chaplain assignments, came to the San Francisco area making his rounds to discuss with chaplains their future duty stations. I sought out this bright and mature pastor to tell him of our research, and how it indicated that the age of drugs was upon us in the Seagoing Services. I stressed that it was a problem that we should not react to with fear by imposing a medical rather than a spiritual diagnosis. The medical route, I pointed out, ultimately would lead to the intervention of law enforcement, not the nurture of souls.

I asserted that by concentrating attention on the medical and legal aspects of substance abuse, and by trying to convince young people how harmful drugs (other than alcohol) are, we are not facing up to the real problem of why people turn to drugs. The drug culture is only one symptom, and only one of many, of a disintegration of generally accepted social, moral, and spiritual values. To tell people they must stop using drugs and then to offer no alternative, I explained, is like telling people in pain to stop using pain-relieving medication without offering them an equivalent. To do this is, at best, insensitive.

Drug use was a symptom of a spiritual void, I told my brother chaplain, that was being experienced by these young people, and I believed it was our responsibility as chaplains, designated spiritual leaders, to respond to this spiritual need. I felt that we could offer an alternative way, by encouraging individuals to undertake a greater self-exploration and more penetrating understanding of themselves.

The result would be to achieve a greater appreciation of their own worth as a basis for integrating social, moral, and spiritual values. It would thereby diminish their desire for drugs and other forms of escape. I told him that I saw the Chaplain Corps, the locus of spiritual leadership in the Navy, as having both a unique opportunity and profound responsibility to respond to the young people whose spiritual hunger was so evident.

Chaplain Hutcheson listened attentively, and told me when I arrived at my next duty station to apply for the pastoral counseling training program in the psychiatric service of the Naval Hospital in Oakland, so that I might deepen my understanding, refine my skills, and prepare a response.

After my tour at the Coast Guard Training Center, and before applying to the hospital training program, I became squadron chaplain to a group of amphibious ships in Norfolk. One sunny afternoon in November while we were underway in the Caribbean, the commanding officer of the Marine detachment on board asked me to deliver to my Marine shipmates a lecture about drug misuse.

The essence of my message was that drugs were self-destructive. On a pastoral level I had heard the personal stories of several of the men whom now I was addressing *en masse*. As I looked into their faces, it occurred to me how foolish were the words coming out of my mouth. Several of these men *were* self-destructive. The danger involved in being a combat Marine was why many men enlisted. In essence, within their personal understanding, I was telling them that drugs were a useful adjunct to their self-destructive path.

Once again, as when I used rock songs as sermon texts, I realized that in order to address the spiritual needs of these young people, we, the leadership, needed to suspend *our* context of values and enter *theirs*, using words that make sense to them.

I could see that it is essential that we place ourselves in the shoes of those whom we want to reach. The use of drugs is a subjective decision by the individual, and therefore not something to be addressed objectively. Again, an element of Credo was coming to the fore: The best way for people to make personal decisions is not to introduce our bias and values, but rather to help them think through their own values. Then the decision each person makes is permanent because it comes from his or her own understanding, and not from that of others.

During our brief stay in Norfolk, Ruth and I also had our first child and son, Timothy. If you are a parent you can understand what a life changing event this was. If, in addition, you come from a chaotic and dangerous childhood, you can further comprehend what an infusion of hope I experienced. Here was my own son, entering the world with his own anticipation, bearing the image of Ruth and me.

For me it was a chance to right some wrongs, to give him the safety, devotion, and love which I seldom experienced. In a way, it was a chance to relive my own childhood in my own flesh and blood, and to enjoy, through him, a childhood free from the very real fears which had dominated my life. I vowed that the cycle would be broken, that I would achieve some element of reconciliation through enjoying his love of life. In retrospect, I can see how I experienced a similar maturation, although less intimate, when I helped broken young men and women thrive in the loving atmosphere of the Credo community.

Heroes In The Seaweed

The fall of 1969 found me in a training capacity on the psychiatric wards of the Oakland Naval Hospital, which were filled with the emotionally and spiritually battered, flown in from the battle front. Oliver Stone captured the essence of their suffering in two powerful films of the 1980's: *Platoon* and *Born on the Fourth of July*; as did Francis Ford Coppola in a more extravagant way in *Apocalypse Now*. Coppola's later documentary, *Heart of Darkness*, described the intensity involved in the making of his film. In it the actor Martin Sheen is filmed actually having a nervous breakdown as he looked in the mirror and saw the destructive side of his own soul.

This level of spiritual intensity was daily fare for all of us on the ward. I will never forget the eerie feeling I had the morning I entered the ward full of traumatized Marines and sailors, only to hear the Beatles new hit, "Here Comes the Sun," echoing through the locked ward from the radios of the patients:

> *Little darling, I feel the ice is slowly melting*
> *Little darling, seems like years since it's been clear*
> *Here comes the sun, Here comes the sun,*
> *I say it's all right.*

I feel the pathos of the situation as if it were yesterday: battle-torn sailors and Marines, spiritually devastated in the jungles of Vietnam, still clinging to hope within a society that at best found them an embarrassment.

I worked with approximately twenty-three psychiatrists on that receiving ward. Only a handful of them were able to bring hope to their patients. Though from competing schools of psychiatric thought, the two most effective doctors, Michael A. Taylor and psychiatric resident Patrick J. Malone, had one thing in common: they were able to convey compassion as well as to apply knowledge. As Pat wrote in a book *The Art of Intimacy* some twenty years later,

> I came to understand that 'having to help' my clients, my 'wanting them to do better,' my 'helping them change things,' was being experienced as non-acceptance of them. And, in a sense they were right. I was gentle, I was close, but I was focused on the goal of 'improving them.' I was not to be of any real use to them until I could accept them as they were. ... It is vitally and fundamentally important to people that

they be accepted as they are, without apologies or ifs, ands, or buts. This is who I am, messed up as I am, but me. Can you care for me? I do not ask for you to approve of me, or agree with me, or think I am right. but do you care for me? You do not even have to let me be as I am, so long as you care for me as who I am.

Healing took place as a young sailor or Marine and his doctor responded to each other as brothers, as well as patient and physician. After their Naval service, Mickey went on to be head of the Department of Psychiatry at the Chicago Medical School; Pat is in practice with his father at the Atlanta Psychiatric Clinic and Institute for Experiential Growth.

For a while I was placed on *Project 49*, a therapeutic community incorporating the Synanon* model whose primary therapeutic approach was one of aggression. Patients, many fresh from the battle front, were put on a "hot seat" and verbally assaulted until their defenses were broken down. Although there was a venting of anger, there was no reconciliation, for I could see no positive spiritual base.

Like cult behavior, the patient was required to be "disciplined-under" a strong leader, and become totally subservient to him. Any man who objected to the humiliation was considered rebellious and untreatable. The misery that the men felt was palpable. I had a better understanding of why they were using drugs, but could see no reason posited by the treatment modality for them to be motivated to stop. I despaired at the moral vacuum which

---

* Synanon was an enclosed, strictly controlled therapeutic community where rigid boundaries were set, and the false realities of the patient-addicts were assaulted by the staff. The belief was that severely addicted people were in such pathological denial that they needed to have their addictive defenses leveled so that they could choose to totally modify their behavior.

typified this therapeutic approach. But at least the staff was trying to help with the tools that they were given.

In contrast, as part of the small talk at a command reception, I remember the wife of the commanding officer of the hospital complaining to me of the destructive nature of the young amputees back from the battlefield. She was astonished that they were kicking in the Coke machines and being generally destructive, and reported with some satisfaction that her husband was effectively putting a stop to this destructive behavior by catching the culprits, heavily fining them, and reducing them in rank. The machines were protected; the souls in pain were repressed.

What was there to say? I wandered off among the guests, the cocktails and hors d' oeuvres, and found myself humming the last verse of "Suzanne" by Leonard Cohen that I had used as my first sermon text as a chaplain. It captured the plight not only of the sailors and Marines in the hospital, but also the similarly bereft hippies who did not have to confront the horror of war to become disillusioned:

> *Now Suzanne takes your hand,*
> *and she leads you to the river.*
> *She is wearing rags and feathers*
> *from Salvation Army counters.*
> *And the sun pours down like honey*
> *on Our Lady of the Harbor.*
> *And she shows you where to look*
> *among the garbage and the flowers.*
> *There are heroes in the seaweed,*
> *there are children in the morning,*
> *They are leaning out for love,*
> *and they will lean that way forever,*
> *While Suzanne holds the mirror.*

Maybe much of society did not think of the youth on the wards and in the streets as heroes, but I felt that the spiritual struggle of many of my young companions as they strove to make sense out of the deteriorating culture was an heroic effort. That they were leaning out for love, I felt acutely, and I wanted to provide them with some small means to discover the love they craved.

The Age Of Aquarius

In conjunction with the ministry to the Naval psychiatric ward, I also worked with Haight-Ashbury residents on the psychiatric ward of the University of California's Langley-Porter Youth Drug Unit. I spent time on the wards with young people who were the wreckage of the self-styled "Age of Aquarius," where greed and selfishness had smothered their naive attempts at initiating an age of love. I discovered that several of the staff were as much a part of the problem as the youth they were treating. I heard from the young patients that farewell parties for the nurses included the use of marijuana. Both staff and patients were confused in their faith and values. Once more I was struck with the hunger for authentic love.

One of the patients I came to know well was a plaintive young woman, the partner of the leader of the Hell's Angels in San Francisco, She would do well during the week days when she was in the ward, but would return on Sunday night after a weekend's pass with bruises on her body. One weekend she invited me to go to a party at a road-house in San Rafael where the various chapters of the Hell's Angels were gathering for an all-night concert featuring Janis Joplin.

I arrived at the party about 2:00 AM, and saw a sea of humanity drinking beer and smoking pot. On the temporary stage off to the side a naked young woman, high on drugs, was dancing erotically, apparently trying to excite the crowd. The cruel reality was that the crowd was completely disinterested in her, even on this the most basic of levels. Soon a scrawny naked young man joined her in an "erotic" display. Again the crowd showed no interest for that which in conventional circles would be shocking. In fact, the couple showed no passion whatever; their sterile eroticism was a reflection of the emptiness on their faces and possibly in their hearts.

Soon Janis stormed on the stage. Outrageous in both dress and in behavior, she frenetically belted out song after song. When her first backup group grew tired of playing, she sang with the next group of musicians until she dropped finally to the floor in exhaustion. Her live concert recording of "Love Is Like a Ball and Chain" captures the essence of the kind of emptiness which pervaded the road-house hundreds of Hell's Angels there, a "community" of isolation:

> *When I want to work for your love, daddy*
> *When I want to try for your love, daddy*
> *I don't understand how come you're gone?*
> *I mean, if you've got a cat for one day, man ...*
> *Say you want a cat for 365 days*
> *You ain't got him for 365 days*
> *You've got him for one day, man*
> *I tell you that one day, man, better be your life.*
> *Because you can cry about the other 364, man*
> *But you are going to lose that one day, man*

> *You gotta call that love. That's what it is!*
> *If you've got it today, man, you don't want it tomorrow*
> *Because you don't need it—*
> *As we discovered on the train, tomorrow never happens*

As I left the road-house with my head throbbing from the crescendo of sounds within which I had been immersed, dawn was breaking over San Francisco Bay. What I left behind was darkness in every sense of the word. Within that darkness were hundreds of the next generation without even the conception of what love might be.

De Colores

The final seminal experience for me in San Francisco was my exposure to the *Cursillo* movement. *Cursillo in Cristianidad* (A Short Course in Christianity) originated among the laity of the Roman Catholic Church in Spain as a means to encourage the men in the parishes to be spiritual leaders, rather than sitting on the sidelines leaving the responsibility for spiritual life of the parish and their children to the women. At that time the women tended to be the guardians of faith and devotion. By default they were left to raise the children, educate them in the faith, and nurture their children's devotional life.

Cursillo was designed to quicken not only the hearts of the lay men, but also to help them be forthcoming with their faith and be committed partners with their wives in the life of their parish. I attended one of the first ones in the United States which was sponsored by the Roman Catholic Archdiocese of San Francisco, and was touched by the spiritual authenticity of the leadership.

Because it was an early expression of the *Cursillo* in the United States, the retreat I attended had not been Americanized, and it retained its strongly monastic and penitential flavor.* Being one with this gathering of men from all walks of life was a stirring experience. The staff were true servants, and our every need was anticipated in order that each of us might be able to concentrate on his inner spiritual journey.

The *Cursillo* was an oasis. Because I had spent so much time among "the garbage and the flowers," it was a comfort to be among people of faith. This gathering of men whom I joined were not so much leaning out for love, as learning how they might be instrument of peace to others. They had a basis for their faith. The *Cursillo* Movement would turn out to be a key resource when I designed the Credo Weekend.

Thorns Among The Flowers

My preparation was now complete. I knew that something had to be done to address the plague which was enveloping our youth.

My immersion in the culture encompassed a broad spectrum. The hospital wards of Vietnam psychiatric casualties; the youth drug unit of "flower children"; the many young people I talked to

---

* Over the ensuing 25 years in the United States *Cursillo* has evolved into several mutations. Today, the gatherings often include men and women together, a far different dynamic than a retreat composed of a homogeneous gathering of men, or of women. In many instances, the Spanish penitential element which causes discomfort for many Americans has been soft pedaled. In fact, I understand that in some areas of the country even the Spanish vocabulary has been eliminated as "foreign." The resulting danger is that the consideration of the pain of the human condition is neglected in the rush to enjoy the emerging fellowship of love. The result can be a shallow joy. I am speaking of particular instances, and not making a sweeping generalization. There are many modern day *cursillistas* who have had their lives genuinely changed and are powerful contributors to the lives of local churches.

on Telegraph Avenue, Berkeley, and Haight Ashbury, San Francisco; the hundreds of youth mesmerized by the rock concerts at the Fillmore and the Avalon; and finally the violence of drugs at the massive outdoor gathering at Altamont became etched in my mind.

This latter was the capstone of my experience. The people of San Francisco were envious of the Woodstock "love-in" concert, which had been held in New York, earlier in the summer. The general feeling was that if New York, with all its "bad vibes," could host such a beautiful event of love and music, then San Francisco was capable of the ultimate expression of the "Age of Aquarius." Mick Jagger and the Rolling Stones said this concert would be their "Christmas present to America." Included on the bill were such groups as the Jefferson Airplane, The Grateful Dead, Country Joe and the Fish, and The Flying Burrito Brothers.

So many people streamed in from all over the nation that successively larger sites for the concert needed to be identified. Finally, the Altamont Speedway was selected. The day of the event was a raw and overcast December morning, with an ominous feeling in the air which reminded me of a landscape in an Ingmar Bergman film. With our young son Tim perched on my shoulders, Ruth and I joined the crowd, numbering in the thousands. The hills were covered with people, many of whom were high on alcohol, acid, and other drugs.

We were packed in, with cars permitted to park on the freeway as a concession to the size of the crowd. Around us people on acid were groaning as a result of "bad trips." It was a frightening time—not at all what we had anticipated. Finally, after a long succession of other groups, Mick Jagger pranced onto the stage for his calculatedly outrageous performance. But soon we could see fighting breaking out at the foot of the stage, and a wave of fear enveloped us all. Thousands of us watched while a man was beaten to death, spilling on to the stage next to the prancing feet of Mick Jagger, who by this time was singing "Sympathy for the Devil" in an attempt to calm the audience. The "Christmas present to America" had become something quite different. It was apocalyptic.

Let Go, Let God

As a result of my medical and cultural exposure I became the primary resource for the Chaplain Corps, and one of only a handful in the naval services with any comprehension of the immediacy of the challenge ahead. Drugs were entering into the main stream of our culture, and things would never be the same again. I felt a strong conviction that I must do everything within my power to help channel this revolutionary energy toward a constructive spiritual end. I felt privileged to be selected by the Chaplain Corps for this year-long residency, and I repaid the confidence the Corps had shown in me by working hard to understand the generation to whom we were called to minister.

But with apparently little value attached to the unique expertise I had just acquired, the Navy issued me orders to go to Okinawa to serve as a conventional chaplain with the Marines. In addition to my regular duties, and with no extra funding or administrative support, I was tasked with the development of a multi-pronged assault on the drug problem. In less than a year, I was expected to accomplish the design and execution of what would have to be a sophisticated and in-depth program.

There I was in San Francisco on the front lines, and sometimes behind the enemy lines, of a struggle for the spirit of a new generation. Since it would be too much to expect that those in the Naval Annex in Alexandria could absorb the scope of the problem, I wrote the chaplain assignment desk a letter. I impressed upon them the complexity and immediacy of the problem. If the Navy were truly serious about confronting this issue, I observed, the response to the drug culture must be my primary duty. I asked that I be assigned to the Marines for three years rather than one, with additional staff support and funding in order to complete the task. Finally, I asked that my tour be an accompanied one. I knew that the next three years would be grueling ones for me, even with the invaluable support of my wife Ruth and our son.

The Chaplain Corps was not responsive. In retrospect, I can understand their reaction, a brash young officer telling his seniors what they ought to do. But this never entered my mind. I was so convinced of the severity of the problem, so aware of the tragedies of the youth around me, that I had to speak out. Those who have viewed the decline and fall of the idealistic heroes of the movies *Platoon*, *Born on the Fourth of July*, and *The Deerhunter* will have an understanding of the moral corrosion which was taking place.

I kept turning the situation over in my mind in order to assure myself that I was not making the request for some selfish motive. I came to the conclusion that if the Navy chose to use my talents I would go anywhere for them, even into a war which deeply disturbed me. On the other hand, if I was to be merely window dressing to mollify some Marine general who wanted something done about "pot," and was assigned to a regular one year tour with no additional resources devoted to addressing the major issue of our youth, then my mission would be doomed to futility.

I had a further problem as well. I knew the devastation of a broken family with an absent father. I knew it personally in my own life, and I knew it in the countless stories of the men I counseled. Conservatively speaking, I would estimate that 90 percent of the troubled men I counseled came from broken families with absent or inadequate fathers. As a Navy chaplain I was willing to accept the sacrifice imposed on our family by our being separated. But I was less willing to jeopardize my family if I was to be sent off on a fool's errand.

With great misgivings, and after much prayer, self examination, and discussion with Ruth, I prepared a letter resigning my commission. I loved going to sea with the sailors, Marines and Coast Guardsmen I served. I felt a part of a wonderful family. But the people on the streets of Berkeley—they were my brothers and sisters too. Any way it turned out, I would always have my own precious family of Ruth and our baby Tim who gave meaning to my life.

Before my letter was acted upon, the new Chief of Chaplains, Francis Garrett, visited the Bay Area. Even though I was preparing to leave the Navy, I made an appointment to see him. I felt strongly for my shipmates and their spiritual struggles. "If I am not meant to be the one with them," I thought, "maybe I can reach the Chief so that he can respond in another way."

I waited in the chapel on Treasure Island, in the middle of San Francisco Bay, to see Chaplain Garrett. It was the same chapel I had visited for solitary prayer many times as a young ensign in the Coast Guard during my first years of faith. The wait was a long one, filled with self-doubt—which is not unusual for a person from my childhood background. Perhaps I am being stubborn, or too zealous, I thought. Again I questioned my motives. Am I using this as a ruse to stay with my family, and to get out of the war? But as I prayed I felt at peace, I felt the love of my spiritual Father.

When it was my time to say my piece, I was pleased to meet the man before me. Frank Garrett was a warm, open Methodist from the South, with a little flavor of the country in him. I explained my convictions, much as I had a year or two before to Chaplain Hutcheson. He listened intently as I tried to help him appreciate the crisis of the spirit we faced.

I gave him copies of two papers from the Bay Area: one was the underground *Berkeley Barb*, the other was the *Rolling Stone*, at that time a radical paper. I asked him to look them over as he flew back to Washington—I wanted him to see first hand. Finally I looked into his eyes and said, "If there is any way I can be of help, even though I won't be in the Navy, I'll be there." Frank put his arm on my shoulder and asked me to wait a few days before I made any decisions.

About 1:00 in the afternoon a few days later a call came to me at home, I think from Chaplain Hutcheson. He told me that the Chaplain Corps had decided to initiate a comprehensive approach to the spiritual and social condition of the men and women of the naval services and their families. Chaplain Jim Williams, who was particularly interested in the self-destructive nature of alcoholism which was rife in the naval services, would head up the Chaplain Corp's approach to alcohol. Chaplain Ray Fitzgerald, one of the pioneers of Clinical Pastoral Education in the Navy, and who came from the perspective of pastoral care, would head up the ministry of marriage and family. (Ray is now chief of the Department of Spiritual Ministry to the National Institutes of Health.)

I was to remain in the Navy to address the problems associated with drug abuse. He hastened to add, that after this assignment I could count on being separated from my family, and that if this was a problem, I did not belong in the Navy.

It is hard to express how grateful I felt. It had taken trust and discipline to do nothing but be open and concerned. It had taken faith in my own value to trust my judgment, but that is all I needed to do. "Trust the process," say some. "Let go and let God," say others. For any person it is difficult, for one from a chaotic childhood it feels dangerous. And now, by trusting my essential integrity, I could remain with my family, and I could devote my energy to serve those with whom I felt so close, my Navy family of sailors, Marines and fellow chaplains.

3

The Launching Of Credo, 1971-1974

San Diego has the highest concentration of sailors and Marines in the Pacific, and I was tasked by the Chaplain Corps to devise a curriculum for chaplains to help them respond to those young men and women involved in drugs and the counter-culture. Because of their understandably limited acquaintance with the problem, some of the chaplain administrators in Washington envisioned my approach as confined to a series of descriptive lectures so that a chaplain could recognize such a sailor or Marine when he or she came for counsel.

But in my eyes this would be missing our vocation as spiritual leaders. I saw my mission in broader terms. Evidence and symptoms of drug use are the tools of the police and the medics. As chaplains we needed to recognize and to respond to the spiritual malaise these young people were experiencing.

The best way to help chaplains and other leaders respond to the spiritual hunger, which was at the base of the sailors' behavior, was first to *broaden* their perspective, so that they were not fixated on the symptom but rather addressed the spiritual cause, a feeling of alienation. After broadening their field of vision, it was important next to *deepen* their vision as well, to help them see that the root cause of alienation and insecurity is a yearning for love.

This yearning, I believe, lies within all of us, whether in the Navy or not. Not only is there no essential difference between the needs of the sailor swabbing the deck, the carrier pilot flying a *Tomcat*, and the captain standing on the bridge, but also there is no difference between the executive, the home-maker, or the telephone repair man. We can best achieve this crucial level of insight by addressing our own inner lives, our own spirituality, so as to be able to respond to the lives of others.

In considering my assigned task, I felt that to teach chaplains how to deal with drugs was essentially a matter of teaching them how to relate more intimately with the alienated youth who were drug users. Many chaplains were ill-prepared because, while they were familiar with administering chapel programs, they felt intimidated by the counter culture which rejected the very programs that the chaplains found useful. Chapel worship and Bible studies presumed a spiritual grounding which the young people lacked. Twenty three years later, in a publication of the Chaplain Corps Resource Board, my vision was validated:

> Over a two month period the chaplain [Jerry Waddell, Naval Station, Annapolis MD] welcomed 50 new personnel to the command. He found that 48 indicated "no preference" on his indoc questionnaire. "No

way!" he thought. After a face to face interview with these same 50, he discovered that, "34 sailors, that is 14 males and 20 females, told me they had received no religious direction as children. They had never, not even once, been inside a church, synagogue, or mosque."

The chaplain contacted Credo Norfolk to arrange for a Personal Growth Retreat [Credo Weekend] for himself, and six of his sailors per month. "Aftercare will take place here, in small groups. ...

"The retreats will give us a common experience and language to talk about spirituality and chapel activities."

Many chaplains harbored numerous misconceptions, as did the people they were called to serve. For example, many chaplains judged an individual sailor's action as wrong — and rejected the sinner along with the sin. By doing so they diminished their ability to see them as part of their flock. At the same time, many of the sailors expected rejection, were wary of both officers and clergy, and did what they could to maintain distance.

I remember riding back on a bus from the first Credo Weekend seated behind a conventional good-hearted chaplain and an unconventional woman sailor. Trying to break the awkward silence between them, the chaplain started up a conversation by pointing out the window at a long-haired young man, and remarking scornfully, "I can't figure out whether that is a man or a woman." The young woman turned with a certain perverse sense of glee and said, "It really doesn't matter, does it, unless you want to fuck him." There was no further communication between them for the rest of the trip.

The chaplain did not realize that for the woman, as well as for many other young sailors and Marines, the chaplain was someone to fear. She later told me that she ordinarily avoided chaplains because of her experience with her father and other men who mistreated her in her childhood; as well as her exposure to judgmental clergy who did not come to her assistance during those trying days.

With such complex issues clouding potentially helpful relationships, I thought, what better way to sweep away misconceptions on the part of both clergy and service personnel than to have them live together in close quarters for a few days, sleep in the same room, use the same bathroom, eat at the same table? Not only would it help the chaplains realize that these youths, whom they were called to serve, were not essentially different from their own sons and daughters; but also it would help the young men and women to see that the chaplains could be caring fathers.* Their shared humanity would be the meeting ground.

My crucial decision was to designate music as the common ground for communication. So often I would hear the leadership say, "I don't understand these kids. They irritate me, and I don't know what they are thinking." "Turn on the radio," I would reply, "It's no mystery. The medium of this generation is music." Cassettes, transistor radios, and stereo technology were making music constantly available. It provided a particular fascination for those in the world of hallucinogenic drugs, such as LSD. "Listen to the Beatles, Bob Dylan, Joan Baez, Jefferson Airplane, The Rolling Stones," I would add, "They express what the youth are concerned about."

Many chaplains listened with incredulity to my recommendation that they listen to the music. Some of the conservatives would

---

*There were no women chaplains at the time.

refuse to listen, dismissing the music as unworthy of consideration. It was, they said, chaotic and demonic. And, in a way they were right. Certainly Janis Joplin sung of the demons within her tortured soul. Moreover, Jimmy Hendrix expressed the moral chaos of America in his deliberately offensive rendition of "The Star Spangled Banner." But there were worse demons let loose at My Lai and Kent State. The challenge of the time was to get people together, living together, even for a few hours. Perhaps through music, I thought, not only could they recognize their common needs, but also their ability to respond to each other out of compassion, rather than fear.

Release Your Song

One cannot overemphasize the importance of music. It cuts through barriers erected in the intellect and goes to the heart. More than words and instruction, music cuts to the core. I remember taking my family to visit my father for the last time on an Alzheimer's ward. We were saddened by the shell of a man who was before us. A world renowned scientist, director of the Nutritional Biochemistry Laboratory at MIT, one of the pioneers in the field of vitamins, my father was now a frail ghost of his former self. All those years of research accompanied by brilliant lectures were gone. In their place was a man expressing incomprehensible sentence fragments, who was frustrated by his incoherence.

In one last attempt to communicate with him, I said, "Dad, your grandson Jonathan is here and he has with him the trumpet you played when you were a boy in high school. He wants to play you a song he has learned." Jonathan, age 12, put the trumpet to his lips and started playing the sweet old song, *You Are My Sunshine*. To my astonishment I saw my father's lips move, and I could hear him singing along quietly, as clearly as any one could. My eyes were moist as I realized that we had connected, perhaps for the last time.

In the movie *Awakening*, Robin Williams plays a compassionate psychiatrist who is determined to break through the horrible barrier of autism. Although his colleagues had tried all other means to help these patients, they had failed. But this doctor insisted on using music, and miraculously he was able to bring some of the patients to life for a while.

On the psychiatric wards of Vietnam casualties, I, more than once, encountered severely troubled servicemen who seemed to find solace playing the piano, or listening to music. One time, as I mentioned earlier, I heard the lyrics of *Here Comes the Sun* echoing down the corridor of the locked ward. Music is as primal as it is powerful.

In the decade of the 1960's, it was more than that. Music was the common language of a whole generation. Because of the advancement of technology which brought the portable radio and cassette, music could be present in the 1960's as never before in history. Just as we in the 1990's find it hard to imagine a time without drugs, or without television for that matter, so it is difficult to conceive of a time when, for the majority who were not musicians, music was confined to the concert hall and the phonograph console. Today, as we drive down the street with our stereo cassette or CD player in our cars, we do not have a second thought as we pass joggers at the side of the road wearing earphones and a wire leading to a Walkman attached to their shorts. All of this came into being in the 1960's, and it has progressed to a point where music is truly ubiquitous.

In the 1960's music emerged as the voice that spoke to the young people in a revolutionary way. Gone were ballads such as Frankie Laine's *Wild Goose*, Doris Day's *A Guy Is A Guy*, or Sarah Vaughan's *Mr. Sandman*. In their place the airways were flooded with social commentaries that were available 24 hours a day. John Lennon's *Give Peace A Chance*, for example, was an articulation of war weariness which constantly entered the minds of the young listeners. So powerful was its message that it has been resurrected today in Bosnia and Israel, as a plea to stop the fighting. Whether or not the messages are encouraging or perverse, they are constantly present. To dismiss the music as immoral or socially destructive does not mean that the songs cease to affect our society.

Getting Underway

In mid-1971 I wrote a Credo *Project Design* as a proposal to the Navy stating that Credo was to be based on the following presuppositions. First, that reconciliation is possible, ". . . Through God's love people can unite as brothers and sisters and be members of one body, instead of destroying themselves." Second, that affirmation of the individual is essential: that each person needs to know that he or she is a sacred being, valuable in God's sight despite his or her multiple imperfections. Third, that through self affirmation, we are able to form that relationship with our Creator and our brothers and sisters which is essential to health.

I met with Chaplains O. Ray Fitzgerald and Jim Williams, who were working on allied projects as part of the over-all program, and shared my convictions. I told them of my experience with *Cursillo*, quickly pointing out that the population we were addressing in the Navy and Marine Corps had at least three significant differences from those who were envisioned by the architects of *Cursillo* in Spain:

First, unlike *Cursillo*, the Credo design should presume no faith on the part of the participants. At the time *Cursillo* was founded, Christianity was the integrating principle of a still-insular Spain. But the culture of the United States was further along the road to fragmentation, so that we could assume neither any common ethical position, nor even a common spiritual metaphor.

Second, the *Cursillo* pattern followed authoritative lectures (*rollos*) that were drawn from an accepted corpus of knowledge (Christian doctrine) and followed by periods of small group and individual reflection. In our case, because the trend of our American youth culture was to distrust *all* authority, it meant that there existed no such thing as an authoritative position which presumed a common ethical understanding existed. The values expressed would have to come out of the common experience of the community on the Credo Weekend.

Third, the most widely accepted metaphor used by contemporary American culture to express their deepest concerns was not scripture, the bed rock of *Cursillo*, but contemporary music. Hence music would become the common language of Credo.

All this notwithstanding, the key ingredient brought by *Cursillo* to Credo (which is also basic to the Twelve Step programs) was its insistence that all people be treated as of equal value, and that the role of the leaders of the retreat was that of servant to the others. Once Ray, Jim, and I thought through the proposed structure, the rest was easy. During the years in the Bay Area I had been immersed in the music scene of the upcoming generation. Immersion that, coupled with my graduate work in literature and my long-standing interest in jazz and the blues, made easy my selection of the music that would coincide with a constructive approach to spirituality. And so the Credo Weekend was born.

The Christening

As with any birth, there is always the question of the name. Just before Christmas in 1970, Ruth and I, and our toddler son Tim, moved into our home in Pacific Beach. I tried out names with Ruth as we unpacked boxes and decorated our tree, with a dog and little child in tow.

One name which appealed to me was *Crux*, for the new program was an attempt to help people get to the crux of their lives and make decisions at the crux, or crossroads, of their lives. Of course, the word had an additional meaning of "the Cross" to those of a Christian sensibility.

However, there was a great problem. The Navy is notorious for acronyms (such as CINCUSNAVEUR, TRAGRUPAC, COMNAVACTS). To suggest to the Navy that *Crux* only meant "crux" would be incomprehensible to them. And there was no word I could manufacture beginning with the letter "X." Xylophone, xanthan gum, xenophobia, I tried them all. Thus *Crux* was dead in the Navy's acronymic waters.

Since we wanted to help people come to decisions about what they did believe, what were their core values, and what was keeping them from feeling whole, I chose the word Credo purely for its objective meaning: Latin for "I believe." As with *crux*, it had an added meaning for those who were people of faith who subscribed to a common creed.

The irony is that Credo turned out to be almost as difficult to fit to an acronym as *Crux* would have been. For a very brief time, a matter of months, I contrived the acronym Credo: *Chaplains'*

Response to the Emerging Drug Order. The cumbersome acronym caught on. In retrospect, we should have stayed with Credo, and forgotten expectation of an acronym. Credo stands by itself. Any contrivance only detracts from the purity of the concept: belief. And the introduction of the word *drug*, with its emotionally charged baggage, clouded the focus of Credo—which was on spirituality, rather than on drug use, the symptom of a lack of spirituality.

Later in the Navy it became (and still is) Credo: *Chaplains Religious Education and Development Operation*. Both are bureaucratic barbarisms of the first water. I think one indication that God has a sense of humor is that my first atrocious attempt at an acronym (referring to the "emerging drug order") follows me like the plague. The point to remember is that Credo is both the name and the concept. All acronyms are merely administrative contrivances.*

I chose Raintree Ranch in Julian, California as the site for the Workshops because it was in a mountainous rural area about an hour away from Credo House in San Diego—far enough so that people had time to "shift gears," yet close enough to be logistically manageable. The area itself was less a ranch than a lodge set within woods and brush.

The core of the first group who went on the Weekend consisted of a gathering of ten sailors who were on their way out of

---

* In the interest of simplicity, the Navy's CREDO (Chaplains Response to the Emerging Drug Order), CREDO (Chaplains Religious Enrichment Development Operation), and the civilian expressions of Credo (as in Credo/Esperanza and Credo Institute) will all appear as "Credo."

the Navy due to misconduct. Their commands were delighted to be rid of them for a few days, and the sailors were pleased to get away from the oppressive atmosphere they found in the transient barracks. A few adventurous chaplains joined them. In order to welcome those people who were wary of institutional religion, we chose to avoid the term *retreat*, which at that time had solely religious connotations, and settled on the term *Workshop*, which was essentially a neutral word.

All of us rode up on a bus together to Raintree Ranch and began the *Workshop* (Weekend). The retreat format Jim Williams and Ray Fitzgerald and I worked out together unfolded just as expected, although the chaplains had more difficulty being candid than the enlisted people. And this was also to be expected. For many clergy, maintaining the public *persona* of a minister, priest or rabbi is second nature. They are apt to feel they have more at stake in maintaining their image than does the sailor whose image is one of "saltiness"—of being a little wild and irresponsible. In fact, the recruiting slogan at the time was "Sailors Have More Fun."

As the hours passed and the group listened to music, talked, ate, and slept in the same berthing area in their sleeping bags, the first indications of mutual acceptance began to emerge. One of the chaplains told of having trouble with a son who was the same age as many in the room. With the help of one of the sailors, the chaplain was able to talk through his frustration. As a result, a young person was able to form an open relationship with an older man, something that sailor had never been able to do before, and the chaplain had new tools with which to approach his son. A young woman felt accepted as an equal within the group. A chaplain talked of his misgivings about the war. Trust was built within what was becoming for some a surrogate family.

In the weeks that followed that first Workshop, Credo House, the staging area for the retreat, became a haven of friendship for the participants. They enjoyed helping with the renovation of the building, some of them spending their off-hours, their liberty time, together rolling on gallons of paint on the many walls.

Setting The Course

On the day after the first Weekend was completed, I traveled across San Diego Bay to Coronado to meet a carrier pilot. He was to be tasked by another part of the Navy to respond to the disillusionment which was becoming more pronounced in the naval services. While waiting to see him, I struck up a conversation with a captain, Charles "Chick" Rauch, who, by chance, was sitting beside me in the waiting room. Absorbed by my enthusiastic account of the Weekend, he urged me to look him up when I went to Washington to report on the progress of Credo. He said that his new office was to be right down the passageway from the Chaplain Corps complex.

Within a matter of days I was called to the Chief of Chaplains office where I reported in detail about the initial success and great potential of the Credo Project. Although the Chaplain Corps administrators expressed interest in the concept of Credo, they were discouraging about the prospect of providing not only substantial funding, but also administrative personnel support. As I mentioned earlier, many of them seemed to hold a restricted view of what the program might do.

So convinced was I of the worth of this new ministry, that I doubt I even considered hearing "no" for an answer. Remembering the invitation Captain Rauch had extended to me in the anteroom in Coronado, I walked into his office, following my conversation with the chaplains, only to find that he was now wearing two stars. He had been selected over many of his seniors to be a rear admiral and subsequently was appointed via a Z-Gram by his good friend Elmo Zumwalt (the Chief of Naval Operations, who had a revolutionary view of how personnel should be treated)) to head what would become the Human Resources arm of the Navy.

Admiral Rauch could call upon resources far in excess of anything the Chaplain Corps had available. In a matter of minutes, he offered ten times the funding that the Chaplain Corps could afford. In addition, he made available six administrative positions to help with the management of Credo. Subsequently, he worked closely with Frank Garrett, the admiral heading the Chaplain Corps with whom I had talked earlier in San Francisco. Thus Admiral Rauch was able to provide the fledgling Credo community with high profile institutional legitimacy. But what truly lent Credo legitimacy were the men and women whose lives were visibly changed by the experience.

As I reviewed each Weekend I saw that the more diverse the mix, the greater was the freedom of interchange. The workshops progressively became more inclusive. First, it was the young "bad actors" who, after attending a Credo Weekend, were acting responsibly on their jobs. Next, it was their older supervisors, who attended Weekends out of curiosity to see what had made such a powerful impact on their crew members. Finally came the wives and husbands of the leadership, who left the Weekends feeling their marriages strengthened.

Perhaps one of the most dramatic examples of the progression of Credo is the story of the inter-relationship of Seaman Charlie Bamforth, a young sailor with office experience; and a naval aviator, Captain Brad Hall, the executive officer of the Naval

Air Rework Facility whose responsibility was to oversee the repair of fighter planes so that they might return to the battle front.

A teenage barbiturate addict, Charlie had failed all conventional treatment and was being discharged from the Navy as "untreatable." I asked my commanding officer if he would assign Charlie to my staff because we needed his secretarial help, and in return I felt that we could help him. "What if he overdoses again?" the captain responded. I replied that in such a case we would take him to the hospital again, but that we hoped the affirmation he would receive from us might make that a moot question. "If Bamforth dies," the captain warned in the dire tones of a professional naval officer, "it won't look good on your fitness report." But Charlie didn't die. In fact, he did quite well. In the process he changed the life of a senior naval officer. Here is an excerpt from Charlie and Brad's account of their Credo encounter:

Charlie Bamforth
"My Credo Experience"

In 1973 I was 19 years old, in the Navy, and lost. I had been using drugs since I was 13, and by the time I was 19 I had been addicted to barbiturates and had gone through several drug rehabilitation programs. The pattern was that I would go through detoxification, take part in a program, and then return to using drugs shortly after leaving the program.

All this changed when I took part in a Credo Weekend. I am not saying that the Weekend itself cured me from my addiction to drugs. It was the beginning of the cure for me. My continued involvement with Credo after the Weekend helped provide me with the tools necessary for me to live a sober life.

The Launching Of Credo, 1971-1974 ◆ 69

I remember my first and second Credo Weekends very well. The first time around I was so intoxicated that I did not get much from the experience. But the one thing I did gain was the knowledge that someone cared, and that there was a possibility for a different lifestyle. It was during the second Credo Weekend that I finally began to make the changes necessary to save my life. I remember that I went on the Weekend because I wanted to be with some friends who were going.

On the evening of the first day, after our group sessions, my friend and I decided to take some LSD. I knew that this was against the rules, but at that time I was not making very wise choices for myself. As a result of taking the acid I was awake all night, walking through the woods. When morning came, and it was time for the group to gather together, I decided I did not want to participate. I was tired, and I was coming down from the drug. I was severely depressed. Instead of joining the group I went upstairs to one of the bedrooms, crawled into a sleeping bag, and tried to shut out everything that was around me.

I heard footsteps coming up the stairs and prepared myself for a confrontation with one of the staff members. I was ready to be chastised for breaking the rules., In fact, I was sure that the staff was going to ask me to leave the retreat center. Instead I saw the leader, Don. His face showed me he was very worried, and concerned. He asked me what was going on, and why I did not want to be a part of the group. I don't remember what I said, but I do remember that I was trying to shock him, to get him off my back so that I could sleep.

Finally I said that I was coming down from taking acid, and that was why I was hiding from the group. I fully expected Don to be angry with me, with the hopes that he would be disgusted and would leave me alone. Instead I noticed something that took me by surprise. Instead of being angry, Don had tears in his eyes. He talked with me, and told me why he felt sad. He said that he knew I was a sensitive person, someone who had a great deal to offer to the world, and for some reason I was killing myself with drugs. He said that it hurt him, because he did not know how to reach me, and that it was the sensitive people like me who died from drug use.

For the first time that I can remember, someone showed me that they cared about me. Not because I was a statistic, or because he was curious about what went on in the mind of a junkie, but because of who I was. He offered to help me! Not only that, but he told me that he loved me and cared about what I was doing to myself.

As the Weekend progressed I joined the group again. As I participated I began to see that the pain and isolation I felt was not abnormal, that other people felt those same feelings. I discovered that I was not the only one in the world who was lost, who felt unloved, worthless. And I gained something very valuable, I gained a sense of hope.

I realized that I did not have to continue to destroy my mind and body with chemicals. That somebody cared about what I was doing, that when I hurt myself I was affecting other people as well. Don's tears stay with me to this day, twenty years later. Whenever I feel like nobody cares, or that I am worthless, I remember those tears and I gain the strength I need to do what is necessary to get out of that depression.

After that Weekend I worked at the Credo House. Don had arranged for me to be temporarily transferred. I had some office skills that Credo put to use, and I worked hard at cleaning up my life. It was not easy. I met a friend, Brad, at Credo who helped me a great deal, along with Don and other staff members. Brad was at that time a captain in the Navy,

The Launching Of Credo, 1971-1974 ◆ 71

and I was the lowest rank of enlisted men. But at Credo this didn't make a difference. My friend was my friend, not a captain. Don and Brad together helped me work through the most difficult time of my life.

There were setbacks. There was a time when I accidentally overdosed on barbiturates and almost died. Other times when I just could not resist the temptation to get high. I was honest with the staff, and when I messed up I admitted it. It was a hard struggle to break free of the drugs. Only someone who has been addicted to something as powerful as drugs can really understand the struggles I went through.

No matter how many times I messed up, how many times I disappointed myself and those who cared about me, the love was always there. In retrospect I guess many of the times that I went back to using drugs was so that I could prove to my friend, Brad, Don, and others that I was a hopeless case. I wanted them to abandon me, to give up because I had given up on myself. But they just would not leave me alone. They would not allow me to feel sorry for myself, nor would they let me push them away from me.

After a period of time, when I was off of drugs, the leader asked me to assist in the Weekends. It was through these experiences that I stopped thinking so much about my own needs, and began to care about other people. By reaching out, in love to others, I was really reaching inward, tapping into the sensitivity and love that is me.

The support from Credo made the difference in my life. It has been eighteen years of being drug free. There are still times when I am tempted, times when I feel depressed and want to use, but Credo has given me the skills necessary to make it through those times.

I am now an ordained minister, serving a mid-sized congregation as pastor. There is no way in this world that

Don, my friend Brad, or I would have dreamed this is what I would be doing 18 years after my first encounter with Credo. Through Credo I was able to get in touch with the wonderful person that God created when He made me. Not only did I discover that person, I learned the tools necessary for that person to grow and blossom.

The following is a companion piece to "My Credo Experience" from the perspective of Charlie's friend, Brad:

Brad Hall
"My Wilderness Journey"

It all began in 1971 when I met Charlie for the first time. I was asked by my Commanding Officer to attend a Credo Weekend as an observer to see if we wanted to send some of our young lads in the Command.

Charlie and I met at that workshop. He was a severe drug abuser; I was a successful Naval aviator/engineer. Charlie was a "loser," I was a "winner."

Charlie went to be cared for, treated, and healed; I went to watch and observe.

There were about 30 young men and women attending, all were going through incredibly difficult life experiences. It was a tough and honest workshop, and I heard stories of early life experiences which not only shocked me, but which often I just could not believe.

The Launching Of Credo, 1971-1974 ◆ 73

By closing time on Sunday I was thoroughly beat, depressed, and confused. Near the end of the time, during a lull in the group meeting, one of the lads turned to me and shouted out, "Well, Brad, what's wrong with you?" I sputtered and stammered out, "Why, nothing." I was so caught by his question I didn't know what to say. But his question was like an arrow which pierced my very soul.

That afternoon we all got on the bus to go home and I sat next to the leader. I was watching the scenery out the window when he turned to me and said, "Brad, what are we going to do about Charlie?" Charlie, the young sailor, was withdrawn through most of the workshop, unable to respond to the world around him. I said, "I don't know, but *you've got a problem there*," and continued to stare out the window all the way home.

Three days later I received a call from the Naval Hospital. God only knows how they got my name, but they called me at home and said, "We have this kid named Charlie in the hospital, recovering from a drug overdose. He was about gone, but we revived him, and he asked for you." I said, "Charlie? Oh, that one." So I put on my best uniform and drove over to the Navy hospital.

Charlie was laid out in the intensive care unit, unkempt, weighing about 85 pounds. They unplugged all of the things that were attached to him and literally handed him to me. I didn't know what to do, so I took him home to my wife, Carole, who, as a nurse, could take care of him if I couldn't. I put him in the family room, laid him on the couch and said, "Carole, you take care of him." I went back to work on my airplanes.

Well she did, of course, and very well. He lay there disheveled for about a week on our new white couch. Every now and then Carole would try to invite him out to have some lunch or dinner, but it was very difficult even to communicate with him.

Then, after a week of having him at home and with our family, Charlie began to come out. He never really spoke, but he did come out and eat a bit, as our two year old Susan chattered away to entertain him.

The next Weekend we had a party at our House. I remember standing in the hallway looking into two rooms at one time. They were divided by a wall and open at one end. In one room were all my Navy friends, dressed and happy, enjoying a wonderful evening. In the other room lay Charlie depressed, sick, and having a lousy evening. I might add that although that room was open for all to see into, not one of my Navy friends said a word about who he was, or why he was there. I didn't realize it at the time but that image of those two rooms mirrored the two sides of what was happening in my life.

Finally, there came a time when I could stand it no longer, so I sent Charlie back to his unit saying he had to do something about himself: "shape up or ship out." Charlie called me, or I called him, or somehow or other we met at the Credo House practically every day for three years. And I have to be honest with you as I tell you this, it wasn't an easy thing for me to do, and it wasn't really what I wanted to do. There were times when I hated it. It was hard to deal with this kid. I never really knew what to do with him, and he kept bringing things up in my life that I didn't want to deal with.

As you might expect, lots of things happened to me and with Charlie over those three years. He began to get well, and finally came out of that incredible shell he lived in for all of his life. ... So did I. Throughout this time, I began to explore what it was that was broken in my life and needed healing. I discovered that in a very real sense even strong, successful naval aviators have a lonely side which cries out for support and wants to participate in life in a deep and meaningful way. I

The Launching Of Credo, 1971-1974 ◆ 75

began to listen, to feel, to relate with people, to explore my faith and my religion. For the first time in my life I opened the Bible and began to read it.

I led a double life for those three years—during the days of my flying and engineering with the Navy; nights and Weekends I was drawn inexorably into the life of Charlie and Credo, and eventually entered the world of my own wilderness journey, on a search for myself and my God.

After this heavy involvement with Credo, the church, and mostly with myself, I got scared. Something was happening to me which I didn't understand and wasn't in my expectations. So I called my Navy Detailer and said, "Get me out of here—I need a new assignment." Well, he did just that, and I wound up with orders to Navy Headquarters in Washington to help develop the new fighter plane—F-18. I was back into the Navy I knew best. I might add that by now Charlie was beginning to do quite well and had even enrolled part-time at San Diego State College.

Carole and I had just settled into our new Virginia house when one early morning, as I was prepping to leave for work, a taxicab rolled up to our front door. Out came the taxi driver, and out came Charlie. "That will be $65," the driver said. It seems Charlie had thumbed his way across the country to "visit" for a while and decided to taxi through the city. We did visit. Indeed it was like an old ghost coming back to haunt me. But now it was clear to me, after that visit, that I wasn't about to shake off Charlie or my Wilderness Journey, or God with a simple move across the country.

The next three years were years of great joy, deep struggle, and decisions. I became quite involved in the ministry of our parish, I took evening courses at the seminary in Alexandria, and eventually explored with a career counselor the possibility of leaving the Navy, which I loved so dearly, and to begin a new career in ministry. Just as I was leaving my office door to pick up my Orders of Retirement from the Navy I was met there by the Director of Flight Operations for NASA and the head astronaut, John Young. They asked if I would consider coming to work with them at NASA, since they heard I was leaving the Navy. It was incredibly tempting, but I said very cavalierly, "Get thee behind me Satan," and I proceeded on down to get my orders.

Finally, in the early morning on July 1, 1977, Carole, Susan, and I loaded up our little green VW and headed off across the country one last time to enter our new life in seminary at Berkeley, California. I should add at this point that just before I left I had received a form letter from Claremont Graduate School and Seminary asking for a recommendation for a young man named Charlie. If I remember it correctly, my response said in essence, "You've got to be kidding!"

What I can say about all this, is very simple and very basic. I learned that when I finally faced up to Charlie's brokenness and struggles I wound up facing mine. There is a wonderful theological 3-liner that goes:

> I sought myself, and myself I could not find.
> I sought my God and He avoided me.
> I sought my brother, and found all three.

I learned that somehow or other we are all in this life together; and though it took five years, it finally dawned on me that my own healing and wholeness, and indeed my salvation, has a lot to do with Charlie's healing and wholeness and his salvation. What I ultimately discovered, of course, is that I didn't save Charlie. He saved me. As Charlie grew up, so did I. As Charlie found new life and God, so did I. It is as simple as that.

The Launching Of Credo, 1971-1974 ◆ 77

In closing, you might be interested to know what happened to Charlie. In May 1980, as I was preparing to graduate from seminary with my Master of Divinity degree, I received a formal invitation from the seminary at Claremont stating that Charlie was graduating with his Doctor of Ministry in Religion. And when I left seminary in June to begin my ministry as an assistant priest at Palo Alto, I received another note from Charlie saying that he was now pastor of not one, but two congregations in Kansas and loving his ministry—where he continues, I am convinced, to save tough, hard-nosed souls like me.

The Rev. Dr. Charles Bamforth is now pastor of a United Church of Christ congregation in Missouri. The Rev. Gordon Bradford Hall is rector of St. Margaret's Episcopal Church in Palm Desert, California and has served as chairman of the board of the Church Divinity School of the Pacific, a part of the Graduate Theological Union in Berkeley, California.

Running On Empty

By the spring of 1972 the Credo Weekends (Workshops) went on at an ever increasing pace. The demand was such that for a brief time I was leading a Weekend from Thursday night to Sunday afternoon. With hardly enough time to refresh my spirit by enjoying the love of my family, I would turn around the next day and lead another from Sunday until Wednesday. In retrospect I can see that I was young, foolish, and driven, for no matter how great the need of others may be, caretakers need first to take care of themselves. To fulfill a caretakers role, I was working myself to the bone and sacrificing my loving relationship with my family, who loved me the most.

The Weekends were remarkable experiences. I remember sitting on the floor of the ranch house living room listening to the Credo tape in which Joan Baez was singing *Where Are You Now, My Son?* Joan recorded the song in Hanoi while feeling the horror of war's impact on children. Through the recording the listener could even hear bombs from American aircraft exploding in the background. I looked around the room and saw several young fliers listening intently: they could have been the ones dropping those bombs whose explosions they heard. Their reaction within the Credo Weekend was pained and searching; theirs was not a self-indulgent navel gazing—they were confronting issues of morality on the most personal of levels.

Between the Weekends, Ruth was always there for me offering love and support in the midst of a grueling schedule. As a mother of a young child, she decided early on that it was best for her not to become immersed in Credo so that she and our home would be for me a haven of refreshment, rather than an extension of my work. The second year we were there we had our second son, Jonathan, who added even more joy to our family. Toward the end of Credo's third year, and after talking with many Credo members who dropped by our home, Ruth began to become integrated into the Credo family—going on Weekends and participating in Credo House activities.

Yet, I found it difficult to separate my Credo family from my own family. I wanted to share with the sailors the beauty of our warm home. Several did come by, playing with our kids and experiencing from Ruth the motherliness lacking in their childhoods, much as I had from Bertha when living with the Ankers. This immersion in a healthy family was good for the lonely and abused sailors.

But, whereas the Ankers had an ongoing and separate life as a dairy family within which I was included, in the case of the Harris family and the Credo family I blurred the lines. Sometimes, in my mind our family existed to serve the emotionally wounded, unaware that I was one of them. In retrospect, I can see the fall-out from my tumultuous childhood: I was more comfortable with people who had experienced similar trauma than I was with my own family who offered me love and acceptance, and often I chose the pain of the trauma to be my primary focus.

The powerful movie, *Fearless*, illustrates the dilemma. *Fearless* is the story of a man who survived a plane crash that so traumatized him that he felt as if he had died. He could relate intimately only to other survivors. To those others who shared his experience he brought comfort and healing: he returned an infant to the arms of a mourning mother; he became father to a young boy who was traveling alone when the plane went down; but he felt distant from his loving wife and their young son. He could relate only through his trauma. As a result, his life was slipping away as he emotionally distanced himself from his family who offered their love to him in his suffering.

He was the loving companion to a grieving Hispanic mother who lost her infant in the crash, but he did not feel close to his wife. He even risked his life so that the grief stricken mother could become whole. But the reason he was so willing to defy death, was that he felt he had died. Finally, his wife convinced the grateful mother that if her helper himself was ever to be whole she needed to treat him as an ordinary man, and not an angel of mercy.

The woman did just that, and as the hero faced himself truthfully, he turned to his wife and said, "You've got to save me." Soon he was stricken, and, but for the mouth to mouth resuscitation of his wife, he would have died. In the last scene as he gasps for the life-giving air which is filling his lungs, he cries to his wife, "*I'm alive!*"

On the Credo Weekends people who have experienced trauma are drawn to each other, and I was certainly one of them. But to the extent that I identified myself with my trauma (in my case, of years gone by), as the hero did in *Fearless*, I was unable fully to receive the nurture which I celebrated within my own family. In the interest of helping others, I cut myself off from normal relationships that would make *me* whole.

A danger is inherent in people who embrace their own struggles as their primary identity. They inflict upon themselves an inaccurate and alienating way of life, as the man did in *Fearless*, and to a lesser extent as I did in Credo. In reality, he and I were more than survivors of trauma, we were full human beings, fathers, and husbands. The irony was that I enabled others to experience on the Credo Weekend that they really were sacred and worthy of love with no strings attached; but as I approached exhaustion from the effort of founding Credo, I found it more difficult to integrate this reality of sacredness into my own self-understanding. I was almost afraid to let go of the pain, because then I would be less effective for others.

Frederick Buechner articulates the situation in which I found myself in his memoir, *Telling Secrets*:

> Love your neighbor as yourself is part of the great commandment. The other way to say it is, Love yourself as your neighbor. Love yourself not in some egocentric self serving sense but love yourself the way you

would love a friend in the sense of taking care of yourself, nourishing yourself, trying to understand, comfort and strengthen yourself. Ministers in particular, people in the caring professions in general, are famous for neglecting themselves with the result that they as people are apt to become in their own way as helpless and crippled as the people they are trying to care for and thus no longer selves who can be of much use to anybody.

A Wolf In Sheep's Clothing?

These were heady times. By late 1973 Credo was seen as useful across the board. I was appointed to the advisory board of the National Council on Drug Abuse. Word of the power of the Credo Weekend soon spread across the San Diego naval community. Credo helped alienated sailors, questioning fliers, young widows, foreign born wives who felt alien in American society, parents who had difficulty understanding their teen-age children, chief petty officers and gunnery sergeants who wanted to be better leaders of the young, and chaplains discovering new ways of living their faith.

I could see that two concerns needed to be addressed before Credo would be on a solid footing. One focused on turf, the second on cost. Some mental heath professionals feared that Credo was actually a religious retreat in the sheep's clothing of a values clarification workshop. They felt that this latter area was their concern, since they were unfettered by religious bias. Their anxiety betrayed their own anti-religious bias, if that is the correct term, for psychology was their religion.

At the same time some evangelical chaplains feared that since the Weekend had no overt evangelistic content, it was actually psychotherapy in the guise of a retreat. So Credo came under assault from both ends, from the aggressive humanists who rejected religion, and, from the equally aggressive religionists who feared secular humanism.

But those professionals and chaplains who actually consented to attend found their fears laid to rest. Rather than observing caregivers competing against each other in an effort to preserve their own orthodoxy, they saw counselor and chaplain, pilot and boatswain's mate working together as brothers and sisters in a common cause.

In addition, the Credo Weekend was soon recognized as cost effective by the management of the Navy since one fighter pilot restored to normal functioning through Credo more than paid for the annual budget of the entire operation. The simple, inexpensive Credo experience increased productivity in the work place for many personnel by replacing malaise with self-respect.

The Healing Community

Central to my concept of Credo is that the Weekend is *never meant to be an end in itself*. It is a foretaste of a new way of living. As an isolated experience the Weekend has no integrity unless it can be integrated into every day living. Therefore, wherever possible the Weekend should not stand in isolation. It needs an anchor, a home base: a place where people can apply what they have experienced on the retreat and can try to live with others in open, trusting relationships. Therefore, a Credo home port, or surrogate family, needed to be available as an area of safety for those who wanted to change the way they related to others and themselves.

Not all of the Credo Weekend participants were low performers in the Navy, by any means. For example, Credo was proud to include Judy Neuffer, the first woman flier in the Navy, as an active member of the family. She was intimately involved in the day-to-day life of the community, as was Carolyn Akter, one of the most senior women line officers. Then there was an unusually caring man, Colonel Fagan, head of security at the vast Marine Corps Base at Camp Pendleton, not to mention, as you know, Captain Brad Hall.

Picking a site for Credo House in San Diego was another subtle decision. On the one hand, the building had to be owned by the Navy—for we did not have the authority or the funds to acquire a civilian property even if it were advisable. On the other hand, many of the people whom we sought to reach distrusted the Navy. If Credo House appeared to be the locus of a heavy-handed military authority, it would preclude any chance of it serving as a home to the spiritually homeless, as a place where they could be with "family."

The solution was an abandoned fire-house in a prime tourist location in downtown San Diego, across from the *Star of India* sailing ship along San Diego Harbor. Although the building was owned by the Navy, it was only partially enclosed by the chain link fence typical of military installations. By cutting a new entrance in the building to provide access from the street, we kept every constituency happy. The conservatives could take comfort that Credo House was a Navy building, subject to Navy security on Navy property. At the same time the alienated sailors, Marines, and pilots could have a sense of autonomy, since they could come and go from their Credo home in civilian clothes without surveillance. Credo House was the locus of our life together. For many, the Weekend was indeed a new way of looking at life. Rather than withdrawal and defensiveness, people on the Weekend experienced the kind of world they could live in with trust and openness.

Because of the personal interest of Admiral Rauch, I was able to have a say in who would be assigned to Credo. To a large extent I was able to assemble a staff who set the tone of Credo House in their personal lives. Walt Scherf, whom I knew as a fellow junior officer on my first sea duty on destroyers, was just completing a naval post graduate school in underwater acoustical engineering, and was assigned to Credo as the administrative officer. Walt was a man's man with an agile mind. He had an acute sensitivity for the environment as well as for the sorrow of the human condition in general, and Vietnam in particular.

Molly Malone, a civilian, oversaw our office administration. A warm, caring and highly competent woman, she came to us from New Bedford, Massachusetts. As with Walt, her warmth was not soft and sentimental, but came from her evident integrity as a woman. Richard Parker spread the word about Credo through slide presentations in the vast Naval complex which was San Diego. A young sailor in his twenties, he had a sensitivity for those who grew up in poorly functioning and abusive families.

A key person was a young man, Peter Chase, who came to Credo under a civilian contract. He became the locus of spirituality of the House. He came to us from Canada where he had been working with troubled adolescents. But his strength was not his clinical experience, rather it was his abiding interest in the life of the Spirit. As he lived his own Credo in a quiet, unobtrusive way, Peter was a source of strength and companionship to many sailors and young officers who were searching for meaning to their lives. His apartment, also along the waterfront only a few minutes from Credo House, became a place where Credo sailors congregated.

Of course, from the beginning there was continual dialogue with Ray Fitgerald over at the hospital, and with Jim Williams who was a part of the Credo operation until the Navy's Alcohol Rehabilitation Center got under way in earnest. Another man who emerged as a mainstay of Credo was Marine Chaplain Skip Hughes, also a graduate of psychiatric training at the Naval Hospital in Oakland, who later became my successor at Credo.

Credo House: A Safe Harbor

Credo House was open every day of the year from 8:00 am until midnight. You may recall that the entrance was directly from the street, so that people could come and go at will. As a visitor entered the converted fire-house, he or she was welcomed by a volunteer Credo family member who manned a desk and phone by the doorway. A small library, where anyone was welcome to browse with no questions asked was situated at the entrance, too.

In the library I tried to have an inclusive collection of works which would deal with all aspects of the human spirit. The books ranged from Western and Eastern spirituality to texts addressing the times in which we lived as well as the impact of drug and alcohol use. Also included were classics from the humanities and a few texts from the social sciences.

As people became quickened with the awareness of their own sacred spirit, I hoped that some would like to explore what that meant for themselves, whether it be expressed by Romanesque art, the reflections of Henri Nouwen, the purity of Greek architecture, Fred Rohe's *The Zen of Running*, the psycho-social insights of Harry Stack Sullivan, wilderness camping, The Bible, Robert Carkhuff's *The Art of Helping*, Thomas Merton, Rollo May, *The Dawn of Western Civilization*, John of the Cross and his *Dark Night of the Soul*, or Viktor Frankl's *Logo Therapy*.

There was also a significant section devoted to the visual arts such as works by El Greco, Albrecht Durer, the Flemish masters, Pablo Picasso, and Georges Rouault. Also included were the scores of contemporary music. A folk guitar lay against one of the easy chairs, waiting for anyone to use.

Past the library was an informally decorated Great Room which could hold 50 people with ease. It had couches draped with India print "tapestries," floor lamps and coffee tables rescued from Navy salvage, and a woven grass mat on the floor from wall to wall. We wanted to have the House resemble an informal home for our Credo family members. One of them, a young steward from one of the repair ships, painted a nine foot high mural reproducing a medieval expression of the outstretched arms of a loving God.

In one corner was a meditation room/chapel with pillows around the low wooden chest which served as an altar. A variety of chaplains who had experienced the Weekend volunteered to help provide daily worship at 7:00 PM for those in the community who found Christian worship an affirming experience. Over the chest were two wrought iron and copper mobiles — one of a cross and animals, the other a star of David, both fashioned in Cuernavaca, Mexico. Several Credo family members were married in the small chapel, or brought their children to be baptized by one of the chaplains they had befriended.

Through the door at the back of the Great Room was yet another large room, which, I understand, sometime in the past was the garage area for two fire engines. In this area we held our family pot luck dinners each month. Having befriended local commercial fishermen whose tuna boats were tied up close to Credo House, some sailors secured from them a fishing net with cork floats which served as a canopy across the high ceiling of the room.

The third room, which formerly housed two more fire trucks, contained large wooden work tables, some potter's wheels, and a kiln. For some of the community, particularly those who were more articulate with their hands than with their mouths, working with clay was a wonderful outlet.

As we had hoped, the Credo House quickly became the center of a community of acceptance. At any one time fliers, widows, Marines, officers, sailors, and their families could be found freely enjoying each other's company. Credo House was a place for companionship and refreshment in the troubled world, a safe harbor to mend broken spirits. Most of the people there were far from home, both figuratively and spiritually.

Certainly An Ember

I remember one Thanksgiving Day when the Credo community had gathered: worship for some, dinner for all. As we were approaching the table laden with roast turkey and all the fixings, and enjoying each other's company, the door burst open and in came John, a very young sailor, in bloody clothes. I recognized him from one of the Weekends of the recent past. Putting my arm on his shoulder, I asked him what had happened.

He told me that he had gotten "high" and had decided to see what it would be like to be like Evel Knievel, the motorcycle stunt driver. John had rented a bike, lost control, and smashed into a wall. He was wounded and scared, and the first place he thought of going to was to his friends at Credo. We washed him off and were thankful to discover that his wounds were superficial. He stayed with us, who served as his family, for the rest of the day.

Twenty years later I received a phone call from John, now 37 years old and happily married with two children. He told me that his experience with Credo was a turning point in his life. "It was not a burning bush experience," he laughingly observed, "but at least it was an ember." Soon he traveled down to Williamsburg to attend another Credo Weekend. This is what he wrote just before he left to return to Massachusetts:

As a young sailor of the ripe old age of 18, I encountered my first Credo Weekend in 1973. At the time I had come from a very abused background, which twenty years later still haunts me. At that time I had no idea the degree to which the abuse affected my behavior, or that people could and do care.

I did not become healed from the Credo experience, but the course of my life was deeply changed forever. I was around people who cared for me, who valued what I had to say, who were committed to me in a way I had never experienced before. I began to recognize my worth, my intelligence, the values which I held deep inside of me, hidden from what I had experienced as a hostile world.

Early on in my youth my father left my mother and five children to a life of welfare and shame, my mother seeking shelter in any man she could find, i.e. a long list of pedophiles, which is my cross to bear. From the first experience of Credo I learned how abnormal all that was (I had some idea before, but I didn't realize that was to affect me so much.).

After leaving the safety of Credo, departing from the Navy and returning home I found it neither to be a home or a place of safety. So the journey began. In the course of twenty years since I have gone to college (I was a high school dropout—they at first were not going to give me my diploma when they discovered I never finished high school), have married and have a family. I also became a very functional alcoholic, and a very dysfunctional man. I lost the love of myself and of others.

For the last three years or so I have been a member of Alcoholics Anonymous, which is basically a place where I could begin to learn how to heal, much as Credo had introduced me to healing so many years before. I found in my searching that it was in fact the Credo experience which allowed me to accept the teachings of AA, the Twelve Steps, and a loving God.

Last week I returned to experience a Credo Weekend once more. It reinforced my belief in God and the feeling that I do not walk the path alone. I have grown and matured over the years, but the love I first experienced at Credo and from Don so many years ago has not changed, but in fact has become stronger. The difference, though, is within myself. I am more willing to experience love for others and myself. The format has changed slightly, but the message is the same.

I do not believe I could have come so far without Credo or the man, Don Harris, without having experienced the need to be loved and to love. I am learning to accept love and to give it back. As I am more able to accept myself I am more able to accept others. Serenity is when you can accept others loving you.

My family life is blessed by the Lord and sometimes I believe Credo and Don were put in my path so that I could truly experience the love of my Creator, even with all my baggage. The Credo experience is that I am not alone, and must return the love I have received. The Weekend cleansed my soul some more so that I could continue on my path. It reinforced my belief that I can live my life as a true Christian. In retrospect, Credo Weekends taught me the basics of Christian belief minus the frills.

All in all, the Credo Project closely followed the original conception. There were few surprises because the concept was elemental. When a safe environment is created on the Weekend, fears subside and love is experienced. When this is followed by a safe locus for activities the newly acknowledged love is translated into the permanence of friendship, the medicine of life.

4

Sea Trials, 1974-1979

The Dark Night Of The Soul

In the summer of 1974, the Navy transferred me from Credo/San Diego to the American detachment at the Spanish Naval Base in Rota, Spain on the Bay of Cádiz. As in so many American enclaves overseas, many of the personnel found safety by remaining within the confines of the military compound. The result was an island of ex-patriates living a constricted social existence. In the United States they would find many of the various travails of family and job diluted because they would be living within the familiar American society with its television, movies and shopping malls. But overseas, these personal problems appear bigger than life because they are experienced in the isolation of a small enclave.

I was exhausted from the struggle to found Credo in San Diego, not only because of the intricate maneuvering necessary to strengthen the sponsorship of the organization, but also due to my involvement with so many men and women on the Weekends. I was succeeded in San Diego by a trusted friend, Chaplain Skip Hughes, and knew that Credo was in good hands. Skip had different gifts than I, but we were of one mind as to what Credo should be. It was healthy for the community to have some new blood and new approaches, thereby taking on a life of its own. I regret that a sabbatical or some "down time" was not available for me as an administrative option, as I was close to "running on empty."

My family couldn't be happier about being able to live in Spain. Ruth had first visited the country in 1967 when she met me in Madrid together with our foster son, Tom, who had joined our family when we settled in Norfolk. I was on leave from the destroyer division which was deployed in the Mediterranean, and the three of us made our initial discovery of the medieval pilgrimage road to Santiago. In 1973, Ruth and I; our two sons Tim and infant Jonathan; and Peter Chase thoroughly explored the *Camino de Santiago,* in a satisfying, if crampacked two week journey. We loved the Spaniards—particularly their personal warmth and their devotion to children.

I looked forward to a time of reflection, and to conventional duties as a chaplain serving a base chapel. Spain, the native soil of many of my personal heroes such as John of the Cross, Teresa of Avila, Ignácio de Loyola, and El Greco seemed to be the perfect place for my spiritual refreshment. But my renewal was not to be in the way I anticipated.

As I was unpacking my books in my office adjacent to the chapel in Rota, a teenaged sailor named Al dropped by. Clearly troubled, he acted "spacey" as he told me of his difficulties. He had been caught by the Spanish customs authorities in Algeciras, a commercial port in southern Spain, bringing in hashish from Morocco. Thus he faced a certain seven-year sentence in a Spanish prison. Al told me that he would remain in custody on the base for up to two years while awaiting the wheels of justice to turn. Then, he said, he anticipated a minimum of five years in prison before he could return to the United States. Al's wife (also a teenager) and two children had left him and returned to Oklahoma.

I was tired and wanted a respite from the cares of the world, but I felt I could not in good conscience send Al away. Before me was a young man who typified what I believed to be true: that those who are experiencing a void may turn to drugs and alcohol as a way to lessen their pain. Because of my experience on psychiatric wards, I sensed that his "driftiness" was not solely caused by illegal drugs and that perhaps his drug use was self-medication for a more serious condition.

Al's isolation was compounded by his arrest by Spanish customs agents. Now "branded" as a drug trafficker within the small base community, he was judged by what he did without a concern for who he was. I offered him my acceptance and friendship, and made a pact with him to see him on a regular basis. I told Al that I could guarantee him nothing as far as the legal situation, but I did assure him of my commitment to him. So I befriended him, daily hearing about the depths of his despondency, and finally getting him to a doctor who confirmed what I had suspected: Al's "driftiness" was associated with a possible psychotic condition.

The result was a mixed blessing. From a legal perspective, Al could not be tried by the Spanish government because he was diagnosed as being mentally ill. Thus his court date was delayed indefinitely until such time as he was declared healthy. No treatment was available, however, since there were no English speaking psychiatrists in the area, and Al was not allowed to leave the country for treatment prior to trial. The paradox was that without treatment he could never stand trial.

The standoff was eventually solved by the death of Franco and an amnesty declared by Don Juan Carlos I, when he became king. To mark his ascent to the throne, Juan Carlos declared a three year amnesty for all prisoners. At that point, as a matter of legal convenience, Al was declared cured. He stood trial, was convicted by the Spanish government, and sentenced to prison. But Al had three years credit for the time spent confined to the base, and another year could be dropped for good behavior. That left only three years to serve—the length of the amnesty. In a word, because he was convicted, he could go free.

During my normal rounds as a chaplain I came to know the prison in Cádiz, for I took seriously the passage in Matthew where the Lord said, *"When I was in prison, you visited me."* (Matt 25: 36) I tried always to see Christ in the face of my sailor brother. The prison to which Al would have been sent resembled the Turkish prison portrayed in the absorbing movie *Midnight Express.* The huge white stucco prison compound on the edge of the Bay of Cádiz was the very one that Columbus entered to assemble his crew for his voyages to America. It was essentially a series of large courtyards filled with all sorts and conditions of men from many different countries.

The prisoners were of various ages and had committed a variety of crimes ranging from assault and murder to smuggling and possession of hashish. Among them there were many young men from England, Holland, Denmark, and the United States who were foolish enough to deal with marijuana and hashish in the days of the uncompromising regime of Francisco Franco. The youth, several of them sailors, were housed with many hardened criminals, a tragedy which is repeated in our own country today.

At first I was not welcomed there by the prison authorities. I had two strikes against me. First, I was an American officer whom they felt was meddling in Spanish affairs. Second, as an Anglican priest I was anathema to the Roman Catholic theocracy which dominated Franco's Spain. The treaty between the United States and Spain allowed non-Roman Catholic worship in English on the base for Americans only. Worship or Bible studies could not be conducted in Spanish, nor were Americans to proselytize any Spanish nationals. It was a time when Protestant churches in Spain were beginning to be tolerated, so long as the worshippers neither identified their buildings as churches, nor publicly advertised their services of worship.

The same treaty, however, guaranteed freedom of religious practice for all American service personnel and their families, even in prison. On this basis I pressed my claim to enter the prison. After explaining to the warden what the American Thanksgiving holiday was, he reluctantly gave me permission to bring Thanksgiving dinner to the American naval prisoners.

The people in the base galley carefully prepared hearty meals for their shipmates. But when I arrived at the prison, the authorities confiscated the meals because I had not provided a statement from the commanding officer taking responsibility for their contents. "We do not want to take responsibility for the food," the Spanish prison official explained, "in case it was improperly prepared and causes food poisoning." In addition, the officials denied me entry to conduct religious services, saying that the meals were all that I was authorized to supply. Since I could do nothing more, I thanked them and returned to my car, waiting for a more propitious occasion. As I left, I could see one of the guards enjoying the turkey.

Forewarned, I came at Christmas time not only with meals for the sailors (with the appropriate documentation from the American commanding officer), but also with material necessary for worship. I was grudgingly admitted. But I was told that I could not use the prison chapel for worship (for fear of desecrating it, I surmised). As an alternative I was ushered to a large cleaning gear locker room which had been designated as the place of worship. It must have been quite a spectacle in the eyes of the prisoners to see an American chaplain in his starched whites moving among them in the large, littered courtyard.

The inmates could readily see that I was handled with dignified distaste; I was, they saw, as unacceptable to the prison authorities as they were. Among the mops and brooms I prepared to celebrate the Eucharist by setting up my communion vessel on a wooden crate. When I looked up, a large and friendly group of Dutch, Norwegians, English, as well as American prisoners had gathered. Thus I stood among "the least of my brethren," bound together in the love of God. How ironic, I thought, that my chalice was a reproduction of a Spanish one used by Fr. Hidalgo, the priest who mobilized the native Mexicans to seek their freedom from Spanish domination. It was a day I will treasure the rest of my life. Fellowship took on a deeper meaning as my brothers and I received communion together.

When I returned to the naval base that afternoon, I had my regular visit with Al and others with whom I had counseling appointments. Al had spread the word around the base that a chaplain had taken him seriously as a person, despite his actions. Soon my appointment calendar was filled with isolated young men and women who were Al's friends. I tried to teach them that they had something of value to give to one another by attending each other. I could see that it was the situation of the Coast Guard Training Center revisited. I needed to have some people to share the load. What better way than Credo?

The executive officer of the American detachment on the base, Captain Charles Stratman, was a compassionate man, concerned for the welfare of his people. When I explained what we were able to do on a Credo Weekend and proposed offering one for the naval community, he not only gave his approval, he also agreed to attend. With his active support, planning for the first Weekend in Spain took place.

Pedro Díaz, the Spanish head of community relations between the Americans and Spaniards, was central to what occurred next. He was a man who enjoyed tackling new projects, and had an affection for Americans and a deep seated Christian faith, nurtured by his experience with *Cursillo* as a layman. To distinguish the retreat from the original Credo program in San Diego we, at Pedro's suggestion, named the experience *Esperanza*, Spanish for "hope." Our effort was funded with a small amount of seed money provided by the Chief of Chaplains John O'Connor (currently Cardinal Archbishop of New York), who was anxious to see if Credo could be viable as a modest program at a local command. It was Pedro who made the arrangements.

Out of respect for the host country, Pedro and I visited the auxiliary bishop of Jerez de la Frontera, Don Rafael Bellido Caro. This young prelate was supportive and even enthusiastic about the Esperanza effort. He said to me:

> Chaplain, the greatest threat to the spirit of my people is materialism. Because my church in the area is iden-

tified with the State and in some ways is so visibly rich, it is more difficult for me to address the problem without appearing hypocritical. You are free of these encumbrances and are in a better position to confront materialism. Therefore I give you my blessing and my prayers. If there is any way that I can assist you, do not hesitate to call on me.

And help he did. When Pedro identified a site for the Weekend at *El Calverio Casa de Ejercicios* in Jerez, Bishop Bellido assured the sisters who ran the retreat house that opening the doors to us was the right thing to do. Soon afterward, when we visited Don Ignacio at *Villa Ballena* to search for a permanent retreat site, Bishop Bellido immediately and strongly endorsed us.

Ruth and I were the only experienced staff members on the first Weekend, but we had no doubt how it would turn out. Participants on the retreat were not only junior officers and enlisted men and women, but also members of the base chapel, including a newlywed, Philana Quick, the choir director. Years later when Credo/Esperanza was established in Colorado, she and her husband Ray would be a key resource for our community.

On this Esperanza Weekend, the participants considered many aspects of their lives. The executive officer, Charlie Stratman, was sorting out the implications of his pending transfer and immanent retirement. A few of the young sailors were struggling with the implications of LSD and hashish use, since Morocco—an unlimited resource for illicit drugs—was only three hours away. Philana was adjusting to being married, to getting settled in Spain, and to life as a Navy enlisted wife.

And, in addition, one of the sailors, Gary Ryan, had a dramatic change of heart, one might even term it a conversion experience on the Weekend. During it he turned from a wasted life of self-destruction and made his first steps away from the drug culture in which he had been involved. After the Weekend, Captain Stratman assigned him to be both a brig counselor and parttime Esperanza staff member.

Because of his history of drug abuse, Gary was effective in working with peers who had run afoul of the military law, and became a dedicated Esperanza spokesman. To be sure, the specter of a well-known drug user becoming involved with Esperanza and the brig was viewed by some as an example of letting a fox into a hen coop. They were skeptical that anyone could make as radical a change of heart as Gary had on the first Esperanza Weekend. The growing involvement in Esperanza of many youths who were known to have been in trouble with the law was viewed with skepticism by the law enforcement community on the base.

Yet the Esperanza Weekends worked remarkably well as the graduates integrated their experiences into the life of the base. Senior officers, doctors, mental health professionals, and chaplains worked together through Credo to build a supportive network throughout the base. The base psychologist, Bill Weiner, who knew Credo from his last duty station as head of treatment at the Naval Drug Rehabilitation Center in San Diego, became a strong supporter of our effort.

Some of the Christian members of the Esperanza family became involved in both Roman Catholic and Protestant Christian education, and were at the forefront in bringing to the base Marriage Encounter, a retreat designed to strengthen Christian marriages. Fifteen years later, Marriage Encounter still thrives at the Naval Base at Rota.

Not only did young enlisted people attend subsequent Weekends, but also foreign national wives came, seeking a means to understand their marriages to American servicemen. Other married people came because their marriages were becoming frayed by the confining atmosphere of the base.

An example is a Navy nurse who was married to a Christian Scientist. Within their household her husband's father was suffering from a physical condition that she was convinced could be alleviated with medicine. She felt helpless to communicate her concern to her husband without offending him, because medication, a essential part of her career, was something which was in conflict with her husband's faith. Whether she suggested medical treatment of her father-in-law or ignored his condition, the situation would cause an underlying stress in their marriage.

But on the Weekend she was able to articulate her feelings. When she returned home, she felt strong enough to talk openly with her husband. In addition, she invited him to attend the following Weekend. And when he returned from the Credo experience, he and his wife were able to share a closeness which they had thought impossible. In time, they worked through their conflict. A year later I received a note from them, pinned to a birth announcement of their first child. It said, "We are a happily married couple now, rejoicing in the child we never thought we would have. Credo saved our marriage."

Not all in Esperanza were drawn from the Navy community. We also had the pleasure of having as a participant both Clarence Hobgood (know as "Hob" to every one on the Weekend), the Episcopal Bishop to the Armed Forces; and Graham Pulkingham, the founder of the international Communities of Celebration, who flew in from his community in Scotland.

One "outsider" who comes to mind was our neighbor, Barry Siggers, an Englishman who lived in El Puerto de Santa Maria while working in Cádiz for an English shipping firm. In addition, Esperanza reached several young Americans who were in the area as one stop in their quest. One, Fred Rohé, was the founder of perhaps the first natural food store in San Francisco. Fred and Sandy and children had met young members of the Christian group, Youth With A Mission (YWAM), when their van had broken down in Morocco. They lived in the community YWAM house outside of Puerto, on the road to Jerez, and then in Dilaram House, the YWAM residence in Chipiona.

In fact, perhaps the most fascinating expression of Credo in Spain may have been the Weekend we held for this young missionary community of YWAM. They were in the area to befriend counter-culture youths, young wanderers, and sailors. They hoped that their personal behavior would be an appealing example of a better, and Christian, way of life, and welcomed those who would like to live within their Christian common household. Among the YWAM community were young men and women from Holland, England, the Isle of Jersey, Brooklyn, Colorado, and Spain.

Their leader, Bob Lichty, attended one of our Weekends with a few of his assistants, and asked if we could present an Esperanza retreat specifically for his YWAM community. In our discussions with Bob and his wife Vicky, we identified a difficult issue that many evangelical Christians experience. Some new Christians mistakenly feel that their acceptance of Jesus Christ as personal Lord and Savior means that all their doubts and problems will be healed. Hence, they are ashamed to admit their continued personal struggles, fearing that to do so will betray a lack of faith and a poor witness to the world. As a result, they find themselves fearful, precisely in the faith which is supposed to set them free. Thus they become less effective in proclaiming the forgiving love of God to others, because they have not accepted themselves as worthy.

Bob Lichty and I agreed that the Esperanza experience might be a way to open the hearts of evangelicals even more to the actuality of God's unconditional love. Then they could more fully enjoy their life together in community, supporting each other in their common faith. The retreat was conducted in four languages at the YWAM community home in Chipiona, a fantastic nineteenth century manse. Emblazoned with Moorish tiles and arches, it was located only three or four blocks from *Villa Ballena*, Don Ignácio's retreat house.

Music, the core of the Credo experience, is an international tongue, and our anthologies of songs easily bridged the language barriers. "This is our journey", Carlos Santana the blues/rock musician observed in an article in the magazine *The Other Side*:

> How do we coexist with one and the whole? I think that comes from spiritual education. ... It is not as complex as it seems. Put children from different parts of the world in a sand box. The fact that they don't speak the same language is not going to stop them from socializing. Add music, the universal language, and we can really begin to see a spiritual coming together.

The Weekend music transcended the fears of the young missionaries as it addressed their inner feelings. Able to be authentic with one another, they talked about where they fell short in the lives they wished to live. As their self-imposed guilt melted, they responded with compassion to the struggles that their brothers and sisters on the Weekend acknowledged and voiced. They emerged from the experience not only with a healthier faith, but also a greater ability to share their love.

The key person on the Weekend was a multi-lingual woman from Amsterdam who, throughout the retreat, patiently translated into English the native languages which were spoken by the other participants. To her missionary companions, she was a living example of quiet, sacrificial service. By electing to help them communicate from the heart, she put her own needs aside. She was a latter day Magdelene, for before her conversion she had been a prostitute.

Love Comes Like A Refugee

> *Every heart to love will come*
> *But like a refugee*
> —Anthem, Leonard Cohen

One of my most satisfying experiences in Spain occurred when I brought the Credo experience to a medium security prison in Jerez de la Frontera. Of course the prison routine would not accommodate a special Weekend for Credo. But there was none of the resistance which we met in Cadiz. The open and sympathetic Spanish chaplain was delighted that interest was shown in the prisoners and arranged for me to meet weekly with approximately nine young convicts for several hours over a period of weeks. The Roman Catholic priest was a true brother.

A diverse group gathered with me and my sailor companion, Gary Ryan, to hear the Credo music and reflect on their broken lives: some were young European men involved in drug trafficking; one was an American Air Force enlisted man; another a young Moroccan man, Benjamin Bouchaib, probably a Muslim. Neither did I know their backgrounds, nor did it matter. Our common denominator was an ability to understand English and a desire to look at our lives. Once again, music transcended cultural differences, and because of the dire circumstances in which the prisoners found themselves, their dialogue with one another was utterly serious.

Since their release from prison, it has been difficult for me to follow up on any of them. After he was fired, the young Moroccan wrote several warm letters to me from Casablanca, but because of the difficulties of forwarding international mail, we have since lost contact. The experience with Esperanza in Spain underlined the universality of the Credo concept. We had moved from sailors, to their leaders, to families, to people of many nations and backgrounds.

Esperanza House

At the beginning, Esperanza had the executive officer of the base as its midwife, but soon the community took on a life of its own, achieving the goal of Credo to encourage people to be each other's keeper. In the process I could see that an elaborate superstructure was not necessary to give birth to a Credo family.

A nucleus of participants, including the executive officer, banded together to establish a center for the Esperanza family. With the help of members of the Seabees (Navy Construction Battalion) who worked on their off hours, an under-used Quonset hut situated next to the Shore Patrol and Spanish security, was transformed into Esperanza House. Esperanza friends learned much about their host country as they scoured the age-old market places of neighboring towns for carpeting and other interior furnishings. Soon there were the Credo/Esperanza family meetings, pot luck dinners, and personal support, as in San Diego. Several Americans brought their Spanish friends.

The presence of Esperanza House in Rota was short lived for two reasons. First, the executive officer who went on the first Weekend was transferred, and the new executive officer had no first-hand experience as to what Esperanza could do. Although his support was positive, he remained detached.

The second reason was more significant: Esperanza became too successful. On the base were a conspicuous group of people working together, with a common desire to help each other live constructive lives. To these members of the Esperanza family the barrier between officer and enlisted made no sense when they were not on duty. Soon, several of us wanted to live what we preached—i.e., living together in a common household, treating each other fraternally rather than hierarchically.

We had been encouraged to form a common household by Graham Pulkingham, an internationally known Anglican renewal figure, who had earlier come to Spain from his community in Scotland to attend an Esperanza Weekend. After experiencing the Weekend with a compatriot, he told me that Esperanza accomplished more in 72 hours than he did in a two-week orientation he had sponsored in Scotland, Houston, and Colorado Springs.

Graham thought that the transitory nature of those in the Navy society might be an impediment to the stability that a Credo community needed. His group, The Community of Celebration, prospered in their common life together, and he felt that Credo could be a significant presence within the Christian community movement.

Several months after his first Esperanza experience, Graham returned to Spain to lead a retreat for those of us considering a life together. At the conclusion of our retreat, we decided to form a common household. Ruth and I and our three young sons, Timothy, Jonathan, and Christopher (born in Spain); Gary, his 16-year-old wife Brenda, and their infant daughter, Heather; and a single sailor, Ken Stahl, shared a common household. We chose to be discreet, living away from the base among the Spaniards, because we were aware that our irregular action might cause some anxiety for the command—particularly since it involved an officer and some enlisted men under one roof.

There were people within the command, whom I will never know, who were uncomfortable with Esperanza's inclusion of some of the less desirable servicemen and women on the base, and they seized upon our community living as a pretext to close the ministry. I have good reason to believe that among them were some of my fellow chaplains, although nothing was ever said to me.

To my amazement, I was told a few years later that one of the chaplains suspected that the reason I was so tenacious in my effort to gain entry to the men in prison was not because of the gospel but because I was running drugs. When dealing with this level of distrust, the only thing which sustained us was our faith, and the witness of all the people around us who had experienced the love of God through Esperanza.

These covert opponents convinced the commanding officer that he would be unwise to tolerate the Credo community, however discreet their behavior. He would appear to be sanctioning fraternization, they suggested, thereby creating a domino effect where single officers and enlisted personnel would chose to live together for other than spiritual reasons. This would undermine good order and discipline.

Within a matter of weeks Gary was given an administrative discharge for the convenience of the government and ordered to leave Spain immediately, with his family following later as flight space became available. Our beleaguered Credo/Esperanza community celebrated Christmas together in November, since Gary would be separated from all of us (including his young wife and infant child) until the New Year.

As I was heading home one day, I was astonished as I drove by the Esperanza House to see a bulldozer gutting the interior of the building. All those hours of volunteer labor erecting partitions, laying down carpet, making a surrogate home, apparently went for naught. Without explanation, the commanding officer took the Esperanza House from us, returning the Quonset hut to the Navy Exchange as a warehouse. Five years after the concept of Credo took form, part of it was now being demolished before my eyes.

Bulldozing Hope

John of the Cross, the sixteenth-century Spanish mystic, had become one of my constant spiritual companions during these first years of Credo. In *The Dark Night of the Soul,* John talked of the various appetites we have—such as those for religious symbols, or institutions—that assist us in our journey toward the love of God. When the desire to satisfy these appetites becomes paramount, John wrote, the "aids" become an impediment in the journey toward God. We are apt to place too much store in these spiritual aids until they become idols, he maintained. We forget that any *thing* is only means to the end, which is intimacy with God. When relying upon a spiritual aid interferes with our reliance on God, He takes that aid away from us, John observed, much as a mother rubs bitter aloes on her breast so that the nursing child may reject this dependency and progress on his path to maturity. When what we relied upon is withdrawn, we do not realize it is for our own good. Thus we experience what John calls "the dark night of the soul."

In a graphic way the Navy bulldozer, as it toppled outward signs of Navy support, was the beginning of such a dark night for me. The silence of my chaplain associates during this destruction was deafening. I had to face the future naked, possessing only my faith and the love I received from Ruth and from a few others. All was taken away. I had to learn to accept the fact that it was good for me to be free from any attachments that stood in the way of my response to God.

During this period I was within the zone of chaplains who were being considered for the rank of commander. Following the chain of command, I routed a letter through my commanding officer to the Chaplain Corps in which I indicated I did not want to be considered for promotion. I was bone-weary and confused. For almost five years I felt I had to keep looking over my shoulder to protect this haven where so many of the poor in spirit were finding hope. To this day I can not understand the fervor of the opposition.

The selection board never received my correspondence, because, without my knowledge, the commanding officer held my letter for five months before forwarding it. In the interim I was selected for advancement. Although I was grateful for the Chaplain Corp's confidence in me, I felt I could not function in such an atmosphere. Tired of the trench warfare that seemed endemic to the system, I declined my selection for commander and tendered my resignation from the regular Navy.

In retrospect, I can see that my decision was clouded by the emotional turmoil that I experienced as a child. It is typical for such people as me to absorb abuse, rather than speaking up about the treatment of myself and my ministry by the command. I loved the Navy, and was firm in the knowledge of the grace that Credo conveyed, but Graham Pulkingham's portrayal of a permanent settlement among people of good will was comforting, and an alternative that had great appeal.

When he heard of my intention, the commanding officer called me into his office to find out why I would sacrifice my naval career for companionship with a recovering teen-age sailor and his family and an expendable petty officer. As he sat behind his massive desk, he looked at me quizzically as if I were Don Quixote. With a broad sweep of his hand toward the American, Navy, and Spanish ensigns on their flag-staffs, he asked, "How can you give up all this?"

As I listened to him I recalled a passage from the Bible which says "king today, corpse tomorrow." In a couple of years this man who currently bore the mantle "Commander, Naval Activities, Spain," would join the ranks of the retired personnel who scan the Navy Exchange for bargains, and look at the energetic young officers and sailors around them, while wistfully remembering the good old days at sea.

I replied that I felt my calling was to continue my service to humanity in another setting. I went on to say, even though I did not know where our community would settle or what its source of income would be, our community would continue to follow where we felt led.

I felt a twinge of anxiety as I said these sincere and somewhat heroic words. What was in store for us? It was one thing for me to say these words about *my* life. But my life was inextricably bound to my beloved family. What did this mean for Ruth? By becoming one in marriage was I involving her in something which was beyond her endurance? We had talked through my decision, so that it was ours. But that meant that she shared the possible pain and uncertainty which would be the result. Was I being grandiose, or was this our calling from God?

What of our sons, including Christopher, who had been born less than a year before? The children were our joy and my solace. For, as they flourished, I could see that the cycle had been broken—out of the ashes of my childhood had come a strong, intact family. And, I believed, the love I received from all of them came from the grace of my loving Father. Was it fair to them? Was I endangering their happiness?

Yet, in the midst of the turmoil of my questioning, something happened which gave me heart. Len Dodson, the senior Navy chaplain in Europe, flew down from London to Rota to see me. Since I knew Chaplain Dodson had been no supporter of Credo in the past, I thought to myself that this was the last person I needed to see, particularly since I suspected that some of the local chaplains had been undermining this ministry, if only through benign neglect.

Late that afternoon in my office, Len talked to me with earnestness and kindness. "Don," he said, "you are a prophet, and I admire you for what you are doing. I confess that I actively opposed Credo when I was back in Washington, and I regret it now that I have seen the fruit of Credo all around me. You are in my prayers, and I will help you any way I can."

Those words from Len Dodson were a healing balm. In the midst of the turmoil a perceived foe became known to me as a spiritual friend. We embraced as brothers, and then departed to do what had to be done. And as the preparations for departure were unfolding, I continued to receive support from John

O'Connor. In a parting letter written to me in November of 1976, he wrote,

> There is still such a thing as a prophet being misunderstood by his people and his times. I can only sincerely hope and continue to pray that the days ahead will provide you with some restful moments and, at least, a moderate degree of well-deserved mental peace and contentment.

5

Pilgrim Credo: The Voyage, 1976-1982

In early December 1976, Ruth and I and our three boys returned to the United States and visited my family in Boston. This was our second Christmas celebration of the year, the first one being in Rota before Gary was separated from his wife and daughter in November. After Christmas, my father and I drove together to Newport, Rhode Island so that I could complete processing out of the active Navy.

There I looked up Ross Trower, now head of the Chaplain's School in Newport. He had been a mentor and father to me during my early forays in Washington in 1971. Knowing that I was a novice in the ways of Washington he had taken a particular interest in me. After a full day of meetings during that formative period for Credo, I would stop by his office and share my dreams and my faith with him. To me Ross was literally a Godsend. So here we were, six years later: faithful Ross and I had an emotional farewell. But, as we parted, I knew I had his blessing. And it was something I treasured during the stormy days ahead.

Driving to Buffalo, we picked up Gary, Brenda, and their toddler, Heather, and continued to Earlham College, in Indiana. There we spent the night with friends who had been active in Credo/San Diego: Dennis, who was finishing his bachelor's degree; his wife, Dana; and their two little girls. They were considering joining our household. He had been a bright sailor active in the field of drug abuse prevention. His wife, Dana, was an equally gifted person who handled well the vicissitudes of being a Navy enlisted wife with two small children and a limited income.

We then proceeded to Fort Collins, Colorado, the home of Ray and Philana Quick, who in Spain had been involved with the chapel community and Esperanza;—thence we went to California via Arizona where two early Credo/San Diego friends, Bud and his wife, Eddie, extended warmth and hospitality.

We chose Santa Cruz because it was in the Episcopal Diocese of California, whose bishop, Kilmer Myers, was one of the heroes of the church because of his earlier work as the "hoodlum priest" in Newark, New Jersey. When the earlier events leading to Credo were unfolding in the Bay Area (while I was stationed with Coast Guard, Alameda, and the Naval Hospital, Oakland), I would periodically visit Kim in his office where we would share our dreams—two of us on a similar quest of bringing the love of God to the abandoned.

Since Kim was a deeply committed follower of St. Francis, I knew that he would be in sympathy with the pilgrimage the community had embarked upon. Kim was the loving man I expected, but he was emotionally drained trying to be a caring pastor, administrator, husband and father at the same time. He must have felt much as I did when, driven by my calling, my body and spirit spent in its pursuit, I had arrived in Spain three years earlier. The ensuing years in Rota were not times of refreshment which I needed, and I yearned for a strong and loyal brother. He and I were glad to see each other, but it turned out that our roles were reversed: I was drawing upon what resources I had left to give him support, rather than his being able to give to me the spiritual nurture I needed.

Our itinerant household found an abandoned Roman Catholic seminary in the hills of Santa Cruz, and received permission to stay there for a while. Our nascent community camped there with sleeping bags, cooking our meals in the commercial kitchen. Soon the Parker family from New Zealand joined us. Richard Parker had been a mainstay of the Credo House in San Diego, and a spiritual companion. In fact, I baptized their first son, Michael, in the Credo House chapel. He and his wife Kathrine, now with their third son about to be born, came from Wellington with their meager belongings and $10.00 in their pockets. Richard felt called to be a part of the Credo community that had changed his life.

Shortly thereafter we were joined by Ken, who had been part of the original Esperanza community in Spain. He was at the end of his enlistment and wanted to start a new life together with his Credo brothers and sisters. We rented a house in the redwoods of Ben Lomond, the town next to Santa Cruz: three couples, six young children (with one on the way), and a single man.

To test the California waters, we sponsored a Credo Weekend involving old friends, including a psychiatrist who had been stationed in Spain with us, a classmate of mine from William & Mary days, as well as Peter Valerio who was one of the original architects of Credo back in Alameda. Also included were friends of Peter and parishioners of the local Episcopal church. Although the Weekend experience was constructive for the participants, I saw no indication that our community would have any long-term support if we settled in the area.

However, encounters with two people especially affected me during this formative period. The first one occurred when I was picking up some milk for the children in our community. By the cash register was the current issue of *The Rolling Stone* with Jeff Bridges on the cover. I remembered the times we had spent in the Coast Guard boot camp, and I was anxious to see how his life was turning out almost ten years later.

Our community was on such a tight budget, that it took some weighing whether buying the magazine was an extravagance. It turned out not to be, for when I read Jeff's interview I came across a passage where he stated that two people had made a deep impression on his life, one was Burgess Meredith, the other was his chaplain at boot camp.

It is hard to convey how affirming that statement was to me. Here I was, camping out in an old school building, feeling the responsibility for a small community with several children, wondering whether this was fair to Ruth and our kids, still aching from the events which had occurred a few months before; and here was my young old friend saying to me that it is worth it.

Back in the formative period of Credo at Coast Guard, Alameda, I had come to know Jeff, then an 18-year-old Coast Guard Reserve recruit. As I explained before, I was seeing a stream of recruits. As is fitting, the five per cent of troubled people consumed 95 percent of my energy. Now and then, for a refreshing change, I would invite a couple of healthy recruits to my office, extend to them my friendship, and talk with them about their future plans.

Jeff was a natural choice as he was one of the faithful members of the recruit chapel congregation worshipping every Sunday. I structured the service so that the first part met the needs of conventional Protestant worship with hymns (led by a recruit choir which swelled to 25 percent of the congregation), prayers, and a sermon. We would then break, and, after greeting the recruits at the door, I would rejoin those who chose to remain for the second part of the service: Holy Communion. Jeff regularly remained.

Jeff and I had good times together in my office, talking about life, families, dreams, and his love of music. We were experiencing the joy of spontaneous friendship; we had no agenda other than to enjoy each other. I even sneaked him off the base so he could hear Janis Joplin, who was just emerging as the singer in the group *Big Brother and the Holding Company*. Many times I have said to him how glad I was that we became friends before he was anything other than another kid from Southern California.

Now, eight years later, prompted by the article in *Rolling Stone*, I gave Jeff a call. Soon we had a reunion, together with his girlfriend, Susan, in his home in the hills of Malibu. It was like old times, with talk about love and marriage, drugs, the War, personal commitment, our spiritual quests: two friends, mutually supportive, seeing only each other's hearts. In the process of reestablishing our relationship it was natural that Susan, whom Jeff loved deeply, was included as well. A few days later, after I had returned to Ben Lomond, Jeff called to ask if Ruth and I could come down and have dinner with Susan and him and talk about their marriage plans. He wanted me to officiate at their wedding.

To this day, I remember the details of that dinner. We dined at a Japanese restaurant, two friends, each one with the person he loved the most. We talked of love and commitment, and how non-supportive of marriage is the world in which we find ourselves. As we looked over possible scripture selections together, Jeff came upon the passage:

> *In the same way, men are also bound to love their wives,*
> *as they love their own bodies.*
> *In loving his wife a man loves himself.*
> —Ephesians 5:28

"This is my goal," he explained, "As an actor, the use of my body is everything, it is my vocation and I provide and care for it. On the other hand," he reflected, "as an actor, my body is my greatest source of temptation. I want this passage read at our wedding as a reminder of what I am pledging to Sue." What a beautiful interpretation Jeff had made of St. Paul's writing.

The subsequent wedding in Jeff's garden was warm and intimate. The mothers of the bride and groom were radiant. Jeff's father, Lloyd, another kind and generous man, took me aside and asked if he could assist in the celebration by administering the chalice of wine at communion. Always attentive to others, Jeff asked me to interpret Holy Communion to the gathering of their friends so that those of their guests who were Jewish would feel at ease.

In my homily I honored our common roots as Christians and Jews by drawing parallels between the Eucharist and the Passover feast. The remarks were received so well that, as the reception wore on, an old Jewish gentleman who was fascinated with the person of Paul/Saul sought me out. We had intermittent conversations throughout the evening. Sue and Jeff's wedding was an experience of love and inclusion, just as was my reunion in

Jeff's home. Jeff and Sue have been happily married for sixteen years and have three daughters who are the joy of their life.

The second key encounter was with Noel Brown, an Anglican priest, who was a scholar of African religions at the University of California at Santa Cruz. At first meeting I felt at home with him and told him of my vision. After telling him how Credo had done so much for the alienated and the outsiders, I spoke of working with college students whom I saw as potential leaders of the future.

Noel implored me not to turn from the poor. For every one person who has the gift and is willing to serve the poor, he said, there are a hundred people who volunteer to serve the privileged and gifted. He told me it would be a misuse of gifts to succumb to the temptation to be with only the best and the brightest. But before Noel and I could deepen our relationship, our itinerant household was invited to come to Fort Collins, Colorado as a companion community to one in Denver and another in Colorado Springs.

Graham Pulkingham, who assisted us in forming our community in Spain, had returned to the United States to help Cardinal Deardon form a lay community in the Roman Catholic Archdiocese of Detroit. Graham called from Detroit to see how the Credo/Esperanza community was progressing. After hearing of the limitations of the support Bishop Myers could provide, he arranged for William Frey, the Episcopal Bishop of Colorado, to welcome us as a community. Frey himself was part of an extended household in Denver, and Graham was affiliated with Community of Celebration outside of Colorado Springs.

We were to be a third household community, under the patronage of St. Luke's Episcopal Church in Fort Collins. I would also serve there as a curate as a means of providing both an income and a spiritual anchor for the household. The fit seemed perfect. Remembering back to the time we stopped by Fort Collins to visit Ray and Philana Quick, our friends from Spain, we recalled meeting the rector of St. Luke's, who seemed a pleasant man.

Our household arrived in Colorado with great anticipation. We quickly settled into the life of the parish. One generous family with two small children put us up in their home until we could work out some other living arrangement. Soon we were joined by Dennis and Dana, whom we had visited in Indiana on our journey westward, and their two little girls.

With the arrival of their family, our community was complete: Ruth and me with three sons aged 8, 5, and 2; Gary and Brenda with their 2-year-old daughter; Richard and Kathrine with sons 5, 3, and one due to be born; Dennis and Dana with their two daughters 7 and 4; and Ken, aged 24—nine adults and nine children. Our goal was not only to bring the Credo experience to others through sponsoring Weekends, but also to set an example of love and inclusion by living the Credo experience on a day to day basis.

We incorporated as the Credo/Esperanza Community and invited our host, William Frey, Episcopal bishop of Colorado, and John J. O'Connor—then Chief of Chaplains—to be on our board of directors. After checking to see if there were a conflict of interest, John accepted with enthusiasm. He told me that he had hopes that our community would be a "mother house" for other Credo expressions, thereby providing a spiritual touchstone for the Credo concept.

Actually, Chaplain O'Connor was about to extend Credo to the Navy at large. In a matter of a few months John asked Chaplain Gordon Paulson to establish the second Navy Credo center in Norfolk. As part of his preparation, Chaplain Paulson was sent to visit Credo/Esperanza in Colorado, so that after talking together he might discern what would be best for the Navy's needs. Gordon told me that there was one fundamental difference in the Norfolk proposal. It was that the Chaplain Corps did not want to follow the Credo House "continuing community" model. Rather, they wished to focus on retreats, with the Weekend as the base—it was eventually to be termed a *Personal Growth Retreat* (PGR).

The shift of emphasis was subtle, but substantial. As implemented in San Diego, the original concept was that the Weekend would be an introduction to what a life of mutual support could bring. The Credo House would be a safe environment where this newly-understood way of life could be lived. In contrast, the focus in Norfolk was not on community but on the individual's personal assessment and growth. At this time, the Navy was less focused on providing an ongoing supportive community, which some felt might become an "underground" church.

To get ahead of the story for a moment, the difference between these two emphases, namely, supportive community vs. individual growth, was bridged recently by my dear friend and colleague, Chaplain George Cooper. We had worked together closely when he assumed the directorate of the Navy Credo/Norfolk, during the early days of Credo Institute in 1990. Today he is chaplain to the USS WASP (LHD-1) and has wedded the two approaches.

I received a card from him the other day which said, "Credo continues on WASP every Tuesday night at 2100!" He continued in a follow-up letter, "But the best thing today is the Credo support group. I have 8-12 sailors coming for our Credo meetings." In this way, the necessity to address acute personal problems of transient personnel, which drives the Navy Norfolk approach, is balanced by the shipboard opportunity for Credo graduates to live together applying the grace they received on their individual Weekends.

A Port In The Storm

When I left active duty, I remained in the inactive reserve as a matter of prudence, although I dismissed any thought that I would advance further. Since I had declined my selection for commander while on active duty, I knew that I would be passed over. Nevertheless, in the course of events my name came up before the reserve selection board, and I was selected once more. Chaplain O'Connor signed my selection for commander in the Naval Reserve. This time I accepted the promotion, feeling grateful that, despite all the turmoil of my time in the Navy, there were still fellow chaplains who understood. I began to have a greater appreciation of my part in the Navy family.

In Fort Collins I worked closely with Louise Stitzel, a Lutheran lay woman with a generous heart who sought to build a partnership between the Mexican migrant farm worker community and the larger Anglo establishment. I served on the board of her agency, *Neighbor to Neighbor*, which was intimately involved in the lives of the Mexican community, helping them with their housing needs and shoring up their family structures.

Louise and I became good friends with one woman, Helen, who was valiantly trying to care for her children and salvage a shaky marriage to a husband who had continual brushes with the law. Louise and I admired her tenacity and her fundamental sense of motherhood and the accompanying responsibilities.

Soon we began to offer Weekend retreats in Fort Collins including members of Mexican migrant worker families, students from Colorado State, and local church people. As before, the disparate levels of society blended on the Weekend and forged trusting bonds of mutual support. Recently I read the words of Carlos Santana, the jazz/rock/blues musician, which echo the feelings I felt from Helen and others in the Mexican community:

> I have a strong and consistent connection with certain things in Mexico. That connection is not really based so much on a nationalistic point of view as much as a spiritual one. I relate to my ancestors, whose roots are deep within me. But in my heart of hearts everyone is my brother and my sister. The geographical place of my birth is incidental. If that means not being patriotic, so be it. It is that vantage point which gives me a better door to enter into the lives of other people.

But the Mexicans were not our primary focus. I remember one Weekend when the son of a local pastor was so motivated to start a new life that, in front of his new Credo family, he turned over a bag of heroin to me. After the Weekend he was anxious to find a group of supportive Christians who could reinforce his spiritual conversion. So, he and Helen came along with Ruth and me and some other Credo/Esperanza community members to a charismatic prayer meeting at the sponsoring upper-class church. But the members of the prayer group were so uncomfortable with their presence that they terminated their worship an hour early, without the customary closing Eucharist, and went home, leaving the rest of us to close up the church hall.

On another Weekend there was a young man who was slated to marry a minister's daughter in a large country club wedding.

During the retreat he questioned the wisdom of what he was about to do. He had just endured a society marriage which had ended in divorce, and decided that it would be prudent to delay his wedding plans until he had sorted out his feelings.

His fiancee was sympathetic, particularly after she in turn had experienced a Credo Weekend. On her retreat she expressed to the others her ambivalent feelings about their forthcoming marriage, and took to heart the advice she received from a streetwise woman who leaned over and looked the young socialite straight in the eye and said, "Listen, honey, get your doubts resolved before your marriage. If you think problems will disappear like magic when you tie the knot, you are going to be very disappointed. That knot can be the beginning of a trap." She continued, "I found my problems with my husband were even worse, because I could see no way out." The couple wisely postponed their wedding.

Perhaps this reinforced some parishioners' suspicion of the unconventional nature of our communal living, that we were some sort of cult—Or, abetted by the sermons I delivered stressing the equality of all people regardless of economic condition, we were communists.

In stark contrast, a sociology professor at Colorado State University saw our commitment to community living as congruent with his utopian socialist views. He was pleased to see such disparate levels of society meeting together as equals and, for a minimal charge to cover utilities, he made available his mountain lodge as a site for the Weekends.

Life Together

Our domestic arrangement, bringing together four families in one household, was a complex undertaking. There were eight parents ranging from 16 to 41 years old, with their nine children all under nine years old. Our base income was the meager stipend I earned as curate of St. Luke's. Since we were largely serving students and the poor, the Weekends barely broke even. The household was forced to live off our individual savings—which, in our case, amounted to something around $10,000. Jeff Bridges visited and helped the community financially, but monetary problems and the lack of cohesion due to differences in faith and maturity made our experiment untenable.

I soon understood why monastic communities are composed of either men or women, but not both together. To try to balance my loyalties to my wife and sons, with those felt toward another family and their children,—not to mention the community's vision—was an enervating and daunting task. Living on the edge of poverty, the strain became overwhelming. On the Weekends we had a glimpse of an ideal way of life, and it was a valid goal on which to focus. But the emotional and economic realities of survival in an unfriendly world had to be factored in as well. We had no conventional administrative superstructure or logistical support. We were on our own.

Our commitment to community living remained strong. We adults met each evening for hours on end in prayer and discussion, sorting out what it meant to live together within this common focus of incarnating the love of God. We were joined by spiritual companions including Lou Stitzel of *Neighbor to Neighbor*, and Gordon Solomon, a veterinary school professor who dreamed of forming a community of his own one day. But the struggle was uphill because of the emotional poverty of some of the younger members who looked to Ruth and me to be their anchor. They should have viewed us as fellow pilgrims drawing from God what finite strength we had, but they were too needy to do so.

As a leader, I found my role complex. Having come from an essentially parent-less family, I was aware of the emotional deficit that an absent or inadequate father or mother causes. This made me particularly empathetic with Gary, Richard, Ken and Dennis,—all of whom came from similar backgrounds of emotional deprivation. What was difficult was that I sensed they often looked to me to fulfill their childhood lack by being the idealized father they never had, (nor had I).

One time, in response to some criticism from Dennis, I said to him, "I'm not perfect." He replied in all seriousness, "*I expect you to be.*" At that moment I knew that not only could I not live up to his expectations of being an ideal father, but also would continually disappoint him. Dennis, like many people, had a rational faith based on rules and structure. His need for clearly defined paternal authority came into conflict with my understanding of leadership.

To this day I strongly feel that, in a community, the dominance of one man or woman, however well intentioned, or the external imposition of law, introduces judgment and the attendant element of fear. The hierarchical form is contrary to the spirit of mutual love and shared responsibility which is at the heart of Credo. It aborts the opportunity for mutual love and compassion.

Just as I was unable to live up to his ideal of a father, I was unwilling to exert the strong hierarchical leadership that Dennis wanted. I sought to help bring about a community with *shared* authority whereby love transcended the law, where at any one moment the decision would be based on the empathy which comes from the love extended by one of the members. In my understanding, Jesus addressed this issue time and time again when talking with the Pharisees. No one, not even a leader, should place his personal "rights" above the welfare of the community. Is not the excessive concern for individual rights a prime source of social chaos today?

Having a few years more experience than the others, I had finally begun to accept that it was futile to search for the father I never had as a child when I needed him. What I missed could never be recovered for myself. Nor could I, by being a surrogate father to my brothers in the community, receive the nurture they never had. Since I would be trying to resolve the unresolvable, I would always fail.

Even today, I falter many times, and catch myself looking for a father in another man. But in my heart I know that what paternal love I need comes unconditionally from God. When I seek divine love from another human, I place an unfair burden on someone who is as imperfect as I am. I was experiencing that kind of burden placed on me by my spiritually needy brothers in the community.

I needed no more burdens placed on my shoulders while I was trying to handle the inherent complexities of community life. What I needed was a friendship of equals: a brother with a heart-to-heart relationship in which we could support one another beyond the context of our traumatic childhoods. I was a married man trying as best I could to be a husband to a loving wife. I was also a father of three sons and was trying with all my heart to be the father to them that I wished my father had been to me. I knew it was best for the other families to go on their way apart from my presence to find some balance on their own. It certainly was best for me, Ruth, and my three sons.

The Demonic

When people individually or collectively misunderstand love, the result is fear. Certainly the Bible is replete with such stories, as is history in general. Fort Collins was a close community at the time, and soon rumors began to fly. To our astonishment, Credo/Esperanza and its leader were termed by some church members as demonic. I even heard that the rector suggested to the lay leadership, and perhaps the bishop, that I should be prevented from functioning as a priest of the church. No one came to our defense, nor was I ever apprised of the evidence.

> *[Jesus said] But if your brother wrongs you,*
> *go and have it out with him at once—just between the two of you*
> *If he will listen to you, you have won back your brother.*
> *But if he will not listen to you, take one or two others with you*
> *so that everything that is said may have the support*
> *of two or three witnesses.*
> —Matt 18: 15-16

When I tried to talk with Gordon, our friend who often had prayed with us in the community and shared our vision, he refused to engage me. He said that he had been warned that I was demonic and that since I was facile with words I could easily confound him.

Our friend Peter Valerio came to visit us. At the time he was the senior layman in his own parish in San Francisco, and had some experience resolving conflict. Peter went and talked with the rector, urging him to meet with me and members of our community, bringing along leading lay leadership from the parish so that we could clear up this misunderstanding. The rector refused to have such a meeting, and to this day has never apprised me of the nature of his charges.

For guidance Ruth and I turned to our bishop, and Credo/Esperanza board member, William Frey. Bishop Frey assured us of his pastoral concern and prayers, but suggested that the appropriate course was for me no longer to work for the rector. He therefore suggested that I resign as curate, citing St. Peter's epistle,

> Servants, accept the authority of your masters with all due submission, not only when they are kind and considerate, but even when they are perverse. For it is a fine thing if a man endure the pain of undeserved suffering because God is in his thoughts. What credit is there in fortitude, when you have done wrong and are beaten for it? But when you have behaved well and suffer for it, your fortitude is a fine thing in the sight of God.
> —I Peter 2: 18-21

The Bishop wanted us as a community to remain as members of the parish, yet to offer no public comment on the accusations and behavior of the rector.

I resigned as curate with a sigh of relief, but it was with some trepidation that we followed the rest of the bishop's direction by remaining in the parish. Sunday Eucharists at St. Luke's became both reassuring and difficult for me. I was heartened at the passing of the peace when many of our friends in the parish community reached out to us with warmth, sensing but not understanding what was taking place. I felt the bond of love as we knelt together at the altar rail.

But the bonds were threatening to the rector. I had chosen to be silent because I did not wish him ill, as it was his parish and I did not want to sow any seeds of discontent. Nevertheless, having to approach the altar to receive communion from the hands of the rector was for me a trial of humility and trust. With a sense of irony I would recall assisting him in the past when he would ritually recite "I wash my hands in innocence." I felt no innocence now as I absorbed the results of his actions. I felt vindicated, but saddened, when within a few months the rector left the parish to enter a psychiatric hospital where he spent a long time in recovery.

Perhaps what strengthened me most was the spirituality of John of the Cross. His words in *Ascent to Mt. Carmel* were fresh in my memory, because the previous Lent I led a day-long silent retreat in the parish. I had presented a series of meditations on the text of *The Dark Night of the Soul*, with the music of Messiaen and Bach that was selected and performed on the parish's French baroque organ by Ray Quick, my Credo companion.

I could identify with the mystic's description of faithful people experiencing dark nights as God cleansed them of past spiritual desires in order that they might mature in their spiritual pilgrimage toward Him. These were dark nights indeed: to have left a career in the Navy and the rubble of Credo House in Spain only to find myself discredited, our community scattered, and our savings spent. I cannot forget one cold winter day when one of my sons asked if I would turn up the thermostat, and I replied, "I can't. We have no money to pay for it."

I am one who evaluates his actions with little mercy. I am apt to internalize any criticism as a confirmation of my dark side. As in the aftermath of Spain, I questioned whether my faith was perverse; and whether it was fair to submit my family to this journey. My wife Ruth was still by my side, but I feared that what she had endured in San Diego, Spain, and now Colorado was too much to ask of anyone.

I remember sorting my thoughts out with a fellow priest, Tom McCormack, who was Roman Catholic chaplain to Colorado State University. With great passion I said to him that the spiritual conflict I faced had occurred because my first responsibility was as a priest. He stopped me short and said, "No, Don, your first responsibility is as a husband and a father. You have been given by God a wife and three children, and those precious people are your first priority." I took this to heart, particularly considering the source: a celibate priest whose celibacy placed the duties of his priesthood above all else.

Soon afterward I read that John O'Connor, Navy Chief of Chaplains and Credo/Esperanza board member, was coming to Denver to address the National Baptist Convention. We met at the end of the convention and while I drove him to the airport I explained to him what was happening with Credo/Esperanza.

Chaplain O'Connor listened intently and then told me that he had just finished reading a five-year study of the results of Credo. He recounted that evaluations were sent to all the participants the Navy could locate. A remarkable number had replied to the extensive questionnaire. Virtually no one had said anything negative. Most of the respondents, Chaplain O'Connor continued, felt the Weekend was one of the most significant experiences in their lives.

He then turned to me and said, "In my eyes Credo is the single program in the Navy which affirms the worth and sacredness of the individual. It complements the traditional ministries of the Chaplain Corps, and I intend to expand Credo service-wide. In addition to expanding Credo centers throughout the Navy,"

Chaplain O'Connor added, "I would like you to help me evaluate what effect Credo might have on new recruits. If we anticipate they will have problems in the fleet," he observed, "what better time to intercede than at the beginning of their careers?"

Chaplain O'Connor said that he wanted me back on active duty to launch this pilot project, but that it would take some doing because in my rank as commander, I would be an expensive acquisition for the Corps. But he said that he could justify my return because I was the architect of that which he was expanding. Hence I would be the natural choice for the experimental Credo with recruits.

I talked over the situation with the members of Credo/Esperanza who had lived in community, as well as our board of directors. All agreed that the best course was to dissolve our community effort and proceed with this new effort to expand Credo. With the agile assistance of Chaplain O'Connor's staff my recall to active duty was accomplished, and I left Colorado with my eldest son Tim. We headed for the Great Lakes Recruit Training Center, near Chicago, with Ruth and the two younger boys following a few days later.

Confronting Fear In A Friendly Port

With our return to the Navy our family life changed radically. Rather than food stamps and day-old bread from outlets, there was a steady and ample income (increased five-fold), and my family was no longer vulnerable to medical expenses. But even more, I was grateful for the spiritual and professional support I received from the Chaplain Corps, quite different from the lonely days of early Credo in San Diego. As I moved to set up the recruit Credo program, I wondered if my fellow chaplains appreciated the security they enjoyed.

Chaplain Tom McPhatter also was assigned to the pilot Credo program for recruits. He had been recalled to active duty for reasons which had nothing to do with the project, and was placed at Credo because it was an available billet. I felt brotherly affection toward Tom as the months went by, but understandably his preoccupation was with the injustices meted out to him and other African-Americans within the Navy and Marine Corps.* We served together for a year, leading Weekends together, but, although he was sympathetic with what the Chaplain Corps was trying to accomplish with recruits, his temperament and interests were incongruent with the project. He was a man of action, not of conciliation.

I confidently approached the task of bringing the Credo philosophy of love, not fear, to recruits because it was a concept I had tried before. Twelve years earlier, at the Coast Guard Training and Supply Center in Alameda, I had encouraged cooperation among recruits. When they agonized about the harsh conditions introduced by the training staff, I helped them to see that this was a necessary process the Coast Guard used to determine a person's ability to respond obediently under the rigors of both combat and search and rescue missions.

But when they complained about how senior recruits humiliated new recruits, that was another story. I was told that the more senior recruits, for example, would slop the food on the tray of the junior recruits making it look inedible. As punishment some recruits were made to eat out of a trough on the floor in front of

---

*He has detailed his struggles in his autobiography, *Caught in the Middle. A Dichotomy of an African American Man (They called him Troublemaker)*, Audacity Books, San Diego 1993

the others who looked on with derision. This created anxiety and division among the recruits.

I asked the recruits what they could do to make life better for each other. This kind of behavior against their fellow recruits, I told them, was within their power to stop. When they had mess duty their fifth week, I pointed out, they could treat their brothers with respect rather than ritualized humiliation. By taking charge of their own lives, that is, they could affect the lives of those whom they touched. In addition. they could offer support in many quiet ways, thereby treating each other as shipmates, rather than as competitors.

In short, I told the recruits, they could change the old attitude by their own choice, setting new standards of behavior which would be the model for those who followed them. If the recruits chose to act in this new way, in five weeks the "old" tradition would be unknown.

And many recruits listened—and effected the change. After a few weeks the old tradition of inflicting pain and humiliation died. The advanced recruits treated the newly-arrived men well. Because the newcomers had no knowledge as to how things operated before, they in turn accepted newer shipmates in a more compassionate way. The result was a more cohesive unit bound together in brotherhood, rather than in fear.

This could only have been accomplished because I had the whole-hearted commitment of the commanding officer, Captain Walt Curwen, who carried this philosophy to the training curriculum itself. I was in his office one day when he called in the training officer to ask whether corporal punishment and humiliation was part of the regimen. When the captain was told that it was, he said that it would stop immediately because it was both wrong and illegal. Because of the strong anti-military atmosphere in the San Francisco Bay area during the Vietnam war, he remarked that he would be hard pressed to explain this behavior to the *San Francisco Chronicle*. When the training officer protested that this was the only way in which to mold men for the Coast Guard, Captain Curwen rejected the statement and had the training officer transferred to another command.

The Great Lakes effort was another story. There had been no preparation of the command for the coming of Credo, and the treatment being proposed for the recruits who were failing under the current system was a different training philosophy, which should have been talked through at length. Because there had been inadequate advance work with the Training Command, Credo was seen as another thing to shoe-horn into their crowded curriculum. It was not clear to them of what benefit Credo would be to the achievement of their training goal. They cooperated at the bidding of an admiral, not because they were convinced that Credo was a good thing.

In fact, Credo's approach to the recruits was the antithesis of the traditional Navy approach to training, where recruits at boot camp bonded because they faced a hostile world of company commanders making difficult demands. The atmosphere of hostility in the training cycle bred fear, and the recruits learned that only by working together could they survive. For the majority of recruits, this was an effective stratagem.

For some young men, however, this atmosphere of fear was their undoing. Because of family experiences fraught with discord and trespassed boundaries, these recruits had little confidence in their selves and their worth. The deliberate pressure administered by the command precipitated the emotional withdrawal of vulnerable recruits rather than bonding with their peers. Their fellow recruits sensed the weakness of those who were falling behind, and realized that these young men were a liability in the unit's drive toward survival through achievement. This rejection by their peers further undermined the vulnerable sailors' ability to belong. In many cases it echoed the rejection the young men had experienced all of their lives, and confirmed their sense of worthlessness, which they were trying to overcome by joining the Navy.

Credo approached these young men from the opposite premise: that affirmation and bonding could best take place for them through an experience of love, not fear. On the Credo Weekend the recruit experienced his sacredness and worth through the response of others who, out of empathy, wanted to help him rather than reject him. The concept was that the recruit returning from the Weekend would find the faith and energy to make it through training and join the fleet because he was armed with this sense of value and support.

We held the retreats in the walnut paneled library of Taylor Hall of the De Koven Foundation, a wonderful ante-bellum building on the shores of Lake Michigan in Racine, Wisconsin. Part of a former college campus, it was now administered by a small band of Episcopal nuns. The sisters, who were as cordial as they were lively and gentle, reflected in their lives the kind of commitment and compassion which was being fostered on the Credo Weekends. The example of their frugality and asceticism was balanced by their joy and warm hospitality.

As is always the case, the Weekends were personally effective for many young men. They had a chance not only to sort out their lives, but also to find some direction, and to be of support to one another. On the Weekend, recruits (many of whom had been damaged by a lifetime of negative reinforcement) regained a measure of self-esteem, only to find their new sense of worth shattered when they returned to recruit training. Hence, the Navy recruit training procedures were quickly undoing whatever Credo was accomplishing, and without the whole-hearted cooperation of the command, we ran the risk of generating confusion within the minds of those whom we were trying to help. Rather than affirming these recruits, we could, in the long term, cause them further harm.

We faced a fundamental conflict. From a recruit training viewpoint the Credo pilot project was unacceptable. It was countering the design of the boot camp curriculum where relationships between the recruits are forged through fear. It was confusing to the recruits to take them from this adversarial atmosphere, substitute the positive reinforcement of love, mutual respect, and care, only to return them to the hostile environment from whence they came.

I discussed this dilemma with Dr. Michael A. Taylor, the head of psychiatry at the Chicago Medical School, an authority who had served with me on the wards at the Naval Hospital in Oakland nine years earlier. His analysis was that the Navy was using an obsolete training philosophy which essentially had not changed since World War I. "Modern scholarship," he observed wryly, "has demonstrated that even in the training of police dogs, encouragement and reward are far more effective instruments for training than fear."

Nevertheless, the two conflicting approaches could not flourish side by side. Dr. Taylor offered to work with the Navy to look at their training process, but even such a study would take months. This being the case, he advised that we stop trying to integrate Credo into such an antithetical system.

On its own, the Chaplain Corps concurred with Dr. Taylor's appraisal, and the Credo operation was transferred from the recruit training area to a place where it might benefit students of the technical schools. When we shifted to the Advanced Schools, which are technical colleges, the conflict generated by fear was absent; here the sailors had a demanding and interesting curriculum and a sense of academic achievement.

Since the Weekend was never intended to stand on its own, but rather designed to give people a glimpse of a new way of life, I followed the original San Diego model and prepared a home base. The Weekends were launched from the Credo Center which was furnished following the philosophy of informality that characterized the Credo House in San Diego. Returning participants, students and staff from the schools, were absorbed into a larger Credo community that gathered at the Center to continue the new way of life they experienced on the Weekend.

With the operation functioning well, I settled into what I anticipated would be a three-year tour. And then I received a telephone call from Ross Trower, now Chief of Chaplains. Mentor in Washington during the formative days of Credo, the man with whom I shared a tearful good-by in Newport when I resigned, and the brother having lunch with Ruth and me when I struggled to identify the proper setting for Credo/Great Lakes, Ross called to tell me that I was to be assigned to *USS SAIPAN*, a large amphibious assault ship home-ported in Norfolk, Virginia.

"You will never be considered for captain," he explained, "if you remain with Credo and do not return to sea." In response, I explained that becoming a captain was not a major concern, but that being back serving the sailors would be reward enough. "I understand that," he replied, "but your opportunity for promotion is a concern of mine. There is no reason you should not at least be considered for captain along with your peers, so I want you to go to sea."

I was moved by what my friend was saying to me. After all these years, he was still by my side. And I was pleased to accept the assignment. The years of Credo had taken their toll of my energy, but even more, I wanted to demonstrate once more the validity and universal application of the Credo concept. I wanted to be far from the program so that whatever was done in San Diego, Norfolk, Great Lakes, and future sites would be because of the design of Credo and not because of any one personality.

The change of assignment affected Ruth and the family tremendously. The years of turmoil, the moves from San Diego to Spain, my resignation and our peripatetic journey with the Credo/Esperanza Community, the precipitous re-entry into the Navy (which necessitated our moving to the Chicago area in the wake of a blizzard), the move to Navy housing—all of this had left my family reeling. The kids even joked about our address in Navy housing, for them "1928 Ranger Court" was "1928 *Stranger* Court." My work absorbed me, enabling me to avoid many emotions. But the work did not enable me to lend all the support Ruth needed. I had Ruth and my work. She had me. We had the saving grace of our sons.

Ruth was still trying to integrate the turbulent events of the past few years, and was welcoming a period of stability at Great Lakes. She had turned to her significant talent in vocal music, singing in the *Cantiones Sacrae* in Evanston, and the newly formed *Camerata Singers* in Lake Forest.

The surprise set of orders meant wrenching Ruth from her musical groups, pulling our children out of school in North Chicago, temporarily settling them in Virginia Beach while I was flown to Spain to sail back with *USS SAIPAN*, and then settling into "permanent" quarters (and a third change of schools in one year for the boys) in Norfolk. In some ways the situation was a repeat of my first orders to sea, except there was much more responsibility for Ruth, as well as more companionship from the children. The boys did well, because Ruth was such an experienced Navy wife by this time.

6

Adrift On An Indifferent Sea, 1982-1989

USS SAIPAN was a refreshing break from Credo. Freed from the creative (and sometimes draining) tension of founding, designing, and administering, I became more spiritually centered. Within a stable framework, I could now be a pastor and teacher. So nourishing was the experience, that, although there were many deployments and weeks away from home, I was able to reaquaint myself with my sacramental grounding..

As mentioned before, I have often thought of a ship at sea as a profane monastery: a monastery in the sense of a band of men brought together through circumstance. They live to the rhythm of the ship's bells, which mark off each four-hour watch, and draw strength from the bonding with brothers embarked on a common mission.

I was under no illusion that SAIPAN was other than profane, since I had gone to sea many times before on a dozen destroyers and amphibious ships. To be sure, there may be a sailor or two on board who were altar boys, but they were more likely to be careful that their current behavior did not betray that fact.

My time onboard was a compelling reinforcement of one of the basic concepts of Credo: that of the beauty of the accidental community where diverse people find themselves living together and learn how to attend one another.

When deployed, my ship carried a complement of 1000 Navy officers and men, plus 2000 Marines—usually accompanied by their own chaplain. As ship's chaplain and senior chaplain, I was responsible for the spiritual well-being of a small city of young men and their leaders. The average age on the ship was approximately 19 years old.

Inclusion And Integrity

Persons who have not experienced the military often fail to consider that many young Marines and sailors are discards from our economic system. Our "all-volunteer force" is a euphemism for a military largely devoid of middle class enlisted personnel. In the past, many joined naval services as an alternative to being drafted into the army, but today the middle class is a smaller portion of the enlisted ranks.

A high percentage of those who enlist see military service as the only viable way they can flee chaotic social backgrounds and "be all that they can be" as the Army recruiting slogan says. Ships are full of these men (and now women), away from home, isolated, trying to keep afloat in the storm of life. Many had abusive relationships with their fathers and mothers. Spiritual orphans, they crave to belong and to be valued. Most have no spiritual home; they are adrift on an indifferent sea.

They were my flock and I their shepherd with an intimacy which could never be approximated in their home neighborhoods—even if they had gone to a place of worship. On a deployment of a combat ship, as a chaplain I lived with the men day and night. I was by their side as they stood watch. I watched movies with them and, following an old Navy custom, prayed with them over the public address system as many of them went to sleep each night. I shared my anxiety with shipmates who were also separated from wives and children. Together, we experienced the boredom of a long cruise and the excitement of a foreign port. I had the joy of informing them when they were new fathers, and had the privilege of helping them work through upsetting news from home. I was their priest and pastor, even if they did not possess an ounce of faith.

The average young man who would seek me out for help and companionship would be from a broken home, with an absent or inadequate father, and minimal constructive family times. The ship was his universe: it provided him food, shelter, companionship, entertainment, job training, income—in a word, security. The captain was his "old man," the petty officer under whom he worked was his older brother or uncle, who could turn out to be friend or foe. The chaplain was potentially the benevolent father to whom a crew member could turn in times of vulnerability and tenderness.

Whether the chaplain fulfilled that role was not a function of the religious denomination he represented, but rather the kind of life he lived, for most of the young men were far from any identity with church or synagogue. In fact, they were far from even self-identity, which is why they joined the service and wore a uniform. Even those who had positive experience with churches in the past still found denominational designations secondary.

They looked to their chaplain, regardless of denomination, as their pastor.

My final cruise on board this "profane monastery" coincided exactly with the primary events of the Christian liturgical year—Lent, from Ash Wednesday leading to Easter. The ship was heading for the Arctic Circle and had only two liberty ports where the ship's complement could go ashore for recreation. I wanted to see if a community could be built on board ship around the Christian story of the unconditional love of God, experienced without the hurdles of institutional religion.

Coming on board with the Marines was a fine young chaplain of strength and integrity. Don Belanus was from the same Reformed tradition I experienced with the Anker family 25 years before. The two of us brought to our shared ministry the strengths of our individual religious traditions. And in the process, we became fast friends and brothers.

On the Sunday before Ash Wednesday, the ship was on-loading 2,000 Marines in North Carolina, and as they settled in their bunks (literally racks or shelves stacked four high) aboard the ship that night, I arranged it so that one of the television options they could elect to watch in their compartments was Part I of Franco Zefferelli's *Jesus of Nazareth*, a sensitively made and authentically portrayed life of Jesus. Parts II and III could be watched on the following nights, Monday and Tuesday.

The next night following the film series was Ash Wednesday and the compartment we set aside for the Ash Wednesday service was overflowing. As I looked into the eyes of these young men and laid my hand upon their brows to administer the ashes I was deeply moved by their yearning for some connection with the love of God, and comforted by my connection with them. Those who were Roman Catholics, Lutherans or Episcopalians were familiar with this rite, but others who received the ashes were Baptists, Pentecostals, and fundamentalists for whom this liturgical act was foreign. In fact, the majority professed no particular church affiliation.

What happened next was astonishing. As the cruise progressed, the crew members themselves began to take responsibility for Morning Prayer and Evening Prayer. A few even gathered at bedtime in my office for the monastic office of Compline. Every evening the library was filled with sailors and Marines who led their own charismatic service. Each Saturday night another group gathered to say the rosary together. Every noon a handful celebrated the Eucharist with me.

On Sunday, there was a Roman Catholic service led by Bob Ryan, the Lay Eucharistic Minister. I invited him to join with the other chaplain and me for an inclusive Christian worship, as well. It included a choir of sailors and Marines, many of whom had no religious background at all. We sang hymns from the whole spectrum of religious traditions—renewal songs with a guitar, stately Lutheran chorales, devout Victorian favorites, sturdy Wesleyan hymns, and even songs from the medieval church.

The climax of worship on the cruise was a celebration of the liturgy of the Easter Vigil, an ancient liturgy of the early church preparing the catechumens who were to be baptized at the first light of Easter. It is a long service complete with 12 psalms, 36 readings of the salvation story from Genesis to John, interspersed with many hymns. Starting after midnight this makeshift congregation, largely composed of sailors and Marines whom few people in society give any significance, worshipped together for over three hours in the ship's training room.

One of the men asked to be baptized. Another man, a Greek Orthodox Marine, had secured some incense in a liberty port, and fashioned an incense pot from a cigarette "butt can." We must have sung over 20 hymns from all the Christian traditions. An Independent Fundamental Baptist shared the reading assignments with a sailor well known for his wildness on the beach. Sailor and Marine, fundamentalist and Roman Catholic, devout and doubting—all experienced a rare example of unity in worship.

Many of us then moved to the weather deck of the ship for an Easter sunrise service with several hundred officers and men joining us. During the night while we were worshipping below-decks, some other sailors, on their own, had fashioned a 15-foot tall cross made of two I-beams and suspended it across the stern of the ship. We were sailing due west, that Easter morning, a day out of North Carolina, and the sun rose directly astern. As it slowly climbed in the sky it was aligned with the suspended cross. The symbolism was dramatic.

The worship was fulfilling that day not because of the fine singing, or the careful presentation, or the beauty of the building. For sailors and Marines sang off-key, and the worship area was makeshift. But for me the beauty was the authentic worship of unassuming people gathered on their own on the open sea.

As is the way in the Navy, the experience would prove as ephemeral as it was indelible. The next day the ship unloaded our 2,000 Marines in North Carolina, tied up at Norfolk, and sent most of the crew on liberty. In almost the twinkling of an eye the community we had fashioned together was gone. Many of us were never to see each other again. But the closeness and intimacy of the spiritual friendships forged among the most unlikely of companions has had a lasting impact.

The Spirituality Of Friendship

The cruise reaffirmed two underlying truths I had discovered in my ministry. The first is that *the spiritual needs of humanity are universal*. Impoverished Cuban-American, devout Irish Catholic lay leader, electronics technician, highly educated physician, abused child of the ghetto, Marine from the backwoods of Georgia—we are all brothers and sisters, made in the image of God.

> *There are heroes in the seaweed,*
> *there are children in the morning*
> *They are leaning out for love and*
> *they will lean that way forever.*
>
> —*Suzanne*, Leonard Cohen

Whether in the seaweed or on the captain's bridge, humans have essentially the same needs and desires.

The second truism is that *when people relate on a spiritual level of friendship, religious strictures disappear*. For a person to comprehend the essence of the Christian story does not require that person to be orthodox in its interpretation. Nor does it mean that a Christian needs to go undercover with his own faith, so as to avoid offending another. When we are communicating truths that are *universal* (that is, they apply to everyone), and *essential* (that is, they convey the core beliefs of the teller), integrity of expression is the highest good.

For example, in Spain I gave the Christian mystical classic *Dark Night of the Soul* to my friend, Bill Weiner, the Jewish lay leader at the naval base. He found John of the Cross nourishing to his spirit, and, even fifteen years later we have referred to *Dark Night* in our conversations. Bill is just as much a practicing Jew now as he was then, and my motivation in giving him the book had nothing to do with either of our religious affiliations.

I gave him the book because things were on my heart that John of the Cross could articulate better than I could. I wanted my friend to understand me better, and I cannot separate my Christian self from the rest of me. The love of God which I have experienced in Jesus is of my essence, and I hope that for any one to see my heart is to see Christ dwelling within me. Bill does not see Jesus within me in the same way I do, but he sees God's love, and here is where we meet. God's love is the essence of my life and his, and it is this love which is our bond as we meet each other as authentically ourselves, Christian and Jew.

So, in the same way, the sailors and Marines who were a part of this remarkable spiritual experience on board USS SAIPAN, were able to sense the presence of love which I believe is of God:

> *God is love; he who dwells in love*
> *is dwelling in God, and God in him.*
> —I John 4:16

The best way I could publicly encourage that love was by using the metaphor that I understood best: the life of Jesus. If I diluted the terminology so as to avoid offending someone who might understand love another way, then I would be offending myself. "The more weakly one stands on the ground of his belief," Viktor Frankl, a Nazi death camp survivor, declared:

> ... the more he clings with both hands to the dogma which separates it from other beliefs; on the other hand, the more firmly one stands on the ground of his faith, the more he has both hands free to reach out to

those of his fellow men who cannot share his belief. The first attitude entails fanaticism; the second, tolerance. Tolerance does not mean that one accepts the belief of another; but it does mean that one respects him as a human being, with the right and freedom of choosing his own way of believing and living.

In the *SAIPAN* experience, those sailors who might have a different understanding of faith were not offended by my actions, because they could see that I meant no offense. They could, as it were, see my heart. In the same way I welcomed being invited to say the rosary by some Roman Catholic sailors and Marines because I understood that their invitation meant no offense, but was rather their expression of inclusion. It was not relevant to me whether the rosary was a metaphor I normally would use. What was relevant was that my companions wanted me, their chaplain, with them as they responded to God in their fashion.

Inclusion and integrity are key concepts of Credo; and they were lived out on a day to day basis on the ship. A ship has an integrity all its own, and crew members carry the identity of the ship: they wear her name on the shoulder of their uniform. Inclusion is not an issue. By government fiat they are ship-mates and it is the responsibility of every crew member to work out what that means, so that life on board may be harmonious. Although a crew member would not typically use this terminology, it means that there is not one person who should be excluded from the realm of brotherhood which is the ship. This inclusion is worked out through the bonding of friendship.

Inclusion also means each person accepting each other's statements and beliefs at face value, without "cleansing" them of something which might cause offense. For when you feel the need to rearrange another person's expressions, you are, in fact, finding the person unacceptable except on your terms. When judgment replaces inclusion, the community is the less for it.

If people, for example, feel they have to watch their word usage in order to be accepted, they are already aliens. For example, for me to know "Dale," for whom the Mormon faith is central to his life, I must allow "Dale" to be himself, a Mormon. Intellectually, I may find it offensive that the Mormons would call me a gentile, not a Christian, but I cannot ask "Dale" to stop expressing that part of himself because it makes me uncomfortable.

This is crucial on a Credo Weekend. People express to the others what is of deepest importance to them, what—if you will—their Credo is. Others on the Weekend may have quite a different understanding. Intellectually they may challenge the validity of the others' observations: but the validity of people is not in their *words*, but in the way they live their *lives*.

I recall being in a small group on one Credo Weekend with Jay, a college graduate in his thirties and Eddie, an uneducated "red-neck" teen-age father who railed against his step-mother, calling her a "Jew Bitch." During a lull in the conversation, Jay said to Eddie, "You know I'm a Jew, don't you?" Eddie, looking at him with surprise, replied, "Yeah, but you're different. I like you." Jay smiled and continued to try to make friends with the boy who was filled with hurt and anger. Jay was able to accept and include Eddie in his life, because he was getting to know Eddie, himself (which included his prejudice), rather than depersonalizing him in order to address the broader issue of anti-Semitism.

Gratitude

While having this spiritually healing time serving the crew of my ship and enjoying their acceptance, my family was harvesting some of the fruits of relative stability and focus. Ruth and I rented a house on a river inlet in Norfolk. We loved to watch our boys playing in the marsh, bringing in pails of crabs which we would drop in a steam pot on the stove. We bought another English setter as a companion to our old setter. Much of the time, however, the young dog was more interested in swimming after canvas back ducks in the estuary than being a companion to the children, or our old setter.

To celebrate this peaceful family time we all flew over to Spain, "space-available" on a Navy cargo plane and spent New Year's Eve in Cordoba and then Three Kings' Day with our old friend Pedro Díaz and his family. After ten years which had been sometimes intimate, but always intense, we were experiencing some refreshing stability. During this time, I gave little thought to the activity of the Chaplain Corps in Washington, and even less to Credo. My focus was on my family and on the sailors who looked to me for spiritual and emotional support. Hence I had no idea that another remarkable event was taking form.

One Friday afternoon, after a long day on the ship pierside in Norfolk, I drove home from the piers to rejoin my family. As I pulled into the driveway I saw all kinds of crepe paper decorations around the front door. On the door was a sign which my family had made. It read, "Congratulations, *Captain* Harris!" I could not believe my eyes.

Various messages had crossed my desk on the ship mentioning that the board was meeting to select captains in the Chaplain Corps, but I did not give them a second thought. I knew that many viewed me as a maverick. I had done the unmentionable by refusing my selection for commander in the regular Navy. I also remembered the senior chaplain in Spain, who looked me straight in the eye and, referring to my perceived incorrigibility, laughingly quoted the song from *Sound of Music*, "How Do You Solve a Problem Called Maria?"

But now I was a captain. After two years of experiencing not only unparalleled spiritual growth on board my ship, but also the beginning of deeper love within my family, once again the Navy formally acknowledged that they greatly valued me for my abilities. I received that which long ago I was convinced I would never get. Although I know I have often used the word *grateful*, that is the only word which describes not only how I felt then, but also feel now.

7

The Hungry Sheep, 1989-1994

My sojourn on *SAIPAN* proved to be a spiritual landmark. From that point forward I was convinced to the bottom of my heart that the bond of love between people who have been, even for a few fleeting moments, in the presence of the Holy Spirit (by whatever name that Spirit may be called) can be passed on by anyone, for love is contagious.

It was not long before our family pulled up stakes and went to Charleston, South Carolina, where my next assignment was as command chaplain at the Naval Hospital in Charleston, South Carolina. There I was active in the inpatient Alcohol Rehabilitation Center. I enjoyed being with people who were addressing the fundamentals of their lives, their personal credos; and was heartened by their willingness to open their hearts to the healing love of their Higher Power. In my experience, the Twelve-Step approach to spirituality has always been an impressive manifestation of the love of God.

In Charleston I also attended the long weekly meetings of the hospital Child Abuse Board, made up of social workers from the local communities and hospital representatives, including the chairman, a pediatrician. Each week I was exposed to a seemingly unrelenting narrative of people trapped in sexual addiction, passing on to their children what had been visited on them. Equally disturbing were some of the persons at the meetings who not only accused, but also sat in judgment. Many of the members of the committee were unable to bring balance and compassion to the meetings, I suspect because of the unresolved anger caused by their personal histories.

In Charleston, I also enjoyed dropping by to see the local Episcopal bishop (as I had in San Francisco and Norfolk) and having stimulating conversations with him. A scholar, author, and former seminary professor, Bishop C. FitzSimons Allison was a find. Since both of us were committed Christians concerned with the fraying of the culture, I felt a kinship with him. I remember one of his wise observations: "When the culture you are in is disintegrating," he said to me in one conversation, "to be behind the times is to be ahead." The stay in Charleston proved to be a time of consolidation, both for myself and our family who enjoyed a marsh-side home close to the open Atlantic, complete with verandahs and live oak trees festooned with Spanish moss—all well "behind the times."

Governors Island, New York City

Two years later, in 1986, I became command chaplain at the largest Coast Guard installation in the United States which is on Governors Island, New York, off the southern tip of Manhattan. I experienced events there which contributed to the growth of my Credo understanding, but they were not an unmixed blessing. On the positive side I gained a continuing appreciation of the value of worship, which, like music, transcends mere words and is able to strike to the heart.

In the nineteenth century, Trinity Episcopal Church, the historic parish on Wall Street in the nation's financial district, built a replica of an English gothic church on Governors Island. The (Protestant) Chapel of St. Cornelius the Centurion was one of thirteen auxiliary chapels which Trinity at one time operated in Manhattan.

As the Episcopal Navy chaplain on Governors Island, I was invited to celebrate the noon Eucharist at Trinity every Monday, thereby maintaining the century-old continuity between the military chapel and its mother church. Trinity's music and liturgy, the edifice, the variety of worshipers who would slip into a pew from Broadway and Wall Street, and most especially the camaraderie I experienced with the lay servers and the staff clergy, was a treat for me after all my years on the move. The vicar, Dick May, with whom I would serve later in Williamsburg, generously included me in many functions.

The time I most remember was an Ash Wednesday when I helped the large staff of Trinity clergy administer ashes. Literally thousands of men and women, only a fraction of them Episcopalians, poured into the church all day long to have priests lay hands on their heads and impose ashes on their foreheads. My eye to eye contact and my hand on the brow of some unknown pilgrim generated within me a deep sense of mystery and fraternity. On a grand scale at Trinity I experienced that same intimacy that I felt with my shipmates at the beginning of the *SAIPAN* cruise—all sorts and conditions of people—all sacred, all leaning out for the solace of a loving God.

Yet at the same time as I experienced the sublime, I also endured the petty: the scandal of religion. As senior chaplain, I had to deal with the complaints of a few parishioners. Some Roman Catholics were offended that the Protestants were using the Catholic garden hose and rakes. Some Jewish personnel were constantly scanning the horizon for any hint of prejudice; exclusivist Episcopalians balked at bringing their service into the nave, the main body of the building, rather than congregating in their elegant side chapel.

This experience of veniality was in stark contrast to the inclusive community I experienced as a member of the spiritual family aboard *SAIPAN*. From some members of the Governors Island religious community I experienced the anti-thesis of the two truths I learned from ship-board experience, namely that when people relate on a spiritual level of friendship, religious strictures disappear, and that the spiritual needs of humanity are universal.

At Governors Island, religious strictures destroyed some friendships; and some sabotaged the spiritual needs of the community. When an atmosphere of denominational barriers is fostered out of fear or distrust, the faithful find it difficult to transcend those artifices to meet each other on the common ground of their need for the love of God.

I shared the pain of my brother Roman Catholic chaplain who felt so alone, unaccepted by some of his post-Vatican II laity who dismissed him as obsolete. Ecumenicism is far more than joint church services and shared study groups, it requires a conversion of hearts so that people can put aside rivalry and see the incarnate God in each other. When individual congregations cannot be loving to those who are their very own, as in the case of the disheartened Catholic chaplain who felt discarded by his flock, then it is quixotic to expect magnanimity in their relations with others. Charity begins at home, and if home is defined in an exclusionary way, it probably will shrivel within its own walls.

I discovered that the four broad gold stripes on my captain's uniform sleeve may have opened some doors, but, to my regret, the gold decidedly closed the door to those young alienated sailors who fear authority. Promotion is a two edged sword. Certainly I could operate on an intellectual level with my peers. I possessed the ability to administer multiple chapel programs. But I was impatient with the conventions of daily living which mask the essence of the human condition.

I yearned for a return to the days of authenticity for my ministry, where I would relate on the level of fundamentals with people who knew not only that they were in trouble, but also were motivated to change. And I mourned my separation from those whose struggles were real, recognized and confronted.

The Hungry Sheep

Too bad, but it's the life you lead
You're so ahead of yourself that you forget what you need
Slow down, you crazy child
Take the phone off the hook and disappear for a while
It's all right if you're going to lose a day or two.
—*Vienna*, Billy Joel

Charles Vaché, the bishop whom I befriended while stationed in Norfolk over the years, told me that the position of Episcopal chaplain to the College of William & Mary was becoming vacant. The chaplaincy was jointly funded by the diocese and Bruton Parish Church, which had historical roots in the College. Bishop Vaché had known me and my ministry for years, and together we talked of what could be done to establish a comprehensive ministry on the campus which was more inclusive than the current conventional approach. When I showed an interest, he encouraged me to apply.

For several weeks I debated retiring from the Navy to become a college chaplain, particularly since the senior leadership of the Chaplain Corps was urging me to stay. After the many storms I had ridden out in my Navy career, it did my heart good to hear, once again, that I was valued. I had achieved significant rank and reputation in the Navy without compromising my ideals.

But this made the vocational decision much more difficult. On the one hand, by remaining on active duty I would be in line for some senior positions (which were apt to be administrative because of my rank), and I would be able to send our three boys through college with no financial worry. On the other hand, I felt acutely my separation from the young men and women of the fleet. It was to them that originally I felt called. Although I had the skills and intellect to be a good administrator and policy maker, I also had a singular gift of being able to get close to the most alienated. One incident, which illustrates the dilemma, pointed to the correct decision.

One noon, while I was in my office putting the last touches on a proposed chapel budget for the next fiscal year, I received a call from an outlying Coast Guard unit in Brooklyn. The commanding officer said that one of his men had just taken his life by jumping out a window. The lifeless broken body lay on the pavement in full view of his shipmates, and the captain needed help addressing the emotional needs of the survivors.

I was there within the hour and promptly blended in with the enlisted people, talking with them heart to heart, sharing their pain. They trusted me, even though they had never seen me before. The work I did with them was constructive, immediate, and authentic. I felt alive again, not enmeshed in negotiations over salaries for the Directors of Religious Education, or sorting out whether the Protestants had the Roman Catholics' Electrolux.

When the incident was over, the commanding officer thanked me for the "professional" job that I had done. "I guess, Chaplain," he said, "I should have referred that man over to you a long time ago. We have not known how to deal with him for months. We tried everything. But because he was not religious, we did not refer him to you. If we had, he might still be alive."

I assured the troubled captain that he did what he thought best, and nothing more could be expected of any one. Yet, at the same time, I thought that he was possibly right. The gulf between the pious and the profane, the highest and the lowest rank, was perceived to be so profound that a life may have been lost purely because of the disconnection of the various "worlds."

With this experience it became clear to me that I should honor my original calling to serve the alienated, and put aside the attractions of the rank I had earned—and the considerable weight this position brings with it. Rank is power conferred by the system of which one is a part. Yet I knew that the real power I had lay in the grace which enabled me to bear the love of God. To a large extent that gift lay fallow. The suicide incident reminded me of that.

My mind flashed back to the commanding officer in Spain sitting behind his flag-flanked mahogany desk, asking me how I could give up "all this," in order to form a spiritual community. I remembered the proud day when, with Ruth and two of my sons looking on, the commanding officer of SAIPAN pinned on my collar the silver eagle captain's insignia. "You used to seek to change the establishment," he joked at the time. "Now you *are* the establishment." I also remembered the humorously humbling comment of my son Tim when he heard I had been selected captain. "Now when we go to the Exchange, Pop," he said with a grin, "you can park up front, next to the disabled."

The Shepherd

With the encouragement of Bishop Vaché I arranged to meet with the parish chaplaincy search committee in Williamsburg. I met with the rector, Dick May, formerly my colleague at Trinity Church, Wall Street; with the current members of the Canterbury Association, the Episcopal student group; and with the lay College Committee of the parish. We explored areas of mutual concern; and I included a detailed booklet about Credo as an example of my approach to ministry.

But each of us saw what we wanted to see. I was viewed as a Navy Captain chaplain—an establishment figure and an alumnus of the College. That I appeared before them in a tweed jacket or a Brooks Bros. suit did not disabuse them of their perception. But their perception was inaccurate. Captain I was; establishment just as surely I was not. The William & Mary chaplaincy I saw as fertile ground for a compassionate outreach to churched and unchurched alike. I could not wait to get involved on all levels, particularly with those students and faculty who found traditional religious resources unappealing.

By including Credo material for the chaplain search committee to look over, I had laid my cards on the table, but I overlooked the fact that my Credo ministry was never addressed in the interviews. I did not want to see as conventional the job for which I was being hired. Both my perception of the search committee's stance, and their understanding of my gifts were equally selective.

After some ambivalence expressed by the rector who told me he had originally envisioned a younger, less seasoned chaplain, the parish extended to me a generous contract. Our family moved to freshly-painted parish quarters close to William & Mary, my alma mater, where our eldest son, Tim, was a sophomore. Ruth soon secured a position as music librarian at the College. No parish could have received a family more graciously.

Yet, it was not long before it became clear to me that although all of us involved in the selection process were people of good will, the words spoken when we talked of chaplaincy meant different things to different people. Because of my experience in the Navy, my understanding of the role of a chaplain was broad and inclusive. While on active duty I was endorsed by the national Episcopal Church to minister to the members of the sea-going services as a body. Therefore, when I was aboard *SAIPAN*, my responsibility was to address the spiritual concerns of all of the ship's company, the profane as well as the pious—with a unique sacramental ministry to those few Episcopalians aboard. Naturally, I conceived of the position "Episcopal chaplain to William & Mary," to mean a chaplain whose duty was to be the Episcopal presence on campus ministering to all the students and faculty of W&M, regardless of their religious affiliation. In the context of this understanding the population I would serve approached 6,000 students, and the accompanying faculty and staff.

Gradually I realized that other people conceived of the chaplaincy as mainly "chaplain to the Episcopalians at William & Mary" (which trimmed the number from 6,000 to the 400 who had indicated their church preference on their freshman forms); or perhaps more accurately, "chaplain to Episcopal students who attend church on Sunday at Bruton Parish" (which narrows the base to perhaps 40—less than 1 percent of the student body).

Although I understood the perception of those who had a more parochial perspective, I also suspected that they were unaware of how the campus world had changed. These loyal church people perceived the chaplaincy to be a parish-based ministry serving the faithful. Because the local lay leadership were believers who regarded the church as important in their own lives, they presumed that the parish had a credibility which the culture, and therefore many students, no longer acknowledges.

In fact, the situation is quite the contrary. The growing unchurched population of our country does not comprehend the value of the institutional church. Recently at William & Mary, a conservative Southern university, approximately two thirds of the incoming freshmen indicated no religious identity on a questionnaire. Among the distinct minority who did indicate an interest in church, the number of incoming students who identified themselves with "mainline" churches numbered only a little over 25 percent.

I was convinced that if the chaplaincy and the visible church continue to concentrate on ecclesiastical (rather than Christian) identity, they would serve a progressively shrinking pool of incoming students. The invisible Church would continue to be found elsewhere in small groups such as those Christians who are members of Alcoholics Anonymous and other Twelve Step expressions. The loving community of God is not confined to those who attend church. In a remarkable address delivered to religious educators, Don Marcelo Gonzalez, Roman Catholic Primate of Spain delivered the same message in 1989:

> We must leave the churches and search for the modern men and women outside of the church wherever they may be.... We cannot limit ourselves to that which we have always done in the parishes; that will be of service to a small group who take refuge in these parishes as a place of sterile consolation. There must be a call to adults, but not in a traditional summons of prayer and feast days. With that we already accomplish nothing.

Although frustrated by what I saw as a myopic vision of the parish which had called me to serve as chaplain to the College, I did the best I could, hoping for a future opportunity to reach many more. I ministered to the handful of Episcopal students in traditional ways. I planned retreats for them, one time using Henri Nouwen's *Out of Solitude,* reflections he delivered to college students at Yale. I hoped to encourage students to begin to move out of a tendency toward narcissism and see themselves as bearers of love to the campus. I encouraged them to take responsibility for planning and executing liturgical events. Together we planned an Easter Vigil at Bruton Parish Church. We used the same leaflets that the *SAIPAN* print shop had produced, but at Bruton Parish there was no need to use an butt can for a thurible.

In addition, I encouraged the students to be an integral part of the parish, while urging the parishioners to take the students seriously as their intellectual and spiritual peers. The real nourishment I provided to some was spiritual friendship.

Yet, I did not feel at peace. All told, I would estimate only 1,000 of the university's 6,000 students had even minimal contact with any spiritual or religious outreach. The church was essentially mute to the other 5,000 who were left alone to look after their emotional and spiritual development in a vacuum. In an article in *Christian Century* William Willemon, the chaplain to Duke University points out why I believed it was essential to be among those who had no contact with faithful adults:

> Increasing numbers of our students have been inadequately parented. They arrive on the campus having missed important aspects of human development—interaction and conflict with their parents over values. They were left to their own devices. These are not people yearning to be left alone by adults. In my first year seminar I ask students to write a short "personal history paper." This past year out of the 16 papers I received, seven mentioned that the most determinative life-changing event for them was their parents' divorce. Only one paper mentioned a father. It was as if these young people were orphans.

When many young people leave home and go to college, they find themselves facing a situation fraught with anxiety. The pressure to succeed is compounded by competitiveness, which further splits students apart. Rather than confronting the difficult social transition, some choose the easy solution to this stress, and shut off or hide. An effective way to hide from the social transition is to become ever more immersed in the intellect, continuing to compile the grades and approval that is rooted in production, not self. As Willemon observes, these students rarely stop long enough to integrate into their lives what they are reading:

> Students seem to believe that the university is merely a step on the way to law school, a necessary evil to be endured before Wall Street. They are here because they want power—power as defined in this society's conventional terms—not because they want Duke to change or themselves to change for the better.*

Another way to feel less powerless is to become immersed in compulsive sex, or drug and alcohol abuse, both of which contribute to depression. What was missing among the classmates was a feeling of responsibility for each other's lives, a responsibility which is at the core of any faith group, Jewish or Christian. In this aspect I felt the students were less mature than the sailors I had known.

For many of the students competitiveness, alienation, distancing from one another was the norm. Many were left by their class-

---

* This is a seminal discussion of student and faculty life which should be required reading for college faculty. William H. Willemon's article, "Reaching and Teaching the Abandoned Generation, " may be found on page 1016 of the 10/20/93 issue of *Christian Century*.

mates to fend for themselves. I read in the student newspaper about a young women being retrieved by the campus police from in front of a fraternity house the morning after she had passed out. How many of her classmates, I thought, had passed her by the night before? I doubt that this would have happened among sailors on liberty together.

One friendly young man, was known by many on the campus because of his sunny smile and generosity. He had an inner circle of friends, and a much broader group of acquaintances who enjoyed his company. In Williamsburg he lived life to the full, and enjoyed taking risks. He particularly relished the free feeling of speeding off on his motorcycle, feeling the wind buffeting his body.

On his twenty-first birthday he indulged in a full day and night of celebration. Knowing him well, his close friends initially kept his keys and helmet from him, because they wanted to keep him from harm. For a while they were their brother's keepers. But as the evening wore on and it was time to head home, they relented. They gave him access to his motorcycle, but decided to follow him home in their car. Of course the motorcycle shot off into the night. When they caught up with their friend, on a road adjacent to the campus, all that was left was his broken body, and a bike smashed against a tree.

In their grief the friends did not know what to do in the next day or two. A local mortician was preparing the remains for shipment back to their friend's home, and consented to have one or two of the young man's closest friends view the body. About one hundred students accompanied the two of them. But viewing the remains of their friend was not satisfying to the students. His friends, who had no apparent grounding in faith, mourned without hope. They remembered that a few weeks before another student had died. No one arranged a service for that other student, only a time when friends gathered with the mourning parents to play some of his favorite rock songs.

Rather than excluding a religious element as in the other situation, the fraternity brothers decided there should be a memorial service in the chapel to coincide with the funeral in their fallen friend's home town. I was asked by the College if I would lead the service.

As I entered the walnut paneled 17th-century Wren Chapel, I noted that the closed altar rail supported a large framed photograph of the young man. Almost an icon, it was flanked by what appeared to be fraternity flags. As I recited the comforting words of Jesus, "I am the resurrection and the life," to a chapel packed with young mourners, it was a strange feeling to wonder if many out there knew what I was talking about. A line from Leonard Cohen's "Please Don't Pass Me By," came to mind: "*I dreamt of a Savior with no one to save.*" The chapel seemed full of pain and confusion.

One by one the young man's closest friends stood up during the service to give some sort of eulogy. Helplessly they tried to express their grief. Many of their reflections lacked even a kernel of hope in a loving God. I will never forget the tall, intelligent fraternity brother who stood in front of the altar facing the people with his house-painter's hat on. Clutching the picture to his breast with an outpouring of sorrow and anger, he was nevertheless unable to affirm anything but the good times they had experienced partying together.

I felt sorrow for the students milling around the sanctuary where I stood at the conclusion of the service. The students left the chapel somberly with little spiritual affirmation evident, except for a few who provided one another a comforting hug. They seemed bereft of faith, with no anchor at all. I am told that many went out to drink later in the day to reminisce once more at the beer hall where last they saw their dead friend. Who has failed them, I asked myself, that they have no hope, only their hunger and pain? "The hungry sheep look up and are not fed," is the way Milton put it. Was the Primate of Spain at all correct in his allegation that the Church had become a place of "sterile consolation?"

The university tries to lend support by providing an extensive professional counseling service to minister to the emotional needs of students. But their skilled counselors are overwhelmed, and because of their heavy caseload, some students who seek their services feel that their contact is both too short and too infrequent. At any rate, the responsibility of the counseling service can only be for acute situations of troubled students. It does not propose to address the spiritual void of the individual or the malaise of the culture.

In this area, therapy needs to come from recognized spiritual resources which can augment the help provided by the discipline of psychology. A few of the students were within the care of a concerned cadre of ministers offering a traditional chaplaincy model, but most were not. An innovative approach is now coming into being through the College of William & Mary School of Education. Established in 1992, *Project Taproot* provides a free drop-in clinic which serves as a training ground for substance abuse counselors. Central to its approach is the provision of a spiritual component in any response to substance abusers. The situation seemed remarkably parallel with that of Credo some 18 years earlier. Could it be, I wondered, that the Credo model could be replicated in a university setting?

With a combination of trepidation and curiosity I decided I would attend a Navy Credo personal growth retreat (PGR) in Norfolk as an anonymous participant. Although for eighteen years I had been the leader, this was the first time that I had ever attended as a participant. I brought along two college students who were military dependents. From a pastoral standpoint I hoped to see whether the Credo approach would be effective with students. But personally, I wanted to see if Credo had survived 18 years of over 100 chaplains interpreting the process as leaders.

My experience as a participant on that Weekend with the Navy confirmed the integrity of the process. The leader, Chaplain Bron Forester, was a caring man of faith. Around me I witnessed many people being transformed by the love borne by their fellow Weekend companions. To be sure, some dilution of the process had occurred. The impact of the musical anthologies had been lessened not only because a "Boom Box" was used rather than high quality stereo components; but also because various people had inserted their favorite songs with little understanding of how the selections should be integrated.

One example was the theme song "Memories" from the Broadway musical *Cats*. Laden with orchestration, it represents a tradition of music quite foreign to most of the people who were listening on the retreat. Although a well intentioned addition, I felt it missed the mark. Nevertheless, audio equipment and music selection was something which could easily be remedied. The inclusion of other songs which were less performances and more authentic expressions of the artists singing them, and the upgrading of the sound equipment would restore the integrity of the process. All in all, I was grateful to find Credo at least as powerful as it had been from the beginning.

Unfortunately, the two Episcopal students I had invited from the Canterbury Association were reluctant to pay substantial attention to their personal lives. Both had alcoholic fathers whose actions had caused deep wounds in their lives. As one of them told me, "I know I have to work on my relationship with my father someday, but my interest now is to get through college with as little added stress as possible. I'll wait until later."

Of course, I knew that never is there a convenient time to deal with deep-seated feelings. Thus, I regretted that they were not ready to seek the freedom from fear and distrust which would make the rest of their school experience more rewarding. Despite their reticence, however, I could see that the two had received benefit from the experience, and I left the Weekend convinced that much could be done for the student body at William & Mary through Credo.

The Drowning Can See

Jesus was a sailor when he walked across the water
And He watched the world go by from his lonely wooden tower.
And when he knew for certain only drowning men would see Him.
—*Suzanne*, Leonard Cohen

It was becoming clear to me that my concern to delve under the conventions of religious life was incompatible with Bruton Parish's vision of ministry. A wintry Saturday night in Virginia Beach brought the contrast in our understanding of ministry into clear focus. Ruth and I had been invited to the retirement ceremony of Bron Forester, the leader of the local Navy Credo unit.

With about one hundred other people, we gathered in the banquet room of one of those anonymous Holiday Inns. After the tired carrot and celery sticks and the steam-tray warmed chicken dish, the time came to bid Bron good-bye.

Having attended many retirement dinners, I settled back expecting to endure platitudes about the chaplain. Instead, I saw a broad spectrum of people express gratitude to Bron for exposing them to a new way of life that had brought them a renewed sense of purpose. One was a retired admiral in his eighties, several times a widower and battling cancer, who was volunteering for several Weekends a year to come along as a helper on the retreats. Another was a young Hispanic sailor who told how thankful he was to be able to return to Credo the help that he had received for his family. A third was a gray-haired pensioner, known as "Mom," who was greeted by all with great affection. After all had spoken their piece, Bron humbly accepted their thanks. The group of 100 people from the most diverse walks of life then spontaneously joined hands around the room and sang, "Amazing Grace."

The next morning I participated in the services at Bruton Parish Church. The setting was beautiful. The eighteenth-century colonial architecture was exquisite. The sun streamed through the clear glass and bathed the enclosed pews. The large choir sang Mozart. The stately progression of the liturgy was done with such taste. That Sunday I mounted the pulpit, as it was my turn to preach. Clothed in appropriate ecclesiastical garb, I looked over the congregation of well-dressed and well-meaning people, and delivered a substantial sermon which I hoped would address their spiritual needs.

There could not have been a greater contrast to the night before, with the rag tag collection of compassionate humanity, many of them unchurched, joining hands to sing a hymn around the cluttered tables and half eaten desserts at the Holiday Inn. For me, it was not a matter of which was better, but rather where I belonged.

Once again, I realized that my calling is to be with those who *know* they are drowning, rather than with those who are treading water. To join with others in a mutual awareness of the immediacy of our need for spiritual grounding enables me to respond directly with intensity and compassion.

Sharing the immediacy of our need for the centering love of God is what happened that night before in Virginia Beach, and it is what occurs on the Weekends. Alan Jones, dean of Grace Cathedral and noted author on spirituality put it this way:

> The Weekend has the ability to take people of all ages, abilities, and walks of life and giving them voice so that they can speak of both their pain and their longing. What impresses me most is the way in which the inarticulate are able to speak. In giving voice to the voiceless, community is born. ... It works across the board with all kinds of people who have come to a point in their lives, because of desperation or insight, where they are willing to risk being "born again" into community.

As a campus chaplain, my response to this awareness of our frailty was to offer three Credo Weekends to the college students. Since I had made friends in the fraternity and sorority circles on campus, as well as within religious organizations, I asked them all to come and bring their friends.

Held in October 1989, the first William & Mary Credo Weekend spanned the spectrum of student society: insiders and outsiders, Greeks and Independents, religious and irreligious, musician and linebacker. One young man was dealing with a vocational decision. A baritone with an outstanding voice, he asked his fellow students on the Weekend what they would think of him if he pursued a career in the arts, and what the implications of that choice would be for his social life.

Another student was wrestling with childhood family problems which were still generating serious conflicts within her as she prepared to graduate. An American woman of African parentage reflected on both the racial and ethnic complexities of her life at college. She explained how she was caught between the black community with whom she shared the color of her skin, and the general American community with whom she shared common aspirations, and how it affected her image of herself. Another talked of his confining life within a fraternity house of 32 other men. An intense student philosopher and composer found the music an effective means to begin to confront the confusion which reigned within him, particularly in his relationships to others.

My only experienced helper, whom I had met at the Navy Credo Weekend, was Maripaul. A widow, she had found her marriage to her jet pilot husband resurrected through their attending Credo Weekends in the Navy, only to lose him a year or so later in a plane crash. An older parishioner of Bruton Parish, Ricks Wilson, also was with us. On the Weekend he realized that he was valued by the young people, even though he felt society in general had put him on the shelf because of his age. A perfectionist Charismatic, who felt safe behind his religious words and attractive appearance, Ricks began what has turned out to be an arduous journey toward authenticity.

Each successive Weekend built on the last. Included were concerned lay people, an executive from Colonial Williamsburg, faculty and more students. Even Joe Girzone, the kindly author of *Joshua*, the best-selling novel about Jesus in modern society, consented to participate. With each Weekend the level of intimacy seemed to grow: some students spoke freely about suicidal thoughts or general depression. Many who attended were trying to find a clearer focus for their lives.

One student, Will Armstrong, later explained how the Weekend affected him:

When I left for college in the summer of 1988 to start my first year at William and Mary, I was scared and excited. I reluctantly reported a full month early for football camp. I had enjoyed the game in high school, but never had very high aspirations to play in college. Looking back, I certainly was not ready to be on my own, but I was so relieved to be out of the realm of my parents' supervision, that I did not acknowledge the responsibility of being independent.

In high school I had experimented with drugs, mainly pot and alcohol, and now in college I wanted my identity to be as a real party animal. I was eager to find others who shared my same desire to "catch a buzz." I had complete freedom. I could stay out all night and skip my classes all the next day, and my parents would never know. I could not believe how easy it was to get wasted.

My pattern of staying up partying all night and sleeping the next day became harder and harder to break. Despite my apathy towards academics, I managed to continue to hang on. I was extremely unhappy with myself, however. My depression worsened the more I used drugs and slept, and my poor performance at school compounded my misery. The guilt I felt towards my family was overwhelming. I wanted to just leave school and never come back, but I certainly did not want to go home to face my parents.

In the fall of 1989, a friend could see that I was hurting, and convinced me to go on some weekend called Credo.

Hesitantly, I attended the Weekend not having any idea what to expect. I was thrown in this environment with several William & Mary students who did not appear to have anything in common with me. As the Weekend unfolded I soon realized how similar we really were. Several others were grappling with the problem of substance abuse, and almost everyone had trouble relating to their parents and meeting the expectations of others. Everyone there knew the academic pressure which can so often be suffocating.

I found that the opportunity to relate to others of different ages and to get out of the college rat race for a Credo Weekend was truly a unique one. The warmth and caring that I felt on that Credo Weekend really changed my life. I was able to put things in perspective, and realize what I really wanted for myself.

Shortly after the Credo Weekend I was forced to leave college because of the poor grades I had compiled while involved with drugs and alcohol. There were some courses I never attended, preferring to stay in my dorm room and use with my friends. But when I left William & Mary I took with me the insight that I had gained on the Weekend. I continued to use drugs for about four months after the Credo Weekend, but it was never really the same. Now that I was back home, drinking and drugging was simply a way to avoid dealing with the realization of my addiction that occurred on the Weekend. The Credo Weekend planted a seed. The seed was the spiritual experience of making genuine friends and finding peace and happiness without the use of chemicals.

A couple of months after failing out of college and returning home, I decided to seek treatment for my addiction. After completing an outpatient substance abuse program, I moved back in with my parents and began rebuilding a loving relationship with my family. Through the help of God, ever-present in my involvement with AA and Credo, I have not felt the need to use drugs or alcohol since.

When I left William & Mary I swore never to return to that dreaded place which caused me so much anguish. Now I realize that it was my self and my addiction, not my surroundings, that caused my despair. I returned to William & Mary because I knew that my friendship with Don and my other Credo friends, and involvement with Credo would provide new friends and support that I needed to stay sober.

It has not been easy returning to college where the social life revolves around drinking. The pressure to pull up my grades in order to graduate was also a heavy burden. My involvement with Credo, however, has been a powerful force in my life and enabled me to accomplish what I set out to do in my recovery. Attending Weekends has refreshed my spirit, giving me a spiritual perspective outside the realm of intellectual discipline. It is keeping me grounded, knowing who I am and what is really important to me in my life. But more than that, Credo is giving me the opportunity to bear the love of God to others, including William & Mary students who are in need just as I am.

The Credo Weekend in Cleveland on the inpatient drug and alcohol ward was a culminating event in my life. The experience of helping my fellow brothers who were dealing with addiction solidified my desire to serve others. I graduated from William & Mary last spring, and providentially, I was invited to stay and get a master's degree in a new program for substance abuse counseling with a spiritual component. I have just completed my first year in graduate school, and I find that Credo still sustains me.

I realize that the training for counseling is essential and I am grateful for the opportunity I have. If someone would have told me five years ago that I would be studying to become a substance abuse counselor in graduate school at William & Mary, and working in substance abuse prevention with disadvantaged youth, I would have laughed hysterically. I also realize that as a counselor, I need to continuously grow in my own recovery. Credo helps me do that, and it also keeps me humble, for I always learn something more valuable that what I read in a textbook from someone on the Weekend with whom I otherwise never would rub elbows.

Credo planted a seed which has grown in my life to proportions that I never dreamed possible. The spiritual void which caused my addiction and depression has been filled with genuine relationships with people and a loving God. The theology of Credo is one of love, plain and simple. My desire is that students and the like can get a taste of this love and change their lives, thereby preventing lots of pain and hardship. I feel blessed that Credo planted a seed which did, and continues to, give me a life of peace and love.

There was no question that Credo could be effective with students. But the problem of defining what kind of ministry the Episcopal Church wanted—parochial or inclusive—remained.

Bishop Vaché directed me to form an Ad Hoc Committee on College Ministry to consider the direction the Episcopal chaplaincy should take at William & Mary. The committee included the current and highly-respected Vice President for Student Affairs at the College, Sam Sadler, who was a United Methodist layman deeply concerned on a national level with the course of his church's campus ministry.

After much study, and a day-long brainstorming session held at the College, the committee recommended that the diocese move the locus of the chaplaincy from Bruton Parish to the campus. But the leadership of Bruton Parish flatly rejected the recommendation, and declared they could not in good conscience provide financial support for such a move should the bishop approve it. It appeared to be a stalemate, and our deliberations futile.

But during the same season that the committee was being assembled, I received a call which cast my ministry in a clearer perspective. Neil Stevenson, one-time Navy Chief of Chaplains, now senior minister at the Williamsburg Presbyterian Church, called to ask my help. He told me of a parishioner of his, Irving Stubbs, who was a unique man with a clear vision.

Irving, Neil told me, was a graduate of Union Theological Seminary in New York and Presbyterian minister, who had married his theological understanding to the systems transformation philosophy of W. Edwards Deming. A leader in the field of executive development, Irving was able to translate the message of the gospel, stripped of its religious accretions, into broadly acceptable terms of quality and personal values formation.

Neil told me that Irving was a close friend and mentor to a remarkable religious leader, Dr. James Forbes, newly appointed senior minister at Riverside Church in Manhattan, and asked if I would work with Irving to bring James Forbes to the William & Mary campus. My resulting friendship with Irving Stubbs has been rewarding to me, and crucial to the development of Credo Institute.

I worked closely with my fellow campus ministers to bring Dr. Forbes to the College. The son of a Pentecostal Holiness bishop in rural North Carolina, Dr. Forbes had been an articulate activist in the struggle for integrated housing in Richmond in the 1960's. Before accepting the call to Riverside, he held the coveted chair for preaching at Union Theological School, New York. The chaplains asked Jim to address the need for building bridges toward community on campus.

When Jim Forbes came to Williamsburg in the Spring of 1990 he met with every conceivable constituency. I was with him when he had lunch with the power structure of the city; when he talked candidly with the black students on campus; when he held a one-hour training session for the dean of students' staff. I heard him lecture eloquently one night to an academic audience. The next night, I heard him preach a moving sermon within a Christian service. He was all things to all people.

What struck me most about this remarkable man was the depth of his love and the vigor of his spirituality. Although I am sure he could have found many reasons to be bitter as an African American confronting the injustices of our society, I detected no hint of anger. He was truly a man who brought peace. Able to meet people where they were, he saw only their hearts. A person might be a civic leader or a minority student, dean or janitor, Christian or atheist. Forbes's only mission to William & Mary was to bring love.

The vitality that Jim's spirituality brings to his presence is contagious. His consistent message is to encourage people to awaken from their sleep and unleash the power of love which is within them. As he read his poem, "Release Your Song" (*see page 192*) that night, it resonated within me with all that I hoped Credo could be. When he talked on the theme "Let My Leaders Go," his words coalesced my thoughts. I could see that I should neither feel regret over the course of my Episcopal chaplaincy, nor should I be constricted by another's definition of ministry.

After talking with my friend Bishop Vaché, I tendered my resignation as Episcopal chaplain to William & Mary. Even though I had earned the respect of my fellow chaplains and was newly elected as moderator of the Campus Ministers United, clearly the parish leadership did not share my view of ministry, and the bishop was not willing to take the radical course of funding the chaplaincy exclusive of local financial support. I needed to step out of the way so that Bruton Parish would have the freedom to appoint another person who more closely conformed to their institutional needs. In turn, I needed the freedom to nurture Credo.

8

Home Port: Credo Institute

It took only a few phone calls to confirm the wisdom of my decision. Peter Valerio and Merrill Berman from San Francisco days; Peter Chase, Brad Hall, Charlie Bamforth, Molly Malone Carroll, Chaplains Phil Jerauld, Vince Carroll, Skip Hughes, Ray Fitzgerald from early San Diego days; Bill Weiner and Alan Jones from San Diego and Esperanza in Spain; Chaplains Bron Forester and Gordon Paulson from Credo/Norfolk; joined with students and faculty, such as David Holmes, a William & Mary religion professor known in the college community as a committed teacher; and some Bruton parishioners, to support the idea of bringing Credo to the civilian world.

As the word got out, I even received phone calls from Navy Credo people whom I had never met, thanking me for getting a civilian Credo underway. Several volunteered to be on the board. Together we pooled our resources to incorporate Credo Institute in August 1990 as a means to bring the Credo experience to the broadest possible audience. Our vision was not only to build a nationwide family of Credo participants and their friends, but also to encourage centers of Credo activity wherever the Spirit leads.

Over these last four years Credo Institute has borne fruit supported only by the free-will contributions of Credo friends. The base of names of people interested in Credo has increased 50 percent, and our Weekends could hardly be more diverse. The following is a description of the various kinds of people we have reached to date.

The Campus

The Weekends have produced lasting results when sponsored by those campus ministries which, although representing certain denominations, seek to support young people in their personal search for meaning. For example, the Episcopal/Lutheran Center at the University of Utah was the site of a Credo Weekend composed of active adult church members, students, and homeless men. The Wesley Foundation of the College of William & Mary used a Credo Weekend for their annual winter retreat for Methodist students.

Students are at an age and circumstance where their concerns about life's meaning are paramount. They are seeking answers which make sense. The concerned older adults who attend the Weekends learn how to care for the next generation by extending the students respect and trust, rather than treating them as perpetual children who need parental guidance. Together they learn that spiritual decisions come from within the individual, and cannot be imposed.

One student on a Weekend for example, spoke of his sexual history. He had been sexually active since the ninth grade, and for the past eight years had been involved with countless women. Now that he was about to graduate and enter the "real world," he was reflecting on how his experience would affect his ability to form a permanent relationship in marriage. On this Weekend he heard from an older woman about her unflagging devotion to her husband who had a degenerative disease. He saw that marital commitment was a reality for her. He also heard from others of the joy they experienced as a result of their long-term marriages and their children leading constructive lives.

In addition, he heard of accounts of sexual abuse from other members of his retreat, and the compulsive sexual acting-out which was the fall out from what had happened to them. Whether marital commitment would be viewed by him as an attainable goal, and how he would chose to deal with the unanticipated fall-out of his compulsive sex is a uniquely personal matter, one that no one else can manage for him.

One lesson learned on the William & Mary Weekends is that the inclusion of older and more experienced people on the Weekend enriched the retreat for all. Students remark that in hearing the stories of older people they realize how much the decisions they make in their youth have long-term implications in their lives. They also find that they gain a better insight into their relationships to their parents or grand parents when they relate to older people on the Weekend. Some retired people on the retreats discover that they are valued by the young for their age and experience. Rather than feeling as if they are put on the shelf as a spare part now that they "are not doing anything," they find that they are valued by others.

The Marginal And Homeless

Some of the most compelling Weekends have been held with this grouping. The stories that the homeless tell reflect early exposure to rejection which has been so severe as to push them to the very fringe of society. Many middle-class people on the retreats, including the students, readily identify with the results of lives of lovelessness, even though their own stories are not as dramatic.

For example, two young women students were on the same Weekend. One, from a leading Mormon family, felt isolated because of the shame she felt concerning the behavior of members of her "upright" family. The other, an Episcopalian from the East, fled an uncomfortable family situation by enrolling in the University of Utah, only to find herself further isolated by being part of a religious minority. From their interaction with the street people on the retreat, the two learned lessons of mutual caring. Transcending religious differences, they exchanged phone numbers so that they could relieve their loneliness through the love and support they could give each other.

The need for compassion that leads to being your brother's keeper is undeniable on a Weekend with the homeless. Recently I talked with a homeless man who had participated in a Weekend. "When I was admitted to the shelter several months ago," he told me,

> I was devastated. I could not face the other men there. In order to stay away I would while away the days by finding a coffee shop and sitting there for hours on end. As my money was depleted I felt more and more trapped. I went on the Credo Weekend as another way to avoid the shelter. Now I am

not ashamed to be in the shelter. I look at the other men with a different eye. I want to reach out to them with the love which I have found.

Wage Earners

The other aspect of bringing together a varied group is that class boundaries are erased, much as they are erased in the accidental community of a warship. When I was a social worker in Long Beach, I would host parties to which I would invite welfare recipients and social workers, Coast Guard officers and enlisted, friends from Dairy Valley, and graduate students. All got along well. So, in the same way on a Weekend, I find it gratifying to see an art dealer enjoying the company of a plumber, or a banker sitting down as a friend with a sculptor who is living alone in a hotel for transients.

Perhaps the most diverse Weekend included a student dancer, a CIA employee, a Salvadoran refugee, a cancer researcher from National Institutes of Health, a knife wielding teen age redneck, a counselor for homeless Vietnam veterans, a retired antiques dealer, a young man fresh out of the Marine Corps, a college professor, an alcoholic former advertising executive from the streets of New York, and a federal judge. The Weekend had a profound effect on several of the participants. One participant, a nautical engineer who runs a small consulting business, wrote:

At the two Credo Weekends that I have attended I have learned many things, mostly about myself. I know that my ability to communicate was somewhat limited, but when I was faced with a young man who just sat there with his head down when I tried to talk to him, I realized I had no ability to get him to talk. I soon ran down and couldn't think of anything to say. Luckily for him, we didn't spend too much time together.

I also learned that even when you don't say much, it can have an impact. While I was floundering around, looking for a question to ask him, I asked him what he would like to do if he could do anything he wanted. His reply was that he would fight. Everybody and anybody, but first his Dad. His voice was pure rage. I asked why he was so angry. He then told me that his father had beaten him brutally all his life.

This young man was 17 years old, married, his wife pregnant, a 15-month old child by her previous partner, he cannot read or write, and he is only occasionally employed as a House painter. He likes to paint pictures, and he told about some of the pictures he has painted. He stated that the last time his father tried to beat him, he beat up his father. He swore he would do it again, as soon as his father got out of jail.

I asked him what he wanted to do with his life. He didn't know. I went on to say that I supposed the first thing he wanted to do was to be not like his father. That was the only thing I said to him that got his attention. His eyes widened and he agreed with me. Vehemently. Later on I told him that everyone needs to make plans for the future. "Even short plans help you to aim your life," I gently urged.

Near the end of the Weekend I was informed that he told another group that he was not going to be like his father, he was going back to school, and he was going to try to be a better husband and father. I swelled up like a big toad. So I also learned that I could plant seeds. I hope fervently that they grow. But even with that small success, I felt a great lack of ability to get close and get down to gut level. That needs working on.

> Credo has taught me that all of us have the same need for love and acceptance from our associates. The highly positioned business person needs love from associates the same as the street person. We had them all at our last Credo Weekend. The more you can love unconditionally, the more you are loved unconditionally. It was wonderful.

The lesson of Credo is that, given the chance, people enjoy crossing boundaries to meet one another. They feel a sense of freedom in these relationships. We despair over Croatians, Bosnians and Serbs not accepting each other, or the antipathy between Northern and Southern Irish, but when, on a Weekend, a Roman Catholic feels akin to a Jew, a born-again Christian embraces a man struggling with sexual abuse, an intellectual confides with a security guard we can see that, as hackneyed as it may sound, the solution begins with us.

Counselors

Dr. Gary Moon, the founder of the Institute of Clinical Theology (ICT), chose to have a Credo Weekend as the introductory retreat for his post-graduate curriculum. The Institute is affiliated with the counseling program of PSI/Georgia State University in Atlanta, although then it was part of Regent University, in Virginia Beach. The Institute offers a two-year post-graduate program in clinical theology for professional counselors who want to deepen their helping skills by adding a spiritual dimension to their psychological training.

The gathering of twenty therapists, ministers, and counselors, some having traveled from as far away as Colorado, came together in Norfolk, Virginia. In many ways the Weekend replicated the experience in Spain when the young people involved with *Youth With A Mission* found a new freedom in the way they lived out their faith. The ICT post-graduate students held in common an evangelical Christian tradition and a desire to be of service.

At first, most of them listened with difficulty to the music of broken humanity. They had come to the Weekend expecting the uplifting songs of their worship tradition. One woman remarked that she felt the music was demonic—and indeed it was. But then upon reflection she realized that the confronting of demons articulated by the likes of Janis Joplin (as well as those within herself), was exactly what the Lord had called her to do as a counselor.

Because they were motivated to live lives of service, the participants steadily moved toward forming an affirming family of faith and love. At the conclusion of the Weekend, I experienced a particularly deep feeling of tranquillity within the community. They had learned the meaning of acceptance and reconciliation, which for some had been little more than concepts they read in the Bible.

When one religious conservative returned from the Weekend, he told me that he confessed to his wife, "I have been a Pharisee for thirty-six years of my life. I have always been right. Dear, how could you stand me?" She replied, "It has been very lonely." The man has now changed the priorities of his life, setting aside excessive church activity so that he could coach his young son's basketball team. His son's chest is swelling with pride, for he has his father back.

In-Patient Substance Abuse Ward

Our experience at the Glenbeigh Psychiatric Hospital in Cleveland was equally as powerful as that with the gathering of Christian counselors. The population we served was just about the antithesis of Regent University graduate students. With little formal education, they ranged in age from 18 to 60 years old. Half were black men, many of them workers in auto assembly plants. One had lost all of his fingers to frost-bite because he had fallen asleep in a drunken stupor in the punishing winter weather of Lake Erie.

The hospital administration assiduously avoided religious expression in the regimen of the patients. There were no Bibles, for example, available for patient use. Nevertheless, the human yearning for dignity and love was, if anything, more tangible there than on any other Weekend I have led. Rhetoric about racial differences and social inequality was never used. Because these drug and alcohol abusers knew that their continued life was at stake, they had little time for the luxury of anger and divisiveness. They unquestioningly accepted us as leaders, although all five of us were white. It made no difference who we appeared to be because they sensed who we were—people who came to love and serve them. The result was a group of people who began to accept that they were sacred and of worth, and who became motivated to fashion a new and constructive way of life.

And now, the experience is being replicated at the Colonial Recovery Center in Newport News, Virginia, with a broader spectrum of people in recovery. In addition to the Weekend, each Sunday I have used the Credo approach to music to transcend the formal structure of worship. By selecting a handful of songs that articulate the worshipers' struggle ("The Beast in Me") and emerging hope ("I'm Like a Soldier Getting over the War"), the congregation has felt a freedom to share their spiritual journey with one another

My five years experience with Credo Institute has confirmed that there is no area where the Weekend is inappropriate. Each Weekend takes on a flavor of its own as defined by those who participate. So long as people of good will are willing to suspend judgment, to grapple with their own fears, and to extend hospitality in trust to others, the spirit of the Weekend does the rest.

III

The Credo Weekend

Release Your Song

There's a song inside of me—
I can hardly wait to see
What it is I have to say,
Or the music I will play.

It's been so long in coming—
First the thought and then some humming,
But before I find my key
Something stifles it in me.

What keeps my song from being sung?
Past hurts, deep fears, a timid tongue?
What makes my freedom come so hard?
A self-made live-in prison guard!

Meanwhile the song still groans in me—
I can't be me 'till it is free.
Debating, calculating, hesitating to sing,
The song could die like a still-born thing.

"Release your song," said the Spirit to me.
"Be free! Be free! It's Jubilee.
Cast out each fearsome song patrol.
Proclaim deliverance to your soul."

The Spirit of life flowed through my blood.
I said "yes"—something broke—it came like a flood.
Up from within; down from above
A kingdom built on the power of love.

Thank God my song has been set free.
The rhythm and the words are right for me.
I'm finally ready to sing out strong.
My soul is saying, "This is my song!"

—James A. Forbes, Jr.

9

The Setting: The World Within Our Selves

As long as we are on earth, the love that unites us will bring suffering by our very contact with one another, because this love is the resetting of a body of broken bones. Even saints cannot live with saints on this earth without some anguish, without some pain at the differences that come between them. There are two things men can do about the pain of disunion with other men—they can love or they can hate. Hatred recoils from the sacrifice and sorrow that are the price of resetting bones. It refuses the pain of reunion.
—Thomas Merton

Resetting The Bones

It takes two to love, mutually giving and receiving. Fear comes from the very element that makes love unique: two cannot unite in a loving relationship if one of the two chooses to be isolated. If we are willing to respond genuinely to each other we are not in control of the result. It does not always turn out as we would like. All sustain wounds when those to whom we reach out are unable or unwilling to fulfill our desire for their love. When the wound heals, a scar is left, reminding us of the risk of being involved with love. If the wound has not healed, the ache is retained.

Nothing is more serious than to be denied the love you seek and need. It engenders a feeling of worthlessness that stems from the internal question, "What is wrong with me that I have been found unworthy of love?" When these feelings are reinforced by continual experiences of being denied love, the person begins to feel defective, spiritually adrift and of low worth.

I speak from my own experience. My father divorced my mother. With no explanation to my brother or me, he left us, his two sons, as well as my mother. He was around the area and was nice to my brother and me during weekend visits with him, but it was not the same. He could not be counted upon to be there when either my brother or I needed him. When as a little boy there was conflict or hurt to contend with, he was no longer present to protect or to mediate.

Often I hear people who are contemplating divorce justify their inclination by saying that their children will be better off when the conflict between the parents is over—when one of the parents leaves. It is true that conflict between parents at home debilitates their children, but often from the child's viewpoint, the abandonment by a parent is even more shattering. For me, each time my father drove away after dropping me off from a weekend together, he was leaving me once again. My father had chosen his own needs over our basic need as his sons to have a father by our side. We felt abandoned.

Statistics provide convincing evidence that many children of divorce fail to thrive. The damage done by the rupture of the family and the abandonment by a parent is often greater than the suffering generated by warring parents who remain with their children. During my years as a Navy chaplain, my advice to parents involved in apparently irreconcilable conflict was to employ all means possible to achieve reconciliation.

In some cases, however, divorce is the only option. Particularly in cases of emotional and physical abuse or addiction, it may be the responsible choice. In these cases, often the children understand, and although they are wounded, they are able to compensate if they are assured of the devotion of the parent with whom they live.

For years, well into my adulthood, I was preoccupied with why my father left me. Twenty years later, when he told me he left because he was afraid my mother was unstable, he confirmed my feeling of abandonment. If his diagnosis of my mother was accurate, I wondered how he could leave us behind.

My brother was so hurt by losing his father that the anger caused by that abandonment significantly impairs his life even fifty years later. Since he makes committed relationships only with difficulty, he has now entered the last phase of his life, still living alone with no family, no children. This was not his choice—it was, as it were, imposed upon him.

Trying To Be Free

> *Like a bird on a wire, like a drunk in a midnight choir,*
> *I have tried in my way to be free.*
> *Like a baby still born, like a beast with his horn*
> *I have torn every one who reached out for me.*
> —Bird on a Wire, Leonard Cohen

The progression is familiar: A sense of low self-esteem leads to an inner emptiness. Since love is based on mutual respect, if you do not respect yourself you are unable to engage in constructive relationships. If you see yourself as unworthy of love, when someone offers you love, you are unable to receive it. Individuals who doubt their worth are alienated from themselves, and therefore from others, from society, and from love extended to them through their neighbors' expression of concern. In the contemporary era of single parents, latch-key children, and confused ideas of love, it is no wonder that so many people feel a void in their hearts and come to Credo. Many feel there is little to trust, including themselves.

The fundamental purpose of the Credo Weekend is to help us accept our own worth. The Weekend creates an atmosphere that breaks the cycle of alienation and rejection, and fosters love. It provides an atmosphere of safety where we can try to trust each other with the needs of our hearts, and experience a compassionate response. This experience of love affirms our worth and frees us to affirm others.

Estrangement

Isn't it a pity, isn't it a shame
How we break each other's hearts,
and cause each other pain.
Forgetting to give back
The love which we've received.
Isn't it a pity?
—Isn't It a Pity, George Harrison

Alienation is something all humans experience. To a degree, every one deals with internal and spiritual estrangement, for separation is an integral part of the human condition. The death of someone close, a broken bond, an involvement in a destructive relationship, may leave us spiritual orphans. Since we depend on the love extended by others to feel whole, relationships that alienate can short-circuit our ability to give and receive love. We contribute to the devaluation of our selves. To be sure, love is stunted in a fragmented family, but it also can be smothered by those who become addicted to deal with their pain. If we numb the cries of our wounded spirits, we numb our relationships with others as well.

Certainly this feeling of isolation is widespread among many who come from broken homes. But it is not unique. Nor is estrangement confined to whole classes of people, racial minorities, the homeless, the sexually abused, and their abusers whom society uniformly marginalizes. My own alienation was masked, but the social alienation of the homeless person, the young drug abuser, or the homosexual, is obvious to the world.

The difference between the homeless or other disenfranchised people and the rest of us is that we live within social structures that allow us to keep spiritual turmoil from public view. Those at the homeless shelter, the rehabilitation center, and the courtroom, however, have no economic veneer behind which to hide. Their cover has been blown, their needs are on display, and their nakedness causes shame.

The immediate response of many is to cover a person's nakedness so that they need not be ashamed. They place a fresh gauze pad on the festering wound, rather than cleaning it. Well meaning people, for example, propose issuing welfare credit cards so that indigents are not demeaned by food stamps. But it is not food stamps that are demeaning. Credit cards do not promote self-acceptance.

Euphemisms abound to buffer harsh words such as *blind, illegitimate, crippled*. Once, when I was an intake worker at the Bureau of Public Assistance in Long Beach, California, I asked an illiterate farm hand whether he was applying for "public assistance." He stared at me for a long time, and then said "You mean welfare?" At the time, it occurred to me, that it was not their dignity we were protecting, but rather our embarrassment that they should have reached this economic state in an abundant society.

Credo encourages personal honesty so that all may experience acceptance just as they are. To gaze at the condition of others is easy, but it is more productive first to understand our own spiritual condition. If we do so with discernment, we soon discover no essential difference between ourselves and the woman at the rescue mission. Alienation does not afflict the abuser alone, nor the homeless mother, nor the AIDS sufferer. It affects the veteran, the questioning student, the compulsive corporate executive, the suburban mother, the care-worn single parent. It affects every one of us.

In American society our identity is what we *do*, rather than *who we are*. Whether it be in the work place, the class room, or even at home, most of us can be very productive without anyone knowing how empty we may feel inside. Solid citizens go to PTA meetings, sell oranges for the school band, read articles about the needy and send checks to an agency.

They never need to be embarrassed by revealing the void they may feel in their own lives. Insecure students compile impressive dossiers of high grades awarded by equally driven professors. Their academic production hides the personal issues that both the student and instructor may face in their personal solitude. Faithful church-goers can even greet their neighbors or pray beside them in a pew and never reveal their spiritual hunger.

The helping professions—religious, medical, and others would endorse the high ideal of acceptance of which I write. But each of them impose categories: clergy/laity; the saved/the lost; physician/patient; counselor/client in which, almost imperceptibly, the servant becomes the master. It is so difficult to put aside this prejudice, but it is vital to do so. We transmit life itself when our judgment is suspended, enabling us to extend our love without conditions.

Excluding Love

In the human understanding of love, one finds an apparent inconsistency. We want to be loved for ourselves to the exclusion of others. We are not satisfied to hear someone we love say to a group, "I love every one here." We would rather that person say,

"Out of all the people here for whom I care, I love you most of all." Yet that desire of ours for exclusive love implies the diminished value of another person. That is the antithesis of pure love, which is *inclusive*. The problem is that we harbor the misconception that love is a quantity like water, which diminishes when it is given out. The more love one person receives, the less is available to another. Hence the assertion: "There is only so much love to go around."

All of us who are parents have faced this situation, at one time or another, with our children. Each child longs for the unconditional love of his parents which will make him feel whole. Children who are insecure about their relationship with a parent are apt to examine how that parent treats a sister or brother. Too much attentiveness to one may be interpreted as rejection by the other. When this occurs, love ceases to be freely given and received, and becomes something to acquire.

In 1965, when Ruth and I were newlyweds, having lived together for only a matter of weeks prior to my deployment, we brought into our new family a love-starved teenager named Tom, who had no other place to go. Tom knew that while in the Coast Guard I had been closely involved in the travails of his large family in Seattle, and felt, therefore, that I was capable of strongly loving him.

But Tom also saw the love which Ruth and I shared as newlyweds, which was of a different quality and intensity than he experienced. Wanting so badly to belong, craving the inclusion that love brings, Tom feared that my love for Ruth would jeopardize his receiving the measure of love he needed to survive. Tom feared that love was a limited commodity and therefore viewed Ruth as a rival who needed to be eliminated for his own emotional safety. In order to belong, he sought to exclude.

As a result, Tom would seize every occasion when he and I would be alone together and "*she*" would be left out. He set up a competition where I had to make a choice between him and Ruth. The tension sowed discord within me, for I wanted to love them both in appropriate ways, and to exclude neither. But when I realized that Tom's relationship with me was one of acquisitiveness, whereas my relationship with Ruth was that of mutual sharing, I knew that the only true love that could exist in such a circumstance was with Ruth. In making this choice, I was not rejecting Tom. He was simply making it impossible for a healthy loving relationship to occur.

It was unhealthy because Tom wanted all the love he needed on demand. But love only reaches fruition when it is *freely* given and received. Tom felt his need for love was such that he dared not give up controlling its receipt. In his decision to exclude another person, Tom hardened his heart, and became less able to receive the love which Ruth and I freely extended to him. It was only as he slowly began to realize that love is not a *quantity*, but an unlimited grace, that he was able to begin to set his fear aside and receive the nurture he craved.

The only way for him to correct his misunderstanding of love as a limited quantity was to let go of all conditions, to take a risk to see what would happen. Only then could he experience love as freely available. In the healthy family children get the love they need and see that that is the case for every one in the household. Love ceases to be an entitlement and becomes a freely offered gift.

I belabor this point because in our era of shrill demands for individual rights many people narrowly define themselves to the exclusion of any one else, and look at others as competitors. Yet our identities must be based on who we are, not the categories into which we are placed. For you can only love *me*, not what I represent. If I accept being categorized as gay or straight, Christian or agnostic, male or female, officer or enlisted, then those who are not within my category become aliens.

Granted, we have to organize our thoughts into categories, that is how we reason and think. Certainly there are significant differences in the genetic makeup of males and females which affect our basic behavior. With other Christians I feel an affinity which is different than with my Jewish brothers and sisters. I enjoy the intimate times I have with my son Tim in a different way than I enjoy the companionship of my other sons, Chris and Jonathan. But to the extent that I compare and contrast categories, I leave out persons.

Sterile Consolation

It is so important that we leave the world of measurements behind when we speak about the life of the Spirit.
—Henri Nouwen

To categorize is to constrict love. Unfortunately, some people seek to be a part of a category in order to feel secure. When they identify with a community of people who are similar in one characteristic, they belong to a defined group. People may classify themselves as Roman Catholics, as Native Americans, as "in recovery," as African Americans. But if they jealously guard that identity to the diminishment of other relationships, they are not so much seeking to be loving as to belong. As they exchange inclusive love for security they lose the benefits of both, for it is only inclusive love which banishes fear.

The traditional public locus of love has been the religious community, be it church, synagogue, or mosque. The more institutional the religious structure is perceived to be, however, the less evident is the community of love within it. An interdependent community of love withers when an institution's need to control its members supplants the concept of mutual support. Control inhibits the freedom of love. The Roman Catholic Primate of Spain recently warned of this phenomenon when he remarked that churches have become "places of sterile consolation."

Although the organized church exists to bring the healing of God's love, many view the institutional form in which it appears with a jaundiced eye. During Christmastide 1992, an accusatory full page ad in the *New York Times* showed a bigger than life woodcut of the head of Jesus and asked Christians a disturbing question: "How can you worship a homeless man on Sunday and ignore one on Monday?" Since exclusion undermines love, it is saddening to see well-meaning church members unconsciously excluding others who appear different.

I remember sitting by the pulpit of a church and watching the ushers set up folding chairs for the overflow crowd. The ushers cordially seated their appropriately dressed visitors, but consistently overlooked two young men neatly dressed in T-shirts, who were among those patiently waiting to be seated. Soon the service began, the others were seated, but not the two young men, who eventually walked away. The ushers were good people oblivious of what they had done. But because the two did not appear to belong, they did not acknowledge them.

It is curious how uncomfortable we are even as we affirm that others are equal in God's eyes. It is the temptation of elitism. People want to feel unique so that they can feel superior. By design people diminish the value of others who are not like them, and they exalt themselves by saying they are gifted, or that they belong, or they are chosen.

When we set ourselves above or apart from others, we are instilling alienation and thereby generating fear. We continue the pain. For if all were gifted, if every one belonged, if all were chosen, then there would be no pride in the distinction. Is not every person sacred, worthy of love?

Yet, Israeli Jews slaughter Arabs, who stone them in return. Hindus demolish Sikh holy places. The Irish bomb each other. Iraqi Sunnis eliminate Iraqi Shiites. Serbian and Croatian Christians "ethnically purify" their country of Bosnian Muslims, and then purge each other. Tragically, religions that are dedicated to enhancing people's awareness of a loving God are also able to close people's hearts to those who are different.

A Third In Our Midst

A friend sees in you nothing but your heart.
—Aelred

On a Credo Weekend, a woman told of bringing her little daughter to Saint Patrick's Cathedral on Fifth Avenue while on her regular shopping trip to Manhattan. When her daughter asked her why there were homeless huddling by the doors, her mother explained that not only did the church welcome all people, but also felt a particular responsibility for the poor. Because of this loving inclusion, she explained, the cold and hungry were offered a place of rest in the church, a sanctuary from the harsh world outside. The young daughter pondered her mother's words.

After receiving communion, her mother hurried back to her pew, afraid for her daughter who was talking to a homeless man. As she approached the two, she heard her little daughter say to the man, "Are you hungry? If you are, there is enough at the altar for everybody." Joy filled the mother's heart.

She was so happy that her daughter understood the essential Christian message of love that she later related the story at her parish prayer group. "But was that homeless person a Catholic?" one of the women reacted with alarm. (In another denomination it might have been, "But was that homeless person saved?" or "Was that person worthy?"). The concern was not for the person, but for the rules—the control.

Credo is sympathetic to what congregations are trying to do. But we hope to help the religious people comprehend more deeply the inclusiveness which is a part of their faith. *Everyone is sacred, even the "unacceptable."* No one is profane. This is the core value of the Credo community, where no one on the Weekend is inherently better or worse.

As an institution the church rarely appears to be a safe place where people can tell their stories, particularly when what has happened is morally unpalatable. For people to feel sacred, they need to experience in real life that what they have done, or what has happened to them, does not diminish their value to others. They need, that is, to be reconciled. There is a particular need for acceptance during a time when the social fabric is frayed and many people, more than you imagine, have been profoundly violated due to the removal of socially imposed boundaries.

Recently I read an absorbing article "Sharing Bread, Sharing Tears" by Martha Barr, a Baptist lay woman, which articulates a calling of the Church that has lain dormant:

Memory is at the center of one of our most cherished acts of Christian worship. Christians gather around a loaf of bread and a cup of wine to eat, drink, and remember Jesus. This is ironic, because as an institution, the church has almost no experience remembering trauma or offering survivors a safe place to tell their stories. Survivors need a place where their bodies are safe and protected. And precisely because trauma breaks the social contract, ruptures the sense of community, and undermines basic trust, survivors need a community within which it is safe to remember and to speak.

Survivors need others to listen, to witness to the trauma, and help reshape the event with meaning, so that the trauma can be integrated into the person's life story. Yet to do this, we the church must be willing to share the pain. Are we willing to hurt in order for another to heal? To side with remembering, not forgetting, is to risk deep pain. For what is at stake is not factual remembering. ... It entails living the trauma over. But only out of such deep remembering can the whole person emerge, reconnected to others, to the world, and to God.

For the church, this will mean hard work. The church does not yet have much experience in supporting and empowering survivors to integrate their traumas. If anything, the experience of the church has been to urge them to be silent and amnesic."

A growing number of people feel alienated from those conventional religious structures within which nurturing love is barely discernible. It is no accident that millions find solace in Twelve Step programs such as AA, yet do not turn to the church or synagogue. On a Credo Weekend, a sailor told me, "Even though I don't drink, each week I go to an AA meeting because I feel loved and accepted just as I am. I never felt that way in my church." In a word, he felt beloved. I feel valued and loved when I am in the company of others who are aware of their loneliness, their feeling of abandonment, and are seeking to live more integrated lives.

Frederick Buechner, a Presbyterian author and minister, writes in a remarkable autobiographical meditation, called *Telling Secrets*:

> What goes on in Twelve Step groups is far closer to what Christ meant his church to be, and what it originally was, than much of what goes on in most churches I know. ...
>
> The Twelve Step groups have slogans, which you can dismiss as hopelessly simplistic or cling on like driftwood in a stormy sea. One of them is Let Go, Let God,— which is so easy to say, and for people like me so far from easy to follow. Let go of the dark which you wrap yourself in like a straight-jacket, and let in the light. Stop trying to protect, to rescue, to judge, to manage the lives around you, your children's lives, the lives of your husband or wife, your friends because that is what you are powerless to do ... leave it to God. It is an astonishing thought. It can be a life-transforming thought. ...
>
> I do not believe these groups are perfect any more than any thing human is perfect, but I believe that

the church has an enormous amount to learn from them. I also believe that what goes on in them is far closer to what Christ meant his church to be, and what it originally was, than what goes on in most churches I know. These groups have no buildings or official leadership or money. They have no rummage sales, altar guilds, no every-member canvas. They have no preachers, no choirs, no liturgy, no real estate. They have no creeds. They have no program. They make you wonder if the best thing that could happen to any church might not be to have its building burn down and lose all its money. Then all the people would have is God and themselves.

Others, who feel like strangers in churches and synagogues surrounded by neighbors who deny their own yearning for community, may seek individual or group therapy as an adjunct or substitute for institutional spirituality. But they move toward wholeness only to the extent that their experiences in therapy are infused with love, as mediated by the group members or therapist.

Although psychological labels can be a useful shorthand, some people become so identified with their perceived "dysfunction" that support groups and popular "group jargon" become their identity. People unwittingly depersonalize themselves as an ACOA (Adult Child Of an Alcoholic), or a member of CODA (Co-dependents Anonymous), or having an MPD (Multiple Personality Disorder) or a PTSD (Post Traumatic Stress Disorder).

Many other people categorize themselves and others indiscriminately through Meyer-Briggs terminology: ENFP's (Extrovert, Intuitive, Feeling, Perceiving) or ISTJ's (Introvert, Sensing,

Thinking, Judging). To the extent they think of themselves as a category rather than an individual, they thereby diminish their chances for love. Seemingly unable to acknowledge their own unique value, they clutch classifications to their hearts as their primary identity. Their sacredness disappears in the crowd.

Credo seeks to confront these short-circuited attempts at identity, by enabling a person to get in touch with the Spirit that lives within him. A person dwells in safety when surrounded by the "family" of love on the Weekend—he is able to "let go" and release his defenses.

When I can feel the compassion of others and their appreciation of the good qualities which are of the essence of our nature, I can let go of fear even more. When I can begin to appreciate my basic worth as being made in the image of God, I am no longer afraid to have friends who see only my heart. Then, laying aside judgment, I am able to see only their hearts:

> *Here we are, you and I,*
> *and I hope a Third in our midst. ...*
> *Come now, beloved, open your heart*
> *and pour into these friendly ears*
> *whatsoever you will*
> *And let us accept gracefully*
> *the boon of this place, time, and leisure*
> —Aelred

Finding A Way In, Not Out

*Woe to him who is alone,
for when he falls he has no one to lift him up*
—Aelred

From the moment we are conceived, we rely on the concern of another. When we come into the world, we are literally in the hands of another, for someone else even has to cut our umbilical cord. We do not even know enough to receive nourishment until our mother offers us her breast. Newborn children thrive in the nursery when they are treasured by the nurses who hold them and talk to them. But babies fail to flourish, and some even die, when a heavy work load limits the care givers' involvement with them. The ingredient of nurturing love is as vital as the air a baby breathes, or the physical nourishment the infant receives.

We learn how to accept that dependency as the many years required for our maturation unfold. In turn, we learn to create an inter-relationship by offering ourselves to meet the needs of others. We realize that other people have emotional needs which may be as great as ours. A mother has an elemental desire to have her child respond with acceptance.

Similarly, I know as a father that I became progressively more involved with each of my newborn sons when he began to move beyond total dependency on his mother and began to include me in his world. My sons and I started to depend on each other—we became interdependent. As they receive the smiles and joy expressed by the new baby, brothers and sisters become included in this circle of love. Through day-to-day experience they come to an understanding that the arrival of the new one does not diminish their share of the affection and care they also need to flourish. This reciprocity, this mutual caring, is the joy of our life from our birth to our death.

The Power Of Love

Some things take so long / But how do I explain?
Not too many people / Can see we're all the same.
Because of all their tears / Their eyes can't hope to see
The beauty that surrounds us / Now isn't it a pity?
—Isn't It a Pity, George Harrison

These lyrics express the fundamental reality of our life together as human beings: *It is not in giving, but in accepting, that we end our isolation.* Our ability to offer love may bring us comfort. But it is the ability to include the love of others within our selves that ends alienation. For in *accepting* we acknowledge our need. We individually become autonomous and whole. John Pretto, who first experienced Credo as a teen-ager, expresses this truth:

> I do not believe I could have come so far without Credo or the man, Don Harris, without having experienced the need to be loved and to love. I am learning to accept love and to give it back. As I am able to accept myself I am abler to accept others. Serenity is when you can accept others loving you.

In the Christian understanding, God is the source of love, and his love is brought to completion in us. But the crucial distinction which scripture makes is that it is not our *giving* love, but our *acceptance* of God's love that is critical. It is not that we love

God, but that God first loved us, and that our hearts are restless until we accept that love. We yearn to receive love so much that we seek it everywhere in order to find harmony in our lives.

But a person's ability to live within the harmony of love is not a primary concern in our mechanistic culture. Rather, a person's worth is defined by whether he or she is found useful to society. Is not one of the first questions asked when one person wants to get to know another, "What do you do?" Many a mother, or a retired person, feels uneasy as they reply, "I don't have a job. I'm at home."

Because our social value is dependent on the definition of others, we choose to appear as we think they want us to be. This attitude even invades homes. How many households are filled with anxiety when they hear an unanticipated guest is about to stop by? The vacuum cleaner and the dust rag are brought out, the lawn is groomed. Finally the mirror is consulted, the hair rearranged, the shirt tucked in so that we will appear "presentable." People rearrange external appearances not only to make the expected guest feel more comfortable, but also to earn a favorable judgment concerning their adequacy. In this context people tend to see others as critics, who, if their expectations are met, will bestow their approval.

Likewise, we become critics of others. For example, we are apt to judge the homeless, inner-city youth, sexual abusers, post-college "slackers," or emotional casualties of Vietnam, based on what they appear to be: useless. But these people have an additional dilemma: for they lack the resources to appear to be what others want to see. They disappoint others and therefore disappoint themselves. Seldom does anyone seek to know what kind of persons they are. Often the poor are simply given labels such as *homeless, welfare mother, inner-city drug kid, drunk, felon*. And then they are discarded.

10

Friendship, The Medicine Of Life

A faithful friend is a sturdy shelter:
he that has found one has found a treasure.
There is nothing so precious as a faithful friend,
and no scales can measure his excellence.
A faithful friend is the medicine of life.
—Ecclesiasticus

Love is reciprocal; it relies upon a mutual giving and receiving. Because it requires response from another person, love can bring great anxiety and even pain to a fearful person. Having to rely on the response of another to contribute to my wholeness means that I am not master of my own destiny. I cannot demand acceptance, no matter how badly I may want to be cared for. The fulfillment of my desire for love is always the decision of another.

In turn, should someone choose to offer me care, that person cannot demand that I accept it. No matter how deeply another may want to be my friend, that person cannot force me to respond in love.

The acceptance of love is a decision I make. It is an option I may freely choose or reject. Each time the offer is made, I make the decision whether or not I will allow myself to be dependent on another and allow the offered love to flow into my soul. It means I must acknowledge that I am not autonomous and self-sufficient, nor will I ever be, from my conception to my death.

The Credo Weekend, through its music anthologies and the candid interactions that it encourages, underscores the essential reality that no one can survive in isolation. We see that we need each other, yet if we want to be loving we cannot control each other. We cannot force anyone to give us the love we need, any more than they can control our willingness to love them or to receive that which they offer. We may be masters of our response, but we are not masters of our needs.

By lowering the threshold of fear, the structure of the Weekend enhances the possibility of our willingness to include others in our lives. Tragically, we may chose to reject the love that we know we need because of fear generated by past disappointments. It is this fear that causes Janis Joplin to call out in agony:

> *Why is half the world crying,*
> *and the other half of the world is crying too,*
> *and they can't get it together?*
> —*Love Is Like a Ball and Chain*, Janis Joplin

When I am able to open my heart to the love offered by another, and that person, in turn, is willing to accept me, then love is complete, and a bond of peace is established. I may experience that life giving unity with my wife, my best friend, my son, my mother or my father, or this may never have been an experience of mine.

This unity of spirit, even if but for a few hours, is the goal of the Credo Weekend. The retreat fosters an atmosphere where friendship on the level of the spirit becomes truly possible. The personal affirmation that comes from that kind of relationship becomes something to be desired in others.

In his treatise *Spiritual Friendship*, Aelred captures the essence of the type of relationships that we foster on the Weekend:

> What happiness, what security, what joy, to have someone to whom you dare to speak in terms of equality as to another self. One to whom you have no fear to confess your failings; one to whom you can unashamedly make known what progress you have made in spiritual life; one in whom you can confide all your plans.

This level of intimacy is not uncommon on a Credo Weekend. Although the experience may be fleeting, it is not illusory. The participants learn that what goes on on the Weekend is as much the "real" world as the fearful and competitive arena from which they came. The Credo Weekend enables those who so choose, to unite with the spirit of an accepting community, and to feel one within mutual acceptance.

During a Weekend this goal of intimacy becomes attainable. The accidents of people's daily lives are placed in the context of their whole being. I will never forget the face of a heart-broken young man who by his actions passed on to his son the curse that so blighted his own life. But there was an unbounded freedom in our relationship, when I was able to connect with him on the level of his sacredness as a unique person. Because I was loving him as a brother, not judging him as a parent might, his relationship to me was stripped of shame and guilt.

Both through follow-up gatherings and informal contacts, relationships born on the Weekend grow. Most of the Weekend participants, by the time the retreat is concluded, feel a close kinship with one another. What their brother or sister experiences, they begin to feel as their own. Together they are able to rejoice in each other's joys, as well as weep with each other in their sorrows.

By encouraging people to know each other as companions in life, the Credo Weekend enables participants to cease judging one another on appearances and social position. On a recent Weekend, a city prosecutor listened to a young man tell the group he had sexually abused his daughters. The attorney's first reaction was to be rejecting and accusatory: "Why aren't you locked up?" he called across the room, "I spend my life catching people like you."

The young man gathered his thoughts for a moment, but then continued to tell his own life's story. He told of a life where he had been abandoned as a child; humiliated and sexually abused by a foster mother and then a homosexual "rescuer." Finally at 16 he found some comfort with a younger girl and together they had several children.

The prosecutor was open enough to experience the anguish which poured from the participant's lips, and said with embarrassment, "You know, I have never thought of men like you as humans." Throughout the rest of their time together on the

Weekend the two reached a greater understanding of each other as fellow human beings trying to make it through life.

Later, the prosecutor told me what an isolated life he led. "As a prosecutor in the court room, I always have to appear to be winning, even if I know I am not. I do it well, so well that it carries over to home, and I never let my wife know of any of my weaknesses. I am pretty unhappy with the situation." A few months later the prosecutor resigned his position and started a new life with his family.

Another person whose life was changed on a Weekend is Lisa. She is a woman of conviction who lived a childhood of sexual abuse, and as an adult then lapsed into a life of multiple addictions. She is now trying to live a constructive life with her son:

The word *Credo* means "I believe," and Credo has made a believer out of me. I am a natural skeptic where organizations are concerned. The more authoritarian and hierarchical one is, the more I distrust it. That Credo was born from a hierarchy like the Navy is nothing short of a miracle to me, because it is the most honestly egalitarian structure I have yet encountered.

The Weekend was unique in many ways. It was casual and remarkably loosely structured. It was facilitated in a non-authoritarian manner by people that participated fully in the process itself. It was loving and respectful and it worked incredibly well. I don't think anyone was turned away who expressed a desire to attend, no matter what the financial situation. I left it wanting to support it in any way I can, feeling that it is the most hopeful, promising, necessary happening of which I am aware.

We were a group of 25 people: women and men, black and white, old and young, penniless and wealthy. We met Friday evening in a lodge in the woods. For about 48 hours we ate, talked, listened to music and each other. I have never heard so much pain expressed at one time. Paradoxically, I have rarely been so happy. It's not that I enjoy seeing people hurting, but this was old pain: weeks, years, decades old. The pains that stay with people and lash out to hurt others unless they are healed. Love heals pain and that is what was happening in front of my eyes and in my own heart.

When I arrived for the Weekend I did what I always do. I looked at people and formed an opinion. This one was a hard-partying college kid, over privileged and arrogant. That one was wacko, best not to get too close. That one looked meek and mealy-mouthed, probably not very interesting, etc., etc., etc. As time went by, however, and these meek, wacko, and arrogant human beings opened their secret hearts to me, I got some humbling insight into the origins of human behaviors. The camaraderie, the group respect and acceptance reached amazing and uplifting proportions. Something holy was happening a lot of the time — probably love.

As a woman I have come to understand the terrible damage done to me, (and many others), by childhood sexual abuse. Dealing with my anger about this has been a major task. One of the most valuable gifts of the Weekend came to me from an abuser. I sat next to and heard and felt the story of a man who had raped a child. I heard the raped child that he had been, and saw the self-hating adult he had become. I felt my difficulty in seeing him as a human rather than a monster. I saw his difficulty, his discomfort, at being seen as a human rather than a monster. I felt healing going on for both of us.

Since the workshop I am looking at people differently. Especially I am seeing men through a filter of what may have been done to them, rather than just what they have done to others. This is not to excuse or suggest tolerance of abuse, but has given me a chance at the understanding and compassion I need for the next stage of my healing.

I learned a lot on this Weekend, things I can't put into words and things I don't want to forget. One thing that I learned is this; patriarchy is not at the heart of the problem in my world. It is hierarchy. It is a system that gives some groups the power to control and use others, whether the power is physical, financial, sexual, or political. In hearing the painful extent of abuse that many children suffer at the hands of their mothers and fathers, I realize that parental power is being abused by people of both genders. And those parents, inexcusable as their behavior is, have stories to explain them. The explanation is always the same: someone who had more power than they abused that power, often over and over again with neither the abuser or the abusee being helped to break the cycle.

There are those that say hierarchy is unavoidable, nature's way, has been forever and will be forever the case. But surely as each of us has power to hurt those vulnerable to us: children, elders, animals, family, friends, the earth itself, we also have the power to nurture and protect them and this is our healthy function.

Hierarchy is loveless. Domination and submission are two sides of the same cold coin, and no love can be bought with it. Only when people are respected as equals is true love and sharing possible. Knowing intellectually that hierarchy hurts everyone is not enough. This intellectual knowledge must be joined to an emotional process and assistance for that process must be readily available. When there is a true opportunity to let down our walls, to feel and share our pain, our vulnerability and our interdependence, healing can occur. The secret starvation of hierarchy can be exposed. The joy of love experienced. I am deeply grateful to the people of Credo Institute, those that arrange and administer and assist and attend, for providing a forum to do work that is desperately needed by so many, and that clearly benefits us all.

Through the Credo experience, Lisa became less preoccupied with how others might hurt her. Her attitude moved from mistrust to compassion. She saw that the hunger for love of even the most lowly of people was hers as well, and that hers and their hunger could be met through trusting human response.

On the Weekend, Lisa could see more clearly that her fear was internal, and that she was held back only by herself. For many participants such as Lisa, as the barriers fall, they feel a rush of joy. They are safe, they are loved, and they are free to share that love with their neighbor.

> *What keeps my song from being sung?*
> *Past hurts, deep fears, a timid tongue.*
> *What makes my freedom come so hard:*
> *A self-made live-in prison guard.*
> —*Release Your Song*, James A. Forbes, Jr.

Credo has no religious ax to grind, no hidden agenda to bring people to the Truth. But from a spiritual perspective one might say that Love moves throughout the community without human manipulation. We are given the power, if so moved, to be wounded healers.

The experience of these people, although therapeutic, is different than psychotherapy which follows a medical model. Psychotherapy views a person in terms of an illness with symptoms that need curing. But the medical context is self-limiting because of the necessity for the client-healer relationship. Even in group therapy an individual is expected to "work on his issues," under the guidance of a professional facilitator.

Credo goes beyond that approach. On the Credo Weekend, individualism and hierarchy dissolve into community. It may well be that a person takes stock of life and draws personal conclusions, one of which may be to seek some professional help, but at the time of the Weekend this self-appraisal occurs within the context of a community of equals. There are no therapists.

The result for people on the Weekend is therapeutic, not because they are sick and need a therapist, but because they realize that they can minister to one another—they find they have the treasure of love and life within their own hearts. The result is religious, not because people are converted to orthodox concepts, but because they experience a love that is greater than the sum of their feeble efforts.

The Credo Weekend neither cures nor converts people. It is an experience which helps many find the happiness of acceptance from a community of people who care; and a better understanding of their neighbors. It brings to the individual a sense of importance and belonging, and a way to live a more purposeful and productive life — all of this while neither accusing, preaching, nor condescending. Credo does not say "You need our help." Rather Credo says "We need each other."

> *The Spirit of life flowed through my blood.*
> *I said "yes"—something broke—it came like a flood.*
> *Up from within; down from above*
> *A kingdom built on the power of Love.*
> —*Release Your Song*, James A. Forbes, Jr.

11

The Structure

> *There is a song inside of me —*
> *I can hardly wait to see*
> *What it is I have to say,*
> *Or the music I will play*
> —Release Your Song, James A. Forbes, Jr.

With this background, I hope you will be able to see how the four icons of hospitality as represented by the loving inclusion of the Anker family, the accidental community of shipboard life, the selfless service of Don Ignacio, and the inclusive love of Aelred of Rievaulx, are reflected in the content of the Credo Weekend. In outline, the Credo evolution has three steps:

1. The Pain of the Human Condition:
   a. Realizing that the absence of life direction and of self respect leads to interior pain
   b. Acknowledging that a lack of love in personal relationships leads to interpersonal pain
   c. Understanding that an absence of responsibility for others leads to social pain

2. Attempts at Resolution: Personal Assessment

3. Reconciliation: Resolution Through Loving Support

The Pain of the Human Condition

It's been so long in coming,
First the thought and then some humming
But before I find my key
Something stifles it in me

The first segment of the Credo Weekend lays the foundation for the experience. It is presented in three parts. Through music and response we establish the reality of the anxiety that we all experience when we are unloving or unloved. Participants sense not only how real is this pain, but also how it is an integral part of each one of us. George Harrison expressed the theme of this segment perfectly in his song "Isn't It a Pity":

> *Isn't it a pity, isn't it a shame*
> *How we break each other's hearts,*
> *and cause each other pain.*
> *Forgetting to give back*
> *The love which we've received.*
> *Isn't it a pity?*

This three-part sequence of music is critical. The acknowledgment of the human condition we hold in common is the bedrock of trust. For when we see that we are essentially the same in our needs and wants, we see that we have nothing to fear from one another. The progression which occupies over half of our time on the Weekend, must not be rushed, though it may be unsettling to find that the revelations of others dovetails with our own private experience.

Too often in our culture we deny the struggles of life and want to move quickly to a more hopeful frame of mind. But it is the awareness of our common journey that enables us to have compassion for our neighbor. Carlos Santana observed,

> There is a way to create music and art and philosophy that gives people the capacity to take a walk and have a real nice cry. At that moment, you have the chance to leave behind what people did to you, or to mend a broken relationship, and to move on instead of carrying those burdens. I believe philosophy connected to spirituality, tone, and colors is the real medicine for tomorrow because it disarms the person who has built up the walls.

It is difficult to enter into a substantial relationship with another human being until we feel safe enough to acknowledge our own struggle and the fear of others which it breeds. For it is necessary for us to be willing to invite persons into *our* lives before they will trust us to enter into theirs. First, we must be able to accept our own vulnerability. Then we need to recognize our common vulnerability as men and women. Only at that point will we permit ourselves to act with others to overcome the barriers that we share in common.

On the Credo Weekend *the sole purpose in surfacing our intimate concerns is to lay the base for a caring community*. It is not for the purpose of establishing an agenda for follow-up therapy sessions in small or large groups. To place the "working of personal issues" to the fore is to betray the trust of the participants who have been assured that the Credo Weekend is not psychotherapy. Problem-solving devalues the nature of the Weekend as a whole, for it inadvertently separates the participants into categories of "sick" and "well."

Attempts At Resolution: Personal Assessment

The climax of the Weekend is the silent walk. Assuring personal solitude in the midst of community is crucial. People need to be left alone with their thoughts and to have time to digest what has occurred in the formative period of the retreat. By integrating the events of the Weekend into their personal understanding, the participants have an opportunity to define their own Credo, understand the source of their own pain, and discover areas in which they may want to move, or seek support within a community of acceptance.

Reconciliation:
Resolution Through Loving Support

For many, the fruit of their meditation is a feeling of compassion. Participants naturally are drawn together in support of one another when they return from the walk. The common concerns expressed within the gathering come into focus upon personal reflection: the prosecutor and the abuser, the judge and the teenage father, have articulated the general anxiety of humanity: loneliness, lack of direction, broken relationships, abandonment.

Finally, as the atmosphere of compassion is realized, participants voice the key discovery of the Weekend: the need for commitment and responsible love. It is at this time that people realize that the compassion which is so evident within the community is greater than the sum of their individual caring. If the initial period concerning the state of the human condition has been thoroughly explored, participants will have little temptation to rely on human resources alone, for the first segment has dealt with the unreliability and inadequacy of humans left to their own devices.

12

The Credo Weekend

Remember to be kind
When the pain of another will serve you to remind
That there are those who feel exiled,
On whom fortune never smiled,
And upon whose lives the heartache has been filed —
They're just looking for another lonely child.
       —The Only Child, Jackson Browne

Credo Institute has evolved a 48-hour format for the Credo Weekend so that it may be available to all. Because the original Navy Credo Weekend takes place over 72 hours, to follow its format would place a burden on full-time students and would exclude hourly wage earners from participation.

The best way for you to experience the Weekend is to walk through it with me. Picture a middle-aged college professor who has decided to go on the Weekend at the urging of a friend.

Day One: Friday Night

My name is Peter and I just finished grading mid-semester exams. It was a long week, and I am looking forward to the Credo Weekend with some anticipation. It will be a chance, my friend has told me, to get away from it all and spend some time with myself. I gather only a few necessities in an overnight bag, since the letter I received told me that all my needs will be tended to. So I leave behind my familiar books, note pad, Walkman and head for the retreat site.

I arrive at the retreat center with anticipation, not knowing exactly what to expect. As I walk in the door I look around and see quite a variety of people: a retired man, some blue collar workers, some women who look like secretaries. One woman is neatly dressed in a polyester pant suit. Another, a man, is wearing wide wale corduroys and a shetland sweater. A couple of others are wearing jeans and T-shirts. Right away I am greeted by several cordial people. One of them, a fairly young woman who could be an office worker, registers me and takes my check. A friendly young man shows me to my assigned bedroom, where I drop my bag. Judging from the book bag and running shoes beside the other bed, it looks as if my roommate is a student "jock."

After returning to the main area, I get a cup of hot coffee and enjoy a slice of home-made banana bread and meander into the meeting room, which is comfortable with subdued lighting and a large circle of chairs. I pick one at random and settle in, trading small talk with others who seem to be as much in the dark as I am.

Soon the leader, Don, welcomes us in an informal fashion. He seems glad to be there, and judging from his smile he certainly enjoys people. He tells us reassuringly of the long history of success of the Credo Weekends. He points out that there are several Credo alumni in the gathering who will help us feel comfortable along the way. He identifies three of the gathering as partners with him. They also look both assured and cordial, with no hint of an authority "trip." Although they have been set apart by being introduced in this way, it seems the only difference between them and us is their experience, and their commitment to serve the rest of us.

They seem fond of the leader, and the four of them work together as if they are close friends. It feels good to have them there, because, although they appear to want to be one with us, they also have an air of responsible concern. I am not reluctant to put myself in their hands. One of them is Kathy, a middle-aged mother, another is Will, a college student, and the third is Ricks, a white haired gentleman with a ruddy complexion.

Kathy explains that we need to eliminate items that might distract us from each other. In particular she explains how much watches, and the schedules they represent, get in the way of friendship. She moves around the circle gathering watches which participants inadvertently may have brought along. I am one of the offenders. I had rushed to get my bag together after leaving the office and saying good-bye to the family. I have very little hesitation dropping my watch into the box. To tell the truth, it was kind of a relief to be rid of my constant companion and warden. It will be an unusual Weekend for me, since I won't have to worry about any schedules.

Next Kathy explains the House rules about smoking, being awakened in the morning, not straying off too far because we don't want to start any session without having every one there. I also like to hear her say that I do not have to say or do anything with which I would be uncomfortable. That will give me a chance to bide my time and get the lay of the land. Reassuring as the leaders are, I must admit that I am a little anxious. The site is unfamiliar, a lot of the people are not "my kind," and I only vaguely understand the program which I am going to undergo. The only reason I have consented to attend is because it was so strongly recommended by my trusted friend.

Will begins by asking us to meet with the last person with whom we were talking before the program began. After fifteen minutes we are instructed to find someone in the group who appears to be quite different—someone with whom it is unlikely that we would otherwise come in contact.

I must admit I feel a twinge of insecurity: "What if the lady over there is offended that I chose her as someone different?", "What if that young guy over there doesn't want to be with me?", I am aware of some of my prejudices: "I certainly have nothing in common with that woman slouched in the green chair, she looks pretty sleazy," or "I am not sure I want to deal with the complications of talking to a black man," or "Those upper class college kids are superficial."

I decide to take a risk and go over to the "floozy," whereupon we spend fifteen minutes talking together. I am surprised to discover how much we have in common. Dolores turns out to be a pretty nice person, actually quite warm and sensitive. We are just beginning to be comfortable with one another, when we are given a challenge by one of the old hands. Will asks us to select another member to join us to make three—which, we are told, one participant of a past

Weekend termed a "tripod." He explains carefully what we must do:

First, Dolores and I are to define the type of person we want to invite to join us. We decide we would like to have an office clerk since that is far from what Dolores appears to be (she is a cosmetics sales lady), and, as for me, I rarely pay attention to clerks when I transact business at a large office.

Second, we are to look around the room and pick a person who most closely meets that profile. Both Dolores and I spot a neatly dressed middle-aged woman who seems a little shy.

Third, we are to decide between ourselves who will do the recruiting, and who will be loyal and "hold down the fort." Dolores seems not only to be self- assured, but also a woman of the world. So I am content to lay back, holding the fort and continuing to get my bearings.

Both Dolores and I like to make quick decisions, and are competitive. So before everyone else is ready, Dolores is about to get a jump on the others and go out and accomplish the task. But Will restrains us. He wants to make sure that the stages are accomplished corporately. He pauses each time to be sure that all of the other participants have reached that stage. When all three steps of preparation are completed, Will asks all of us to stand so we may feel free to move about. Finally, he gives the signal, emphasizing that the result may only be groups of three, not four or more; and instructing each group of three that upon formation we should spread out away from the general gathering so as to minimize confusion among those still seeking to form their groups.

I can see right off that from a mathematical standpoint the exercise is impossible to accomplish without some breaking their word and abandoning others: two cannot become three without breaking up another pair. I do not want to be one of those who are abandoned. So I begin to think whether I want to remain with Dolores, or is this a chance to move on to someone else who might be more interesting. No, I don't want to do that to Dolores, but what about her? Might she want to move on, leaving me holding the bag? She seems quite self-possessed and garrulous. If I am not sure of her loyalty, should I be loyal to Dolores and risk being left alone? I place a great stock in keeping my word, so I guess I will take the risk. I have done it many times before. I would rather be disappointed in her than to disappoint myself by choosing to be unreliable.

As things turn out, Dolores is very actively recruiting Peggy, the clerk, so I find it easy when I am recruited by a student to refuse his overtures and maintain my obligation to my partner. Soon the two come back and we have our "tripod." But as I look around the room I see that the more the rules are followed, the more likely one or two people will be left out.

In particular, I notice a young Hispanic guy, Paco, who is dressed like a New Yorker from the Upper West Side. He is quite out of place here. Hence, others seem to be veering away from him, not wanting to deal with him at all. Is the group going to deal with him? How must he be feeling? I am sure that this is not a new situation with him. So I bring him to the attention of Dolores and Peggy, and together we decide that Paco's feelings are more important than the rules and we welcome him into our group. There are disapproving glances from a couple of others, but there is a sign of gratitude on his face. Together we get busy getting to know a little more about each other.

I can see how the Weekend is going to progress. The leaders do not discuss the problems involved in the exercise. Instead, they let us discover the solution among ourselves.

The questions that come up remain implicit and discussion does not make them explicit. We feel them rather than analyzing them. This is particularly important for Paco who does not have a command of the English language. And it is important to me, because my life in the classroom is spent analyzing and intellectualizing. If I am going to be close to Paco, he has to know how I feel, not how I view things. Otherwise, because he lacks my schooling he will feel inferior, and I will lose the chance to learn from him. I can see now that I will have to be myself, without the defenses of my scholarly vocabulary. The time flies, and I guess after a half an hour we are asked to take a break.

When I return from having a cup of coffee, Don introduces another key to the Weekend: being my brother's keeper. Not only does he ask us to concentrate on ourselves, but he also asks us to draw the name of another person in the room as we head for bed in silence at the conclusion of the music. We are asked to become a silent "brother's keeper" of another in the room. In this way the depth of isolation is counterbalanced with caring.

And when you've found another soul who sees into your own,
Take good care of each other.
When you are thinking you're alone,
be aware of each other.
When you are looking for something of your own
Take good care of each other.
—The Only Child, Jackson Browne

But before we go to bed, Ricks introduces what turns out to be a key ingredient in the Weekend: the music anthology. He tells us that we are about to hear a selection of nine or ten songs which are played with no comment. He stresses that the music is not intended to be a concert, nor to satisfy the listeners; rather, it is to encourage personal reflection. He urges us to pay attention to the words, but even more than that, to try to place ourselves in the heart of the artists—experiencing their feelings and emotions, their view of life evident in their music.

As I settle in my chair to listen to the first set of music, I try to suspend my analytical nature and go with the music. It seems to address the alienation we all feel as human beings; expressing the pain caused by self-doubt and isolation. I hear the grating voice of Janis Joplin asking, "Why is half the world crying when the other half of the world is crying too?" John Lennon reflects, "How can I give love when I do not know what love is?" Kris Kristofferson describes his life as a heavy drinker getting up on Sunday morning to put on his "cleanest dirty shirt." All these are feelings some one of us in the room have experienced. As a whole, the selections help us recall when we have felt emotionally and spiritually alone.

I am quite a follower of Kris Kristofferson, a Rhodes scholar turned country balladeer. I remember reading the album notes telling how Kris wrote "Sunday Morning Coming Down" in the condemned tenement apartment in which he lived. His wife and daughter had left him to return to California. Kris reflected, "Sunday was the worst day of the week if you didn't have a family. The bars were closed until one in the afternoon so if you had no family, there was nothing to do all morning. I was just writing about what I was going through then." It was his own autobiography as he fell from being a Rhodes scholar to a fallen down drunk:

> *Well, I woke up Sunday morning*
> *With no way to hold my head that didn't hurt.*
> *And the beer I had for breakfast wasn't bad,*
> *So I had one more for dessert*

I heard John Lennon articulate the all-consuming dilemma of his life which ended in self-contempt and constant self medication with drugs:

> I'm stoned. I'm stoned
> Every day of my life,
> I just manage to survive
> I just want to stay alive.
> —*I'm Scared*, John Lennon

As I listen to song after song, it strikes me how willing the artists are to reveal themselves. Janis, Kris, and John are singing from their souls to the world about their alienation and loneliness.

I begin to feel the root cause of their loneliness, a lack of unconditional love. And I can relate to times in my life when I felt as they did. As I glance around the room at the faces of my fellow retreat members, I can see that they are not alone in their loneliness. I feel a bond with these individuals and these artists that transcends age, sex, social position, race, or religion. I am identifying with the human condition.

The music is played without comment, one song after another—a collage of what it feels to be alone and adrift. When the selection of songs is completed, we are all very quiet. We have been exposed to the depths of personal anguish. It is late on Friday evening, and most of us have just completed a week of work. Silently we file out, drawing the name of an as yet unknown companion over whom we will watch for the Weekend. I check the name to be sure I did not draw my own name, and read the name "Tom." I can't recall any one with that name, but then again my mind is preoccupied with what has been summoned up by the music. So it is off to bed in silence, with all kinds of thoughts swirling around in my mind. I am tempted to talk to my young roommate, but then decide that I will go along with what I am asked to do.

Day Two: Saturday

Early the next morning I am awakened by a knock on my door. I glance on my wrist to check the time, but, of course, there is no watch there. Then I realize that it really doesn't matter since I have no schedule to keep, and the leaders seem to have things in hand. So I walk over to the breakfast area and am delighted with the wholesome fare: oatmeal with brown sugar and raisins, English muffins, juice and coffee. I chat with a couple of people I have not met before and then head for the living room where we will be gathering.

When we are all together a new set of music is played. I sense that each part of the Credo Weekend builds on the previous section. After experiencing the isolation of Friday night we eat together on Saturday morning before gathering for more of the music anthologies. In the same way each segment of the music builds on the previous one. From what I experienced, I would say that the music on Friday night centered on internal pain. This new set of songs seems to me to be moving from complete self-absorption to a slightly more detached description of the state of personal alienation.

This one, "Cheap Is How I Feel," which I am told later was written by a Canadian group, Cowboy Junkies, made quite an impression on me:

> It's not the smell in here that gets to me; it's the lights
> I hate the shadows that they cast,
> And the sound of clinking bottles is one sure thing
> I'll always drag with me from my past.

> *I think I'll find a pair of eyes tonight, to fall into*
> *and maybe strike a deal*
> *Your body for my soul, fair swap*
> *'cause cheap is how I feel.*

When the music finishes, Dolores, Peggy and Paco and I get together once more. We all talk about the music we have heard, what happened during the activities of the previous evening, why we decided to come on the Weekend, and what we expect to get out of it. As I suspected, Paco expected to be left out of the formation of the small groups. He has felt like an outsider all of his life. Being the only Hispanic in our gathering, he was sure no one would want to be with him.

Dolores says that she is here because she is having a rough time raising her teen-aged daughters by herself. The Weekend is the first chance she has had in a long time not only to leave all that behind, but also to have a chance to talk things over with some other adults. Peggy says that a good friend attended an earlier Weekend and came back to work refreshed. She is a clerk in a government office, but has not been able to make many friends since she moved here from a little town in West Virginia.

I tell them how fascinated I am with the fact that I am getting involved with some of the songs. It is the kind of music I scan past on the car radio, but I am beginning to see why some of my students would take it seriously. I am glad to see that the Credo alumni, so to speak, have joined most of the other tripods. The last thing I want to be is supervised or judged by my performance. It is kind of a funny thing to say, since that is what I do to my students every day. I'll have to think about that.

In about 20 or 30 minutes the whole group is reconvened. Kathy asks each group of three to appoint a spokesman who will tell the rest of us how they came together, as well as what the group talked about. The other tripod members are introduced by name, and they share their reflections, as well. At last I will have a chance to figure out who Tom is—the name I drew the night before. It is an entertaining time as people recall the confusion of our first formation. But there are also seeds of more important feelings as people talk about their anxiety in the situation.

Finally, there is a short break during which time I go over to get to know Tom, who turns out to be my roommate. He seems to be a really nice guy, honest and open. Maybe not the brightest person I have met, but I begin to realize that judging people that way is unfair. Being honest and open is a much more valuable trait in the long run, than being intelligent. He is going to be an easy person for me to be a "brother's keeper."

Upon return from the break, Will announces the configuration of our small groups of about six or seven, and where we will spend the rest of the daylight hours together. Although our quartet is dispersed into other groups, it's all right, for I know we will have some time to be together later on. It's curious that I even worry about that, since none of them are the types of people that I would run into at the college. I am glad to see that the "grandfather" Ricks, whom I noticed when I arrived, is going to be in my group. As he openly talks about himself to us I can see that they really mean it when they say that what comes out of this Weekend will be determined by all of us. Ricks is no professional facilitator maintaining distance in order to control. He is one of us, and I am delighted.

His concern seems simply to encourage an open environment where all are listened to without interruption and every one has a chance to share. He is listening with empathy to what all of us are expressing. Now and then he gently asks clarifying questions, drawing a shy person out, encouraging another who is having a hard time putting into words what she wants to say. As a result of his caring, Ricks assures that no participant dominates our session; no one assumes other people's problems while neglecting one's own needs. He deflects Mark's intrusive comments, since as a self-assured man he believes he can provide quick solutions to a woman in the group in order to lessen his own anxiety. I am glad to see that, for I do not want the group cast into the mold of problem solving. I am here to listen attentively to others, and I hope they will treat me the same way. We are here to care about each other, not to offer cures.

When we all break for lunch, I am surprised to find myself once again quite as absorbed in the stories of others, as I was listening to the singers. It is not the intimate details of another's life which fascinate me, but rather how close some of their experiences are to mine, even though we live worlds apart. For example, I hear Tom tell of the anguish he feels about not having a father when he grew up, and how his search for a father and manhood got him into a lot of trouble when he was in the Marine Corps. I can see in my own life how the absence of my father—who deserted my family when I was eight years old, causes me to be over-competitive as I try to prove my worth as a man to my colleagues. I certainly do not do so through bar room brawls or through demonstrations of my physical strength. Although I am more apt to prove my manhood with my mind. I see that I can be just as violent in my own way as is Tom in his.

Lunch time is very enjoyable. I check back and see how Paco is doing, and am pleased to see that he has made a friend. Dolores is her own incorrigible self carrying on with some people in the corner. I decide I will sit down with Peggy and introduce her to Martha who is a similarly shy person in my new group. Soon we are all talking together, and after a while I slip away to go for a walk alone by the shore.

Saturday afternoon begins with more music. The music continues to build on a theme. The morning's music dealt with internal alienation in relation to others, and now the afternoon selections concentrate on the results of failed relationships, such as Cat's In the Cradle referring to father-son indifference, Motherless Child, or Tainted Love. The music deals with interpersonal relations, the relations between lovers, friends, parents and children, and the difficulties that people experience trying to form these kind of loving bonds. The song which particularly reaches me in the heart is a reflective piece, "Men," by the articulate guitarist Louden Wainwright III:

> When the ship is sinking and they lower the life boats
> And hand out the life jackets; men keep on their coats.
> The women and the children are the ones who must go first
> And the men who try to save their skins
> are cowards and are cursed.
> Every man's a captain, men know how to drown
> Man the lifeboats if there's room; otherwise go down.
>
> And it's the same when there's a war on,
> it's the men go off to fight
> Women and children are civilians;
> when they're killed it's not right.
> Men kill men in uniform, it's the way war goes
> When they run they're cowards,
> when they stay they are heroes.
> Every man's a general, they all go off to war
> The battlefield is the man's world;
> cannon fodder is what they're for.

It's the men who have the power,
it's the men who have the might
And the world's a place of horror
because each man thinks he is right.

A man's home is his castle, so the family let him in
But what's important in the kingdom
is the women and children
A husband and a father, every man's a king
But he's really just a drone: gathers no honey, has no sting
Have pity on the general, the king, and the captain
They know they are expendable, after all, they're men.

After the music segment, we get together again in our small groups. I hardly get seated before I pour out all my feelings about being both a father, and a son, and how hard it is these days to understand what it is to be a man. That sets off a variety of reactions. Ricks deftly keeps us in focus and averts intellectual discussions on the virtues and vices of feminism. He knows that what I am talking about is not an intellectual exercise on my part. Neither is the response of Tom, who confides in us that he was regularly beaten by his father.

I have mixed reactions when I hear what he says. I guess the first one is surprise, since he is to me such a fine, well-put-together person. Then I chide myself for thinking anything different about him—of course he is a fine person, despite what happened to him. Then comes an overwhelming feeling of compassion and sorrow that anyone should have his or her life stained in this way. I want to reach out and affirm him with a pat on the back, but then, if he has the honesty and trust to let us, his companions, into his heart he really doesn't need comfort. I am so grateful that he is here and that I am his guardian angel. You know, two things are becoming quite clear: first, we never know what another's burdens are. Second, to judge people by their actions is foolish.

We move on to some less charged areas of interest. A woman named Joy is wrestling with the decision as to whether to uproot her family and move to St. Louis where an advancement in the company would take her. Would the move be fair to her husband and to the kids? How would her husband handle such a proposal? Tony, who is an electrician in his late 20's, is considering whether to go back to college, even though he has a wife and two kids and is making fairly good money. Harry is talking about how his tour in Vietnam has affected him and his family, even after all these years.

It has been a long and emotional day, and I am glad that we conclude well before dinner time so that we may have an opportunity for personal reflection. It is also a time when I can look up Paco and spend some time with him, for he is not in my group. As it turns out, Dolores comes over and asks me to take a walk with her. For all of her outward hardness, I am discovering that she is quite a gentle soul. I am glad I have the chance to spend some time with her because I don't want to be confined to the friendships I am making in my particular small group. The way I look at it, the purpose of our small group is to prepare us for more openness with the community as a whole. I know it has for me. My focus is now outward, not inward.

At supper time there is a natural mingling of all the participants, with the old hands sitting with their new friends whom they have gotten to know during the day. We have no more need for small groups, and it is now time to start bringing us all together as one. After supper on Saturday evening, there is time to hang out together. I am feeling very comfortable among all the people here. I have no facade to maintain, and I realize for the first time in a long while how constricting it is for me to have to live up to what other people think a professor should be. Here no one knows what my occupation is. They only know me for myself. It is very freeing. I look forward to getting together with my new friends for some more music.

We are now settling into our places in the familiar room where we listen to the music together. While others move around the room, sitting in a different place each time, I more or less sit in the same place through all of the sessions. The next musical anthology follows the outward expansion from introspection to empathy for others in their struggles. The evening music presents two related glimpses of life, one of which highlights the panorama of social disruption in America which leads to feelings of helplessness, anger, or cynicism. It considers inner city angst, alcoholism, the frustration of racial and gender conflict. I hear a poignant a cappella song, "Behind the Wall" by Tracey Chapman, as a black woman caught in the slums where she has to raise her children:

Last night I heard the screaming, loud voices behind the wall.
Another sleepless night for me
— it won't do no good for me to call the police.
Always come late, if they come at all

The other glimpses consider the other side of the coin: social relationships and attendant responsibility—such as the inevitability of middle age, the sterility of a tired marriage, the emptiness experienced by Vietnam survivors, grandparents, the plight of old people who have lost sustaining relationships and the care of the aging. One in particular grips me. It is a recording of the voices of old people in a rest home in New York City who talk about their chronic coughs, their bitter sweet loneliness without their mates who have died:

> I still sleep on my side of the bed.
> He used to sneak in, in the middle of the night, though

Perhaps the most poignant voice I hear is that of an old woman with a thick Bronx accent:

> An old person without money is pathetic

And then I think of my aged mother who is living with our family now, and what it must be like for her. Then there is the song "Tower of Song" by Leonard Cohen that captures what I, as a middle-aged person, am just becoming aware of:

> Well, my friends are gone and my hair is gray
> I ache in the places where I used to play.
> And I'm crazy for love, but I'm not coming on.
> I'm just paying my rent everyday in the Tower of Song.
>
> I said to Hank Williams: How lonely does it get?
> Hank Williams hasn't answered yet.
> But I hear him coughing all night long,
> A hundred floors above me in the Tower of Song.

The tape concludes with "Please Don't Pass Me By," a haunting song I had never heard before. Another poignant cry by Leonard Cohen:

> Now, I know that you are sitting there
> deep in your velvet seats.
> And you're thinking
> "He's up there singing something that he thinks about
> but I'll never have to sing that song."

*But I promise you, my friends,
that you're going to be singing this song.
It may not be tonight. It may not be tomorrow.
But one day, you'll be on your knees.*

*And I want you to know the words when that time comes,
because you're going to have to sing it to yourself,
or to another, or to a brother.
You're going to have to learn to sing this song. It goes:*

*O, please don't pass me by. Please don't pass me by.
I'm blind, but you can see; I'm blinded totally.
Please don't pass me by.*

The repetitive nature of Cohen's singing reminds me of the style of a black preacher who builds to a crescendo as he delivers his message to the congregation. My mind flashes back to a time when my family and I attended such a church in Memphis and left feeling exhilarated by the warmth and immediacy of the congregation. As my focus returns to the song, I can see how Cohen skillfully builds to an awareness that we are all cripples, all wounded, all in need of love, that none of us is immune to the human predicament, no matter how secure we may feel at the present.

The song is a summary. It brings together all that I have become aware of this Weekend in my time in the various groups. I think once again of wary Paco, of gracious Ricks, of feisty Dolores, of strong Tom, and indeed, of myself. We all experience isolation and vulnerability as humans when at any time we feel deprived of that which is our life blood: love mediated through others. It doesn't matter whether we are a struggling single parent living in an apartment, or a professor with a Ph.D. standing in a classroom teaching the insights of John Milton.

When the music is done, we discuss our feelings and concerns in an even more open way. Personally I am realizing that this really is a safe place to be. It feels good to be able to let down my guard with no pressure to say anything I don't want to. By now there are no apparent leaders, for our initial companions are full participants in the discussion, still attentive to the needs of others—but then again, so am I. I find myself asking clarifying questions to help the others who might not be as articulate as I am.

The evening discussion is the key transition point of the Weekend. We are all beginning to care for one another as a response to the alienation we have heard. My passive observation of the personal needs of someone like Paco is transformed into a desire to actively respond to others. I can see that I am not alone in this transformation. Before my eyes I see our family beginning to take form through our sharing of feelings, aspirations, and thoughts which we hold in common. In small groups, by varying people in particular ways, we have all acknowledged and described the problem of alienation; now we all are together as fellow sojourners on life's journey. It is the beginning of genuine caring, and for me the Weekend is no longer an exercise, it is an experience of real life. Our evening together is open-ended, but is not exhausting. We are not together to wear down each other's defenses, but rather to patiently accept any words our brothers and sisters may want to express, making sure that we pass no one by.

As the community session comes to a close, we are free to do as we wish. For some it is a time to seek out another whose life may particularly resonate with theirs: taking a walk into the night with a new found companion. Others are congregating around the coffee pot to continue discussions they have had before. I end up talking with my roommate Tom while preparing for bed after a long day. Although we are both tired, I must admit that neither of us are anxious to fall asleep, so we talk for quite a while into the night. As Tom tells me of his hopes, dreams, and struggles, I smile to myself. For I remember that thirty years ago, I was asking myself similar questions. It is refreshing to put myself into the consciousness of youth once more. They have so much ahead of them—so much potential.

I can see how this long preparation (the Weekend has well passed the half-way mark) is absolutely critical. It is the bedrock of all the trust we are building. Although I have been comfortable with the living conditions of the Weekend, I have felt impatience in lingering with the discomfort of life for such an extended period of time: I see now that the building of trust must not be rushed, as unsettling as we may find the revelations of others.

Day Three: Sunday

Sunday morning breakfast is a time of renewed anticipation. Much is on my mind, yet at the same time I feel refreshed, and among friends. As usual, our alumni companions sit where they would like, not as a separate group, for this time there is no separation. We are one emerging community of trust. Several of us want to linger over breakfast, even though we have been told that there is a great deal more to accomplish. Kathy tells us that it is best to reconvene the group sooner than later so that there is ample time in the morning to accomplish what is the climax of the Weekend.

Before the music is played, Kathy observes that we will observe a variation from the customary pattern. She asks us to take a solitary one hour walk after the music set has been completed. During this time we are asked to talk to no one else, to bring no diversions such as a notebook or reading material, and to spend the time reflecting on what we have learned and experienced. When we complete the walk, we are to return to the gathering area and sit in silence until every one else returns. As if she were reading my mind, Kathy reminds us that this is not a time to return to our bedrooms, go to the bathroom, or take a nap. The thought had crossed my mind after Tom and my long talk into the night!

For some of the people here, such as Tom and Paco, I am sure that the idea of meditating for an hour with no distractions is a foreign one. We live in a culture of external sensory overload. The younger participants, particularly, may initially feel at a loss, since there is nothing to do except be by themselves. I can see why the walk is so crucial. After many hours spent hearing from others of the struggles and joys of their lives, it is important for me to integrate what I have learned into my understanding of myself. I hope the fruit of this reflection will be a deeper level of trust and the opening of friendship. I would speculate that, for others, the idea of being by themselves is uncomfortable because they have so much going on in their minds and hearts. Kathy, who introduces this evolution, acknowledges these causes of anxiety, but stresses how very important it is that we take time to be with our selves for a period of personal reflection.

The music begins, and rather than suggesting thoughts I might have, it deftly reflects how I am feeling at this moment. I find the music encourages my own inner reflection, rather than telling me how I ought to feel. (Actually, I never feel an element of "oughtness" while I am here.) I begin to focus on what it takes to be myself. I want to feel freer to welcome others into my life. But to do that I see that I need to be more at home within himself—I need to discover the center of my life which is in my own heart. The music recalls some of the areas of conflict that have been touched on during earlier times, and is more philosophical in tone—e.g., Jefferson Airplane's You're Only as Pretty as You Feel, and Bob Dylan's You've Gotta Serve Somebody.

I am moved particularly by Jackson Browne's song "To A Dancer." I remember reading many years ago that the author wrote this song while grieving over the unanticipated suicide of his beloved wife. Within the context of community which is bringing refreshment to me here, I find that it is also true that:

> No matter how close to yours
> Another's steps have grown,
> In the end there's one dance
> You'll do alone.

After the music, the walk begins with people slipping on their jackets and leaving the building in silence. During that time, we talk to no one. We are here to deal with our thoughts, with our feelings. In this sense, the walk is based on a proven tradition, cutting across cultural lines, that of meditation. Most of us know of examples of vision quests, contemplative prayer and the like.

And so, this is the first time in the Weekend when I have been free to sort out my thoughts and feelings in solitude. For me it is quite an experience—actually, the turning point of the Weekend. I recall parts of the lives of many of my companions here and relate them to my own. As I experience once more the emotions expressed on the Weekend, I feel as if all our lives are joined. Against this backdrop of humanity, I start making decisions about my own life and my family.

I find the walk to be an integrating experience for me. It is an important time to bring some order to all that I have felt and heard. I realize that until I can achieve some calm to the complexity around me, I am not going to be able to develop a higher degree of intimacy and trust within the gathering. For I know from experience that when my soul is particularly restless, when I feel driven by thousands of different and often conflicting ideas and worries of this world, I find it impossible to create the room and space where someone else can enter freely.

I am finding that this Credo experience is lessening my anxiety about approaching my own center where I can take the time to concentrate on the stirrings of my own soul. What is coming through to me with no equivocation is that to be alive means to be loved. I realize now that I am free to let others, such as Dolores and Paco, enter into the intimate part of my life which I make available to them. I can allow them to be themselves without fear. As I feel more at home with myself, my presence is no longer threatening and demanding, but inviting.

In about an hour Will starts rounding us up. He silently motions to those within view to return. As we get back together, it turn out that a couple of people are still missing, Will asks quietly whether any of us has seen Betty and Mark. I can see that he is reluctant to send any of us out to fetch them. Although it is important that we do not resume before every one returns, Will wants to avoid a mass exodus of search parties. They, in turn, might end up among the missing and further disrupt the atmosphere of the contemplative group. It is better to wait patiently and silently.

Soon the stragglers are back with us. Now, Don asks to hear from each person about what he is experiencing and specifically what were his thoughts while on the walk. For some, a few words may suffice, he tells us. Yet if any one wants to pour out what is on his or her heart for twenty minutes, that is all right too. I can see that this is a rare opportunity for everyone to express anything they want, for it will be received by the others without judgment.

As one person after another shares personal reflections, I feel a general feeling of compassion. I see that my initial reticence in talking to Dolores was merely a matter of appearance and stereotype. Her concern about her kids is identical to mine. The frustration of Bill, the naval aviator, with the military bureaucracy is remarkably similar to the problems I grapple with when trying to deal with the department head and provost of my university. When I feel with Tony and Susan the pain they carry with them because of child abuse I experience great sadness,. I am so grateful that neither I, nor my kids, have to carry that burden.

But, the most memorable moment I guess, occurs when Dave, a high school teacher, returns from his walk and pours out to all of us, his friends, his realization that he was living a life which was completely unsatisfying. For the next several moments he reviews his life and both the circumstances and the idealism which led to his being a teacher. During the quiet time, he tells us, he has resolved to leave suburban secondary school teaching and go live with the poor in Appalachia.

I see how foolish it was for me to be wary of many of these people when I arrived here on Friday night, for in their essentials they are just like me. The traumas to do with love and trust are so much the same for all of us. When I first met him, I thought of Dave as kind of dumb and tacky, certainly below my station in life. But now he expresses a conviction and devotion to teaching that I lost long ago as I settled into my tenured position. His statement to the Credo family jogs my heart a little.

Friday evening seems so long ago, even though it is a matter of hours. My fear of other people, and their fear of me, is dissolving, and the seeds of community are germinating. I feel a calm expectation throughout the room. We are beginning to enjoy the rare and astonishing freedom of being ourselves within a caring family. Friendship has taken root and the tentative feelings that each of us has for the other are, in fact, the seeds of love: the fountain and source of all friendship.

After we hear from everyone, the feeling of intimacy and compassion is strong. We have bound ourselves to one another because of the profound sense of trust which we have forged. The final lunch that we share together is one filled with joy and anticipation. As we enter the dining room we see that rather than having the meal served buffet style, our table has been set. There is a tasteful centerpiece of flowers, full carafes are strategically place about the table, and a golden crusty round loaf of sourdough bread sits in a basket in front of Don's plate.

We happily gather around the table for our meal is prepared and served by other members of the Credo family. Don, the leader, addresses the newly formed community, and places in context what we are experiencing as we break bread together. He points out that before there was any codified religion, there existed an incontrovertible law of the desert which stated that anyone was bound to welcome any stranger to his table. Major religions, drawing on that which is elemental in human relationships, codify this law of hospitality, and within their own communities attach a specific sacred meaning to the common meal, e.g., the Seder meal for Jews, or Communion for Christians. The Early Church also celebrated an Agape Feast, a loving meal together after their sacred Eucharist feast. But the action of welcoming the stranger and offering the hospitality of the table, Don explains, predates any organized religious practice.

In some cases it actually was a matter of life and death, Don observes, for the traveler without food and shelter would surely perish if left alone to fend for himself in the wilderness. He goes on to say that in medieval Europe there was a similar understanding of hospitality where one was bound to open one's House and table to the wayfarer. I hadn't thought of it before, but Don suggests that in a pallid form we reenact this action when we join someone for coffee, or when as a host we offer a Coke to a visitor to our home.

I can see that his is a long way of saying how appropriate it is for our emerging Credo community to gather together at lunch to celebrate as one our bond of love. Here we are, the emerging community enjoying each other around one large table, spread with lunch meats, bread, cookies. One of the other leaders suggests that we reveal to each other who we were looking after as "brother's keepers" during the Weekend. I was pleased to find out that Ricks drew my name. I hope this is the beginning of a long friendship with him.

As we settle down from the excitement of telling one another who was whose guardian, Don draws together the experience of Credo through a concise review of what has happened, making explicit the structure which was hitherto implicit: the progression of the music from internal, to interpersonal, to social alienation and thence to social responsibility; and the response of caring and trust founded on hope. He explains that this musical pattern underscores our progression from an isolated person on Friday night, to a duo, trio, small group, large group, and community.

Don extends the metaphor of what we as a family are experiencing. Before him, he explains, is a loaf of bread and carafes of grape juice. He mentions that bread and fruit juice/ water are the essentials of life for the body: bread representing the nourishment that rich and poor alike must have, and juice/water representing the essential ingredient for all human life. In the same way, Don continues, love is essential to all spiritual life. Just as bread and water are essential to our physical well being, so is love essential to our whole being, which includes the spiritual as well as the physical. But love cannot stand on its own. It is only effective when there is a response. Love given must be accepted. Love accepted must be returned. At this time Don tears off a piece of the round loaf and gives it to his neighbor, asking the community to celebrate with him the bond of love we are experiencing by offering a morsel of bread to the person by their side.

Joe, a common laborer, calls me by name, looks me in the eye and gives me some bread. He has had quite a life, I think to myself, how glad I am to know him. As I turn to place some bread in Paco's hand, I am very moved. He has quite a struggle ahead of him, and I am glad he knows that I am there should he need a helping hand. It is quite remarkable what has gone on in the past day and a half.

Returning from lunch we gather for the final set of music on the theme of mutual support and celebration. I like hearing Aretha Franklin as she talked to the audience in the Fillmore in San Francisco: "Ladies and gentlemen. I would like to say before we leave that you have been much more than I ever could have expected. I'd like to leave you singing:

> *Reach out and touch somebody's hand*
> *Make this a better world if you can ...*
> *Why don't you make it a better world?*

Turn around and touch your brother and your sister
Extend your hands.
Need I say more than that ? No ...
Come on, and reach out for your brother's hand
—Reach Out and Touch, Nickolas Ashford
and Valerie Simpson

When the wonderful set of music is completed, we remain together face to face, feeling free to say what we would like within the inclusiveness of a true community. We unite ourselves to the spirits of others and of the many make one. There is neither distrust to be dreaded, nor correction to cause pain. Friends find satisfaction upholding one another.

The Weekend draws to a close too quickly, but before we disperse into the world Ricks addresses our transition into the world by involving all of us in the following considerations:

1. We discuss the difficulty of transition back into the less than perfect world where the type of candid discussion that became the backbone of the Weekend is not expected.
2. We suggest that because of the difficulty of this transition for some of us, and our desire to build on new friendships, we need to be able to call on one another during this period. Ricks smiles and says that he has thought of that already and distributes preliminary rosters with everyone's name, address, and phone numbers to be checked by the group for accuracy.
3. We arrive at a general consensus as to a time and location of two reunions. I know I want to keep track of my new friends' lives, and I am eager to support them. The follow-up is an effective way to make sure that the experience of our Weekend is translated into

long term relationships. I don't want the Weekend to be an isolated experience.
4. Kathy explains the reality of Credo as an informal international movement and emphasizes that the success of Credo, and the success of the next scheduled Weekend is heavily dependent on our word of mouth and genuine grass roots support.
5. Finally, we are given an evaluation sheet to be filled out at the site, and brochures, decals and newsletters, tapes, books, stationery are all made available to us.

I am feeling so refreshed from the experience, so warmed by the caring of others, that I want to go home and spread the word. I want to draw my wife to this Credo experience of healing love. Kathy announces the date of the next Credo Weekend in our area. I might even approach the English department secretary who seems to be leading a solitary life.

After a few parting hugs and laughs, we of a new Credo family go out to our separate worlds with new found resources for love and acceptance. Long forgotten is the distinction I made between others and the designated Credo companions which seemed so apparent at the beginning of our time together. We all have the same needs. Each of us has the ability to help and be helped. We are one in spiritual friendship, and the change in our hearts is permanent. As I return to the every day world of university teaching, my attitude is different, and it sends a message to all those students that I am truly trying to care for them—like I dreamed I would twenty five years ago when I started out fresh.

A New Way Of Life

Is it not a foretaste of blessedness to love and then to be loved? Let him lay bare his mind and heart even to their sinews and marrow. Then let a man so attach himself to his friends that all levity be absent and all joy be present.

—Aelred

The Credo Weekend is not a flash in the pan, but rather the introduction to a new way of life. As new lives are fashioned, other lives are touched: a wife, a little boy, a father-in-law, a companion in a homeless shelter. At the second follow-up several want to be a part of another retreat which would include their friends. Thus a new Weekend is born. Some who are new Credo family members will serve as companions to this new gathering. They are not expected to be therapists, evangelists or instructors—rather they are asked to be neighbors who are thirsting for an answer to the loneliness of the human condition, and once found, want to bring hope and love to others.

An excerpt from a telephone call received from Ray, a homeless man whom I had met five months before at a Credo Weekend in Salt Lake City, illustrates what can happen. Although he was constantly on the road as an itinerant T-shirt vendor, he was able to find some self-respect through the Weekend:

It is remarkable how often in the course of a week I bring up the subject of Credo.

It has changed the way I look at myself, and allowed me to stop and think about my worth. God has a purpose for me. I do not know what it is, but I think I want to give back what I have received in Credo.

I have a hard time describing to others what Credo is. Of the twenty people I keep in touch with on the road, seventeen are involved with some group: AA, NA etc. I have always thought of a group as a crutch. Credo is not a group nor is it a crutch. It is a loose knit family which is there when you want it. For me it is important that it is loose because if it were too tight I would not be there. As it is, I can count on my Credo friends. All I need to do is to call, any time, day or night. I guess you could call me sort of a gypsy, we are always on the move and never take time to reflect. Credo gave me time to reflect, time to smell the roses.

I sent some money to Bill for Credo. I think everyone who has been on the Weekend should. Do you remember Tony? He was only with us a few hours on Friday night. You know he has the AIDS virus. I am going to be there for him, either financially or in person. I might even settle a while in there. You know Donna has a food program there, maybe I could help her. I have a lot to be thankful for, and I want to give back what I have received.

I don't want to beat a dead horse, Don, but Credo has changed my life. If you can give me enough notice I would like to go through the Weekend again. Two weeks before and after a major sporting event you know that I will be there selling T-shirts. Right now I am leaving in a half an hour, but I can't stop by because I am traveling to Florida with some other people. Maybe in the next month or so I will be heading north and I will look you up. Maybe we can go to dinner.

13

Companion And Leader

"Release your song," said the Spirit to me.
"Be free! Be free! It's jubilee.
Cast out each fearsome song patrol.
Proclaim deliverance to your soul!"
—Release Your Song, James A. Forbes, Jr.

The Credo Weekend is a school of love, a school where we learn from each other. When we feel loved, we feel sacred, and when love is withheld we are *desecrated*. We are *consecrated* when love is extended to us by another, and we consecrate one another by sharing our love—whether it be with our families, our neighbors, those who are alone, or when we are in the close contact of the Weekend. As imperfect as those may be who return to help on a subsequent retreat, it is their calling to affirm the dignity of each person.

The primary qualities for an effective helper are humility and compassion. Those who have been on the retreat before set an example for the new Weekend participants. As the newly formed retreat family assumes a life of its own, the helpers are seen as brothers and sisters, not as parents. The ideal for helpers is to be so much servants of the new participants, that as the new community emerges other people become at least as significant as the helpers were at the start.

On the Credo Weekend every human being is treated as sacred and valued regardless of that person's station in life, his or her credentials, or the actions that a person has done or not done. This is the uncompromising assertion of the Credo. On the retreat, if a person's value is compromised in any way, however subtle, the Credo Weekend is the less for it. This sanctity is revealed in the two pillars of the Weekend: the music and the participation of Credo friends from earlier Weekends.

The music presents an anthology of artists whose music expresses valued reflections. Not only each Weekend participant, but also each performer is honored as a channel through whom the Spirit may speak. As is typical on any Credo Weekend, included among the artists is the broad spectrum of humanity: a Rhodes scholar, a woman who destroyed herself with heroin, a man who wrote sublime expressions of his faith, a somewhat jaded secular Jew from whose lips come profound theological truths, a down-and-out alcoholic, a social activist, a lesbian, a man who is recovering from his wife's suicide, another who celebrates the presence of love in his life, an ex convict, a greedy song writer, an uneducated blues singer.

None of these categories serve as a basis for judgment of a person's worth. What is vital is what comes from their hearts—some secure in their faith, others mangled by the vicissitudes of life, all of them "leaning out for love," as Leonard Cohen would say. In short, the musicians, as it were, are an extension of the Weekend.

The other pillar of the retreat is the person who returns to the Credo Weekend as a helper. The motivation of that person is as crucial as the music. There is nothing more critical to the Credo process than the motivation of the staff. Throughout the years many words have been used to describe that role, and I have used some of them in this text: team member, companion, facilitator, staff member, leader. All of these descriptions are fraught with danger because the words come from a society which thinks hierarchically, not inclusively. Perhaps it is even an inevitable part of human nature to think in terms of rank, to want to set another person or one's self apart as superior.

Returning to be a part of the nucleus of another Weekend is both humbling and gratifying. Helpers are humbled when they accept that all they have to offer is themselves, and gratified to know that that is enough. When Credo family members return for another Weekend, their responsibility to the new participants is nothing more or less than to be truly themselves. It means the helpers strive to lower as many of their own barriers as they can so that the love which flows through them can be experienced and valued by their neighbors on the Weekend.

Weekend staff members want to relate on the level of the spirit and have no need to keep their own experience of life hidden. Credo companions need no veneer on the Weekend since the function of a veneer is to hide a less valued substance beneath. On the Weekend who is lesser? There is nothing about any of us that makes us "lesser." The helpers are who they are, and there is nothing wrong with that.

In the same way, there is no room for "professional distance," since no Weekend companion is coming as a professional. Surgeons can perform skillful operations even when their private lives are disrupted, because what they have to offer is only their technical skill. Credo companions cannot do this and be successful, for they are offering their whole selves to others, not just their technical skills.

Many times people are reluctant to speak because they recall experiences where they felt devalued. Rather than avoiding this anxiety, Credo Weekend companions confront it, by extending hands of friendship so that all may feel safe enough to articulate the fears they find within themselves. They hope that participants who are distressed will be reassured as they come within the embrace of a friendly secure "family." By their actions the Credo helpers show that rather than finding a *way out* of their pain, the way *lies within*, through friendship and love—first in our own hearts and then to the hearts of the others.

For this reason, Credo Weekend volunteers need to consider their motivation carefully. Are they sure that they are wanting to attend to others and are not returning to the Weekend for personal help? Although there is no question that in giving we receive, in helping others we ourselves are helped, if the helper's life at the time of the Weekend is fragile, and he or she has a strong need for emotional support, then that person is not in the best position to be of much help in guiding others. It would be better for that person to wait until he or she is on firmer ground.

The concept of being a wounded healer is easily misunderstood. Human beings are not helped by people who merely share the same problems. Making our own wounds a source of healing, therefore, does not call for sharing of superficial personal pains but rather it calls for a consistent willingness to see one's own pain and suffering as rising from the depth of the human condition which we all share. Tim Wiford, a Credo/William & Mary graduate wrote:

> The Credo experience left me with a sense that we are all broken, and that we all share similar hopes and fears. I could see that our brokenness is a door to love and friendship through that common ground. Suddenly my pain was useful: I could use it as a resource for building meaningful relationships.

The Credo Weekend succeeds because the spirit of love is greater than all of us combined—it is not dependent on any of the companions. No individual has that power, and therefore no one person has the responsibility to make Credo work. The helpers are all companions on the Weekend with their different gifts employed to prepare the table. One may be used to bring in the food. Another may solely attend others. It is the spirit of love which alone provides the nourishment.

Returning Credo family members can relax when they accept that healing is not their gift, that they are powerless even to help themselves. The success of Credo is not on anyone's shoulders. Helpers are asked to be sensitive to the needs of others, to be open to ways in which people may be cared for. They are asked to model interdependence and caring as they work as one with other Credo family members.

Most of all, they are asked to be open to how the spirit of love can be conveyed *through* them, rather than *by* them. It takes faith in their own value, to trust their own judgments during the Weekend—to do nothing but be themselves, but that is all they need to do. "Trust the Process," say some. "Let go and let God," say others.

The position of being an experienced friend on another Credo Weekend is not for every one. Some excellent people, particularly educators, clergy and therapists, so identify themselves in terms of their professional vocation, that it is difficult for them to put aside this identity for which they have worked so hard. I have known many fine, compassionate people who are unable to shift from being valued as a skilled helper to be known purely for their personal selves. They struggle to accept the paradigm shift where the "dysfunctional" (their word) person is their equal.

But, to be an effective helper on a Weekend a person must embrace this egalitarian position, not just think of it as an ideal. All of us start out life the same: sacred; and no matter what blesses or befalls, all of us remain the same: sacred. All are the beloved. Someone showed enough interest to help us claim life during those first hours and years when we were fully dependent. Since that beginning, each of us have had experiences that form the way we respond to others today.

The tenor of the retreat is easily compromised by Credo family members who succumb to the temptation of believing themselves to be "ordained," set apart, keepers of the trust. For them to be a member of a team means that they are chosen, and have gifts which make them superior. They become Gnostics, priding themselves as keepers of the mystery of Credo which they are dispensing to the new initiates. Others cast themselves as staff facilitators—part of an organization which is bringing healing to others in need, often overlooking their own brokenness. To assume a title may be a way of belonging, of being different. It is also a way of alienating others.

Love is a not matter of belonging, it is a matter of including. There is a clear distinction between wanting safety and seeking intimacy. Volunteer companions on a Credo Weekend must be willing to set aside their desire for security in order to accept every retreat participant as a fellow wayfarer in this life: loyal wife or adulterer; devoted teacher or hustler; true believer or spiritual derelict. What helpers have to offer during the retreat is not their personal skills or their own truths, but rather their compassion. Only then may the retreat diminish fear and thereby enable love to come to fruition.

Building Community

He who loves community destroys community.
He who loves individuals builds community.
—Dietrich Bonhoeffer

It is easier, as people who have been on the Weekend before, to take the risk of vulnerability and love than it is for the newcomers. The Credo veterans are aware of the wonderful things that happen on the Weekend when this state of trust between individuals is achieved and a community is formed. Nevertheless the aim of the Weekend should not be *community*, but rather *intimacy*. Community is the *fruit* of our intimate friendship, it is not the goal. The helpers act as a midwife to the birth of community, through intimacy of exchange within a safe environment. Henri Nouwen, in *The Wounded Healer*, conceives of the healing role of the companion as that of hospitality.

> Hospitality is the virtue which allows us to break through the narrowness of our own fears and to open our Houses to the stranger, with the intuition that salvation comes to us in the form of a tired traveler. It

requires, first of all, the host feel at home in his own House, and secondly that he create a free and fearless place for the unexpected visitor.

By their hospitality and openness, the Weekend companions assist the birth of community. They encourage unity based on the shared confession of our basic brokenness and on a shared hope. This hope, in turn, leads far beyond the boundaries of human togetherness; it leads to the reality of love, the source of life itself. The others on the retreat learn from the willingness of Weekend companions to open their houses, as it were, to the stranger. Faced with such a responsibility, experienced companions approach the Weekend with humility, and with a desire to do what is loving.

Right or Wrong

When Weekend helpers are comfortable with the spirituality of the Credo Weekend, they recast questions of what is right or wrong, into what is hospitable, what is loving. The responsibility rests squarely on the companion to determine whether his or her actions are loving, and therefore right. Their individual consciences become their guides. Who can better read what is the motivation of an individual soul than that individual? There is no objectively right or wrong action. The yardstick for all the actions of a companion should be whether they are loving.

The goal of the retreat is shared leadership so that each person's particular gifts may come to the fore and be honored by others. Some would feel more comfortable if they were given very specific cue cards, as it were, so that they would say nothing "wrong."

Others would tend to look to the leader for prior approval of their actions. In each case, the person is shifting the responsibility to the author of the cue cards, on the one hand, or the leader, on the other. This desire is based on fear of failure, fear of self. Each person, however, has a particular aspect of his life where he or she may provide leadership.

> *Just do the steps that you've been shown*
> *By everyone you've ever known*
> *Until the dance becomes your very own.*
> —*For a Dancer*, Jackson Browne

Subjective Leadership

This is not to say that there is no leader. In my experience in living with sixteen others in the intentional community of Credo/Esperanza, I learned that there is no such thing as a leaderless group. The convener of the Weekend, the leader, should be confirming, having a comprehensive understanding of the Weekend format and what practical items need to be addressed. The leader brings into harmony the offering of all the companions and the other participants by maintaining a broad overview and a sensitivity to the movement of the Spirit within the gathering. The responsibility of the overall leader of the Weekend, then, is not to tell fellow companions what to do, and certainly not to take responsibility away from them. Rather, the leader's job is to enhance movement to the common goal of trust and compassion.

So also, each Weekend companion needs to comprehend the charisma, the spiritual essence, of the Weekend. Objectively nothing much happens on a Weekend, nor is anyone burdened with many tasks. Essentially, a group of people sit around listening to recordings at scheduled intervals and then talk about whatever crosses their minds. But the charisma of Credo is the spirit of love which meanders through it like a refreshing breeze. It is the subjective atmosphere that allows people feel safe and attended to, thereby freeing them to say whatever they feel.

Because the Credo Weekend is subjective, rather than objective, the leader's fundamental understanding is internal, not external: it resides in the leader's heart. Let me give you an idea of what I mean by subjective.

A couple of summers ago I returned to Spain with my son, Jonathan. We visited *El Mesquita*, the great mosque in Cordoba. Built at the zenith of the Muslim culture, it now has streams of tourists with their strollers and cameras, and there was not a faithful Muslim worshipper to be seen. Nevertheless, the feeling that Jonathan and I experienced was one of awe, of transcendence: we were in the presence of something deeply holy, crafted centuries ago by the faithful.

My objective description of the strollers and the cameras misses the point. But words miss the point, too. I have tried to understand the essence of Islam by reading books. I only began to understand the depth of Islam when I suspended that objective data, and became absorbed in the subjective nuances of being in the midst of that mosque.

Let me cite more familiar examples. The Lincoln Memorial captures the essence of American idealism; the Vietnam Memorial captures the essence of America's sorrow about her fallen sons and daughters; St. Peter's Basilica in Rome embodies the essence of Roman Catholicism; Francis of Assisi is the essence of Jesus' message.

Are these examples right or are they wrong? I am sure you see that this is a meaningless question because it is taking objective considerations (the definition of right and wrong) and applying them to something beyond the rational plane. When we are able to suspend the objective—the "shoulds" and "musts," the correct and the incorrect—then we are able to comprehend the totality of what we seek to understand. We are able to see its *charisma*: its spiritual essence.

On the Credo Weekend each step helps the participants get in touch with their interior feelings, and provides the foundation for building the type of community that encourages a participant to share openly. The leadership goal on the Credo Weekend is to become a servant to the new participants by modeling loving behavior. Through the Credo companions the participants will see that all participants are to be equally respected, each one valued as they speak from their hearts. This is compellingly illustrated in the testimony of Ricks Wilson, a veteran Credo Weekend companion:

My family comes from a country town in Virginia, and have been there for generations. I had the blessing of a family that loved and cared and encouraged one another most of the time. In 1942 I joined the Navy along with thousands of other young men, and spent three of my four years in the Pacific. As a sailor I lived with a broad cross-section of men and learned how self esteem can be either built or destroyed by those by whom we are surrounded. I learned a lot about living life that I had never known.

Some of the situations in which I found myself were confusing. My self esteem went up and down during those Navy days and I can understand the problems with dealing with low self esteem. Oh, how I could have used the help of Credo then, but Credo was not to come into being for another 26 years, and the help I received from that fellowship did not come until 18 years after that.

Credo did come to the Navy in 1971, brought by a young chaplain who knows human pain and how to relate to those suffering from neglect, lovelessness, and all the known abuses. God gave Don the vision for helping those fellow humans. Along the way many thousands of seemingly hopeless lives have been and are being turned around and saved. I got to know Don when he came to my parish to be Episcopal chaplain to the College. I listened to his stories about helping "throw away" sailors and officers, and I knew I wanted to have a part in his vision of a civilian branch. My spiritual life and my faith in Jesus Christ was strong, and I shared it with any one who would listen. Don had a true but willing neophyte on his hands!

I asked to go on the first Weekend with William & Mary students, back in 1989. Don hesitated a moment, and then said, "You can go, Ricks, so long as you promise to keep quiet and listen." As I have matured in my understanding I can see there is good reason for that. I have learned more about the value of living like Christ, rather than talking and instructing.

A milestone in my path to spiritual wholeness occurred on my third Weekend. I am a loving and caring person by nature, and while I can't match the horror stories lived by many (thank God), I went to offer love and to support their efforts to renew their lives and find healing.

This was put to the test when I heard that there would be in attendance some men who had sexually abused their children. I was appalled at even the thought of doing such a thing, and considered bowing out of the retreat so that I would not have to face them.

But I came on Credo to learn, and found myself sitting beside a tall, very nice looking young man who said very little at first, although his eyes were full of suffering. Then, in his deep need, his heart opened and quietly, with tears welling in his eyes, he told of how he had sexually abused his own son. He was desperate for help and was in the care of a counselor. He longed for forgiveness and strength to resist this damning urge.

I was afraid my heart would break under the weight of sharing his pain. I thought of the scripture, "The sins of the father are visited on the son for generation unto generation." It seems that he was abused by his father. To my surprise, without a second thought I put my arm around my "untouchable" brother. The man's agony was genuine, and I was there for him.

He experienced love and help from a group of people that day, who would hear him and see him make a few more steps along the road to recovery: understanding, self-forgiveness, and, God willing, eventual healing. "This is what Jesus would have done," I thought to myself. God loves the broken man and so do I. The face of that young man comes into my mind often, and I pray for the death of his plague and a new life for him and his son.

Another milestone was when Credo was asked to provide a Weekend with 25 patients in a drug de-toxification ward of a psychiatric hospital in Cleveland. Four of us drove up together from Williamsburg, and we were put up in the home of Susan, a neat gal with the same focus. On the ward there were a few women, and a mix of blacks, whites and native Americans—all from blue collar backgrounds. Alcohol abuse, heroin, cocaine, pot, it was all there.

I always found myself sitting beside a middle-aged man who had lost all of his fingers from the first joint down, on both hands. His hands were frozen one night when he was drunk and sleeping in a doorway. Near the end of that time we had together, I took the stubs of my black brother's hands in mine while we sang along to Bob Dylan's You've Gotta Serve Somebody. I believe Christ was there in that room and lives were helped because five people offered their love and caring.

Credo has opened new vistas for me. I have come a long way from my childhood in the countryside of Virginia, and from my many years as an antiques dealer, bringing to others the joy of 18th Century furniture. All those years were wonderful, but now I am alive and awake to the needs of others I never knew before. I know that I do not have many more years to live, but for as long as possible I want to continue to learn and to share the love that God has given me.

I guess we won't know the time on earth when everything is "loverly," as Eliza Dolittle sang about in My Fair Lady; human needs are not confined to any socio-economic group —they are the same for the very rich and the very poor alike. We are dealing with a poverty of spirit. But we can help make things better if we give our love away.

The Passion

Some Christian Credo companions have told me that a helpful way for them to visualize the Credo Weekend is through the analogy of Holy Week. In his life Jesus experienced the extremes of the situations recalled during the first portion of the Credo. During the first night, participants are trying to recapture in their own lives some of the same feelings of pain and isolation which occurred during Judas's betrayal, Jesus' arrest, His agony in the garden, His desertion by all of his followers, and the desolation of his crucifixion when he cried, "My God, why have you forsaken me?"

After the crucifixion came Saturday. During this period, his followers, the soldiers, Pilate, the crowds, most likely tried to evaluate the meaning of all that had occurred as it applied to their individual lives. So those on the Credo Weekend spend time sorting out what they have uncovered about the state of their lives and the lives of others.

Finally came Sunday, the day of the Resurrection, when Jesus was with his people once more. His loving presence was felt among his followers who had gathered together to try to find some consolation and meaning regarding these unsettling events. He talked with them, but more importantly He gave them the Comforter, the Holy Spirit, so they could have the insight and the strength to understand what had happened and to pass on this new life to others. So also we hope that in the final part of the Credo many may feel the presence of God; and that through the Holy Spirit their lives will take on new meaning and direction.

For the Christian helper, then, Credo may well mean walking the path to Calvary. It may be a useful image for the Christian Credo companions to retain as they attend to others on their journey. Remember that Calvary was a necessary part of the process. Without the experience of the suffering and rejection, the impact of the resurrection would have been lost. Helpers may be tempted to avoid the discomfort, as Peter did when he attacked the arresting soldiers. But they must be on guard for that. Without Good Friday there is no Easter.

On the other hand, life is not all Good Friday. One must be careful not to be morbid, wallowing in suffering. The angel at the tomb said, "Why do you seek the living among the dead?"

(Luke 24:5) Remember what we are looking for in this Credo workshop:

> *I want to bring you some spiritual gift to make you strong;*
> *or rather I want to be among you to receive encouragement myself*
> *through the influence of your faith on me as of mine on you.*
> —Romans I: 11-12

The Credo helpers are not facilitators in a marathon psychotherapy session. They are looking to share their spiritual gifts so that all are mutually made whole.

One final caution for active Christians who are to be helpers. Although you may understand Credo in terms of Christ's passion, many do not. *Nor do they have to* in order to be receptive to love's action in their lives. Although you may experience the joy of Jesus' love in your heart, many do not. Do not try to force God's hand. Take to heart this quotation by Cardinal Suhard. It is the heart of the Credo approach. Please honor this. This is not the only valid approach, to be sure. But it is the one we are committed to use.

> *To be a witness does not consist in engaging in propaganda,*
> *nor even stirring people up, but in being a living mystery.*
> *It means to live in such a way that one's life would not make sense*
> *if God did not exist.*
> —Cardinal Suhard

14

The Partnership Of Credo

Certainly there are many other ways than Credo to seek wholeness, and many of us have spent our lives successfully applying these insights for the benefit of our selves and others. No approach is all-encompassing, any approach is limited both by its definition, and by the boundaries that are defined. Any definition provides a stumbling-block for some people. Christian symbolism or the vocabulary of the social sciences, for example, is illuminating for some, and decidedly negative for others.

The usual comparisons which people draw when they hear of the Credo Weekend are with self-help meetings, group therapy, or religious retreats. There are elements of all of these in the Credo Weekend. Indeed the Weekend does help people help themselves; it is therapeutic; and it does awaken their desire for deeper spiritual understanding. We at Credo wholeheartedly endorse these other approaches, for Credo is not a substitute or rival to any of them. Rather, we hope Credo *complements* them, and extends the boundaries of these other helpful approaches to human wholeness.

In common with many religious retreats and self-help programs, Credo affirms that the final responsibility for growth and health lies with the individual, and that one's spiritual life (whether or not it is religiously defined) is the foundation of any long term move toward wholeness. Together with self-help programs and many religious retreats, Credo affirms that involvement with other people is a key ingredient in helping one's self. However, Credo places emphasis on the loving presence of the community *as a whole*, and does not focus on a specific problem as a source of bonding, as do many Twelve Step groups.

Twelve Step Fellowships

The Twelve Step spirituality articulated in 1936 by Bill W. and his friends in the Oxford Group, found its fruition in Alcoholics Anonymous. It is the most significant wave of spirituality in the twentieth century. Like Credo (and I would add, like Jesus), AA is singularly egalitarian. The list of famous people who have found serenity within the Twelve Steps is impressive.

But most important are the thousands of anonymous heroes who are known only to God and their recovering friends, who with conviction follow "the Program" and are redeemed from lives of addiction. They are the unsung saints of our addictive culture. Their spirituality is the leaven of our loaf and the hope of our society. Many of them lend their lives and spirituality to churches and synagogues, and some to Credo. They enrich the broad Credo family by their presence and, in turn, are nourished by the diversity of Credo family members who may be of quite different orientation.

Credo differs from a specific Twelve Step meeting by focusing on the universal brokenness embracing all of us in our spiritual struggles, rather than a particular addiction. As a matter of fact, most compulsive people are multiply addicted and when one addiction is stymied, they shift to another means of numbing the pain. Bill W., for example, found his sexual behavior a source of great pain. Pulitzer prize-winning author Nan Robertson describes this story in her book *Getting Better: Inside Alcoholics Anonymous*:

> Wilson's marriage to Lois Burnham in 1918 lasted until his death at the age of seventy-five in 1971. She believed in him fiercely and tended his flame. Yet, particularly during his sober decades in AA in the forties, fifties and sixties, Bill Wilson was a compulsive womanizer. His ... behavior filled him with guilt, according to old-timers close to him, but he continued to stray off the reservation. His last and most serious love affair ... began when he was in his sixties. She was important to him until the end of his life.

Bill W., like all of us, had a valiant struggle to keep his spiritual focus. Thus it follows that dozens of variations of the Twelve Step program acknowledge multiple compulsions and address everything from substance abuse, sexual abuse and addiction, to overeating and anorexia. The Twelve Step Program restores the capacity for meaningful relationships by helping a person develop a more palpable and constructive set of personal beliefs.

The comprehensive spirituality of the Credo Weekend addresses the root cause of all of these addictions, a spiritual void, and serves as a useful companion to those who are facing specific issues in their lives. Credo works hand in hand with the process of self-acceptance and increased ability to accept love. It helps addicts affirm that they are sacred and worthwhile human beings. On the Weekend the addicts experience love and acceptance by people who know them as they are, and they experience their needs being met by the compassion and care of others, now that they have felt safe enough to express their needs.

The Weekend provides an opportunity for all of us, should we chose, to talk openly about our spirituality in an accepting atmosphere where there is no fear of being rejected. So often today, in this age of pluralism we can be intimidated by being in the presence of so many others who may hold beliefs that are in conflict with ours. We are not in a time where there are generally accepted standards. Incredible as it may seem, even in seminaries, where one might assume there is a common body of belief, people are reluctant to share something as intimate as their core beliefs. Frederick Buechner, in *Telling Secrets*, reported a remarkable instance:

> Harvard Divinity School was proud, and justly so, of what it called pluralism—feminists, theists, liberation theologians, all pursuing truth together—but the price that pluralism cost was dramatized one day in a way that I have never forgotten. I had been speaking candidly and personally about my own faith and how I had tried over the years to express it in language. At the same time I had been trying to get the class to respond in kind. For the most part none of them were responding at all but just sitting there taking it in without saying a word.

Finally I had to tell them what I thought. I said they reminded me of dead fish lying on cracked ice in a fish store window with their round blank eyes. There I was making a fool of myself spilling out to them the secrets of my heart, and there they were, not telling me what they believed about anything beneath the level of their various causes. It was at this point that a black African student got up and spoke. "The reason I do not say anything about what I believe," he said in his stately African English, "is that I'm afraid it will be shot down."

At least for a moment we all saw, I think, that the danger of pluralism is that it becomes factionalism, and that if factions grind their separate axes too vociferously, something mutual, precious, and human is in danger of being drowned out and lost.

The Credo Weekend fosters the reality of something mutual, precious, and human, as do the Twelve Step meetings. Because of its approach, Credo may provide for some individuals an even broader canvas to integrate their second and third Steps, which are concerned with the existence of a Higher Power, and the turning of one's life over to God as personally understood. An example of this is the experience of an employee of Old Dominion University.

Mary is a person who for many years has been committed to the Twelve Step way of life. But she found a nagging barrier as she meditated on the steps to do with turning herself over to God. On the Credo Weekend she told us that when she was younger, and a devout Roman Catholic, she visited her church to pray, only to be molested by an altar boy, who, in an involuted and perverse way, convinced her that their sexual experience was linked with spirituality. She had never returned to any church since, and felt spiritually impoverished.

On the Credo Weekend Mary ruminated over her beliefs and values, seeking in some way to transcend the block which had stultified her progress toward becoming a whole woman. While on the Sunday morning meditative walk she found herself walking by the very church where the abuse had happened.

When she came back to tell her fellow Weekend participants about the fruit of her hour's meditation, Mary told them that she decided to slip into the church and sit quietly for a while. "Soon," she reported, "I felt an overwhelming peace, a burden being lifted from my shoulders, as if I were in the presence of God. Now," she said with a visible sense of relief, "I can move ahead to work my Program with a renewed belief in my Higher Power."

Credo welcomes the privilege to be a partner with those who have found the Twelve Step approach to be meaningful in their lives. We hope that we can be an added resource to these our brothers and sisters in the spiritual search we share.

Group Psychotherapy

Group psychotherapy focuses on areas of dysfunction and provides valuable insight. Under the guidance of a trained counselor, people gain from the affinity they feel with fellow sufferers. When they listen to someone else tell of experiences and feelings that mirror their own, the group member contradicts a lifetime of being certain that no one will ever be able to understand.

The common experiences provide a basis for understanding, sharing, and connecting. They are a foundation for figuring out how to approach recovery. As with the Twelve Step Fellowship, group therapy focuses on specific areas of conflict (sometimes defined as mental illness) rather than addressing the general plight of the human soul. Psychotherapy, moreover, follows a medical model where there is a delineation between therapist/doctor and clients/patients. In Credo we are all viewed as one.

Group and individual therapy are appropriate and even vital approaches to personal wholeness. Personally I have made great breakthroughs in my recovery with the help of a skilled therapist to whom I owe a deep debt of gratitude. Credo can be a partner with a therapist, helping the patient make personal discoveries so that his or her therapy may proceed with a clearer focus. Credo was invited to offer a Weekend on the inpatient substance abuse ward of Glenbeigh Psychiatric Hospital in Cleveland.

The retreat augmented the hospital's medical focus on the individual pathology of the patients, and the Twelve Step awareness of the patients, by addressing the collective sickness of society in which the patients live. In effect, Credo constructed a micro-society of caring friends which included patients, hospital staff, and concerned neighbors, and offered an alternative of love.

Religious Retreats

The Credo perspective is akin to that of a traditional Judeo/Christian retreat, in that such a retreat focuses on the alienation of all humanity from the love of God. Like the Credo Weekend, the religious retreat is comprehensive rather than specific, affirming that the individual is ultimately responsible for his or her own growth and health, and that one's spirituality is the keystone for any permanent healing. Since there is this affinity between Credo's approach and Bible-based theology, some people fear that Credo presumes to be a substitute for organized religion.

There are many responsible Christians, Muslims and Jews who ask this question for good reason. Some secular self-help organizations deny the need for a relationship with a personal God. These alternative groups represent an understanding of life that teaches that self-realization, or peace of mind, may be achieved autonomously. This is antithetical to the devout Christian or Jew whose central beliefs revolve around the intimate presence of God in their lives. To my understanding, the self-actualizing philosophy also flies in the face of the first three steps of the Twelve Step Programs whose keystone is our powerlessness as individuals to effect our recovery.

Credo has an affinity with the spiritual basis of religious retreats, yet differs because of its inclusiveness. There is no doctrine endorsed to the exclusion of others, and whatever religious expression occurs on the Weekend comes from the personal experiences of the participants. The Credo Weekend does not presume to provide any answers. Its only purpose is to provide an atmosphere where neighbors may feel the presence of the Spirit of love in their lives. How they integrate that experience is purely a personal decision, and not Credo's responsibility.

Credo focuses on the human condition and the need for the healing of love and friendship. Self-realization cannot come independently, but only through setting self-interest aside in order to be able to accept and give love to others. Credo provides an atmosphere where love is experienced through members of the emerging community. A young man recently released from prison for child abuse, tearfully said that for him Credo was BLT—Basic Love Training. This love within the community is sensed by the participants to be greater than the sum of the compassion offered by each individual there. It is the experience of this love which causes many to hunger for its source.

Our hope is that the Weekend will open doors for people so that they may seek appropriate avenues to approach love's source and satisfy their hunger. These avenues vary from person to person. Some Credo graduates become more vital to their support groups; others are restored to active involvement in their Twelve Step walk; others find themselves more focused in their psychotherapy; others make initial steps in discovering their personal spirituality; still others make a deeper commitment to their religious tradition. I am told that Al Koeneman, when he was chief of Navy chaplains, observed that for many, Credo is the "front porch of the church." That is an apt image, but I hope that it will mature into the servant's entrance.

Just as Credo is not a substitute for support groups or psychotherapy, it emphatically is not a para-church competing with faith-groups. The Credo approach is one of service to others—not one of competition. If Credo is able to assist someone in finding a loving community of support which brings them life and purpose, wherever that may be, then our mission is fulfilled.

Some people are uncomfortable with the terminology used by traditional religion, even though they may share the same perspective as that of many religions that love is the source of life and brings healing through friendship in community. Where the rub comes for some is when formal religion defines the community of love as uniquely its own. For them, because this institutional religious paradigm is so specific, it is less inclusive than they would desire.

Love is greater than any institutional understanding. Credo helps people see that love is the essence of life without defining how this may be expressed by any organization. Credo is a vehicle of love for those who, as John Milton described, "look up and are not fed." At the same time, Credo serves as an experience for those within religious fellowships who seek to share their love in a new and powerful way.

Credo might be termed a school in love and friendship. It is not a congregation, a community of faithful, nor does it ever intend to be. Credo only introduces people to the possibility of loving friendship, and helps believers be better witnesses to their faith in their lives. Credo is open to all, however they define themselves. By trying to bring humanity together on an intimate level, Credo becomes a partner with all loving approaches to spiritual health.

Part IV

The Need For Credo:

Love Is The Only Engine Of Survival

The Future

You don't know me from the wind
you never will, you never did
I'm the little jew that wrote the bible.
I've seen nations rise and fall
I've heard their stories, heard them all
but love's the only engine of survival.

Your servant here, he has been told
to say it clear, to say it cold:
It's over, it ain't going any further.
And now the wheels of heaven stop
you feel the devil's riding crop
Get ready for the future: It is murder.

There'll be the breaking of the ancient western code,
Your private life will suddenly explode ...

Things are going to slide in all directions
Won't be nothing, nothing you can measure anymore.
The blizzard of the world has crossed the threshold
and it has overturned the order of the soul.

When they said repent, I wonder what they meant.
When they said repent, I wonder what they meant.
When they said repent, I wonder what they meant

—Leonard Cohen

15

A Famine Of The Spirit

> *A time is coming, says my Lord God,*
> *when I will send a famine on the land:*
> *not a hunger for bread or a thirst for water,*
> *but for hearing the words of the Lord.*
> *Men shall wander from sea to sea*
> *and from north to east to seek the word of the Lord*
> *But they will not find it.*
> —Amos 8:11-12

You and I, I am convinced, are in just such a time of spiritual famine—a famine of the heart as serious as any African tragedy you see on CNN. It is hard to accept such a diagnosis, and even more difficult to face this reality. But unless we address this spiritual famine face to face in all its aspects we remain in denial. By refusing to name the demons which affect our life together we choose to remain in their power, and can experience no reconciliation.

As distressing as this exploratory surgery may be, I ask you to bear with me. I am not writing these words in despair, for I believe there is healing once we acknowledge what is staring us in the face. "We have to create, to sow eyes which enable us to see," a contemporary Russian composer observes. "Yet today there are less and less of these unclouded eyes. They have been clouded with indifference."

Healing comes when we suspend our desire for a way out from that which is not ours to control. We need to open our hearts trusting in the benevolence of God so that we may give and receive love. When we seek to understand the shadow side of both our culture and our selves, God gives us the grace to transcend our condition by accepting His invincible love.

The introduction of this book put forth my understanding of the human condition: the tension between love and fear which is the fabric of every human life. I referred to the life of Jesus as a universal metaphor, a paradigm of this struggle of love to conquer fear—a constant part of being human. In the narrative I have reported the cycles which occur naturally in our lives as we die to one security in order to live for another. Our attempts to adjust to the stages of our lives may yield either constructive or tragic results. This is the human pilgrimage.

In the same way, the tension between love and fear, life and death, is reflected in the social and political systems that we construct. As in our personal lives, these systems also have stages. A society moves from a sense of order and vitality generating a feeling of well being, toward an awareness of the chaotic and intense, inviting fear. The fear, in turn, generates a yearning for order, and the cycle repeats.

Part I described four images, or icons, in which the reflection of love expressed in hospitality brought meaning to my life: the graciousness of a dairyman's family grounded in welcoming, accepting faith; the bonding in mutual support experienced in the accidental community of a ship's crew; the spiritual intimacy of a Spanish nobleman who met each person as a reflection of God's sacredness; and the unconditional acceptance of a monk within whose community all were honored.

Presenting these concepts in terms of personal images is no editorial contrivance. I extrapolate meaning in my life by placing events in the context of a metaphor, an image, a symbolic perception. In my particular personal history, which began within a chaotic family with blurred boundaries, I have been attracted to the Spanish culture as one of my personal metaphors.

For me, Spain represents the counterpoints of passion and reserve; a deep community commitment to family and children, in harmony with an individual sense of dignity of what it is to be a man, and what it is to be a woman. In a recent interview, King Juan Carlos reflects the basic Spanish grounding in the family:

> Having children—and you know as well as I do—gives their parents constant anxiety, but great joy and happiness too. It's wonderful to see them growing up day by day; to try to find out their tastes and learnings so that you can understand and encourage them better.

As unusual as it may seem, Spanish culture has frequently exhibited a metaphor of the cycles which were congruent with my own life, and with my source of hope.

As a solitary boy, alone at home for hours on end after school, I poured over pictures of the works of El Greco. Unconsciously I experienced the tension in his work, the polarity of ecstasy and order: the passionate excesses of El Greco's saints enveloped in what John of the Cross termed "the living flame of love," counterbalanced by the brittle stability of Counter-Reformation Spanish Catholicism.

From 1974 through 1976, my family resided in Spain. These were the years just before and jusr after the death of Francisco Franco. We experienced in that culture the tension between social order and individual freedom. During his tenure as head of state, *El Caudillo* Franco relentlessly imposed order. As a result our family enjoyed the sense of social and physical safety this limitation of personal autonomy brought. Hence, we never gave a thought to locking our house. Ruth and I never feared walking about the city at night.

In the events of day-to-day living. we experienced this atmosphere of trust and order. One day, for example, while Ruth and I were driving with our foster son in a remote part of Spain a boy turned his bicycle into the path of my slow-moving automobile, and his head struck the hood of the car. I carried the unconscious boy to the doctor in the village. Filled with dread, we waited in our car.

After a while the village priest came by and asked, "Why are you waiting here? You can do nothing to heal the boy. My parishioners who saw the accident tell me that it was not your fault, so go in peace. We want you to enjoy your holiday, the boy is in God's hands." We were not only astonished at the priest's concern for us, but also his commitment to simple justice. Thankfully, while we were digesting what the priest had said, a smiling villager came out and told us that the boy was conscious and doing well.

Another time, while we were living in the very center of the Spanish port city of El Puerto de Santa Maria, a stranger knocked on our door and handed me my costly camera which I had carelessly left on the top of our car parked on the main street. The Spaniard had no expectation of reward, it was done out of neighborly concern.

The whole neighborhood celebrated our little sons, showering them with affection and admiration. The woman who operated a tiny snack shop down the street from us gave them *caramelos* (candies) as if our children were her own. We had no worry about boundaries being crossed, nor about our children being hurt. In a real way the neighborhood was part of our extended family.

But, after Franco's death, Spanish society reacted against the rigid and intrusive social strictures. "Freedom" was celebrated by the dismantling of many imposed limits. But for some freedom was license to rob homes with apparent impunity, to engage in hitherto forbidden sexual conduct, to ingest illegal drugs. And because their individual freedoms were exercised outside generally accepted boundaries, they caused social harm.

As a result, our freedom was restricted. Ruth and I no longer felt the freedom to go out into the city streets at night. With Franco we were "free" to watch nothing but rituals on the television during Holy Week; without Franco we are now free to watch a national talk show hosted by a transvestite. This new polarity eschewed the ecstasy and order typical of the mystics and Roman Catholicism. Rather, it gave birth to license and disorder, in the interests of individual freedom.

But cycles continue on their course; first living on the extremes of anarchy with a civil war bathed in blood on the one hand, then forty years of imposed order on the other, folowed by the excesses of individualism (anarchy, once more). At the present time, the Spanish people are achieving a personal balance reflected in the words of Juan Carlos, their constitutional monarch:

> It's true that we are different in Spain. When Vaclav Havel came to visit me in Palma De Mallorca, I took him out one morning to a bar where every one greeted me as if I were an old acquaintance. Havel couldn't get over it. What surprised him even more was seeing me pay for our drinks, even though the proprietor wanted us to be his guests. "Doing anything like this is absolutely out of the question in Prague," the Czech president told me. [Queen] Dona Sofia took some time to become accustomed to our ways, too; they must have struck her as rather strange. Personally, I've always thought them perfectly normal. I am the king, but I'm also a human being, and a Spaniard into the bargain, and I don't think putting yourself upon a pedestal is enough to inspire respect.

Ruth and I experienced that harmonious change toward individual dignity and collective responsibility about twenty years later. In 1993 we revisited Galicia, one of our favorite parts of Spain, joining our son Jonathan and thousands of other youthful pilgrims. Like our son, many had walked hundreds of miles along the pilgrimage route and gathered at the holy city of Santiago de Compostela, the burial place of St. James.

To be sure, the polarity was still there. Before a throng in the cathedral the Primate of Spain was delivering an extraordinary sermon from the tomb of St. James, yet his voice had to compete with the cacophony of fire-crackers bursting in the plaza. But a balance was there as well: religion and revelry, community generosity and individual responsibility.

On the climactic eve of the feast day, Brad Hall, the man whose life was so changed in the early days of Credo, joined Ruth, Jonathan, and me in the plaza packed with thousands of young pilgrims. There was no fighting, drunkenness, or pickpocketing. We witnessed neither license nor oppression. I enjoyed a sense of well being which I rarely experience in America.

16

The Cradle Of The Best And The Worst

*It's coming to America first, the cradle of the best and the worst.
It's here they've got the range, and the machinery for change
and it's here they got the spiritual thirst.
It's here the family's broken, and it's here the lonely say
that the heart has got to open in a fundamental way.*

—Democracy Is Coming to the USA, Leonard Cohen

I find it hard to stay the course I need to maintain for my spiritual health in a society that has lost its bearings. For me, this incongruence is the most disturbing dimension of our current culture. The excitement and danger of an entire society living on the edge is stimulating. But I face the inevitable changes within myself without the safety of a cohesive culture. Because a lack of boundaries in my early childhood caused me to suffer, I acutely feel my personal vulnerability in a society where limits are ignored.

All of us are bound to experience some degree of disorientation and alienation in such inharmonious times as now, regardless of our personal background. Many generally accepted social and personal values are now being called into question, fueled by the irresponsible behavior of some of our political and religious leaders.

In a period of cynicism such as ours, we have passively permitted a questioning minority to diminish our values. The majority have become fair game for any sophisticated pressure group. In the interest of a poly-cultural ideal, where the interests of the politically active minority become primary, we stand by while the values of the prevalent culture are selectively repressed.

For example, the United States is a country where a high percentage of citizens publicly worship each week. Yet the values that millions of people affirm each week in their place of worship are belittled by those who dismiss them as expressions of "the Religious Right." When the deep-seated beliefs of the majority are dismissed as trivial by the cultural elite, an undercurrent of abandonment, resentment, and anger is generated. My hunch is that we will reap a whirlwind.

My commitment to spiritual equilibrium will not be reinforced in a society which is out of control. Within myself I feel divided—in conflict with what I intuitively know is right: As I was absorbed by the television coverage of our electronic victory over Iraq in the Gulf, I was conscious of the mayhem we were visiting on the innocent. As I became engrossed in the Clarence Thomas hearings in the Senate, which were concerned with his worthiness to sit on the Supreme Court, I was aware that the mean-spirited character assassinations by the senate inquisitors compounded the abuse of all parties involved in this spectacle.

Alice In Wonderland

I'm sentimental, if you know what I mean;
I love the country, but I can't stand the scene.
And I'm neither left nor right, I'm just staying home tonight,
getting lost in that hopeless little screen.

—*Democracy Is Coming to the USA*, Leonard Cohen

Often I feel as though I am a guest at the Mad Hatter's Tea Party. I opened a church magazine only to read that a Christian theological school in New York now feels obligated to provide seminary living quarters to homosexual seminarian couples, while refusing seminary housing to unmarried heterosexual couples.

As each day passes, a new item in my daily life seems to be consigned to danger, articulated by a culture which is dominated by fear. Last Christmas the local hardware store displayed a sign that read, "Mace: the perfect stocking stuffer." The television carried an advertisement warning "If you feel safe walking down the street, you're just not looking." The expression of fear was palpable.

A few days after the Memorial Day weekend, a time not only for family cook-outs, but also of peak sales for frankfurters, the Weekend guide section of the local newspaper carried a banner headline that read, "Hot Dogs Linked to Leukemia in Kids." According to the article, a survey indicated that children who eat more than 12 hot dogs per month have nine times the normal risk of developing childhood leukemia, and children born to women who eat at least one hot dog per month during pregnancy have double the normal risk of developing brain tumors, (as do children whose fathers ate hot dogs before conception). Even the innocent joy of having a cookout with one's family is dimmed by warnings.

A while back I opened the welcoming letter from my son Jonathan's college. On the first page was an essay warning of dire consequences to those students who do not buy supplemental health insurance. It implied that should my son waive the proffered insurance and later have to apply for public medical assistance, medical care might be denied.

Next, I picked up the wallet sized sexual-assault card which had tumbled out of the envelope into my lap. It had a precautionary reminder to my son that if he was sexually assaulted he was not to wash himself, thereby destroying possible criminal evidence derived from the residue of blood or semen. The tone of the communication from the college was not welcoming, it was frightening.

As a man, I am disturbed by the fear-laden view of manhood, which seems to be a muffled, yet constant drum beat. In Charleston I heard the male chairman tell members of a hospital sexual abuse review panel that no responsible person should ever allow a boy to be a baby sitter. He was talking about my sons, and I knew to the core of my being that his view was distorted. What was that pediatrician saying about *himself* as a man? What was he saying about all men? What was he saying about me?

When a woman is excused of responsibility for her actions in severing the penis of her husband and is vindicated in the courtroom, our view of manhood seems askew. When two young men are excused by many citizens from the responsibility for viciously murdering their parents who allegedly abused them, violence seems to be accepted as the male norm.

The plague of AIDS is addressed by issuing free condoms to adolescents in high school so that they may have "safe sex," even though it is clear that promiscuity is corrosive, both to the young people involved and the society they are preparing to enter as adults. College administrators sanction the issuing of whistles to protect daughters from young male classmates (who could be my sons).

In all of these situations I see the image of a predatory male animal—not a valued father, son, partner or husband. And such prophecies can be self-fulfilling. A young man, deprived of any affirmation of his sanctity, can easily accept the view consistently expressed by some in society that to be a man means to be feared, not to be celebrated. Such a self-image can lead him into the trap of self-rejection and addiction.

And so the lingering question: Are we not as a society introducing a new hurdle for any couple seeking to bond in marriage? The young woman is taught that she had best be wary. She senses it is wiser to reinforce her autonomy rather than to affirm her unity in marriage. Therefore, she finds it difficult to weigh the advantage of the economic autonomy a "substantial" career brings, against her natural desire to raise a family—particularly when motherhood is described as bondage. Politically strident cries of "right to life" and "right to choose" are bound to bring confusion to her as she addresses the critical decision of the moral use of her body, which scripture refers to as more than a body: it is the temple of the Holy Spirit.

Control From Without

But I'm stubborn as those garbage bags that Time cannot decay.
I'm junk but I'm still holding up this little wild bouquet:
Democracy is coming to the USA

—*Democracy Is Coming to the USA*, Leonard Cohen

As a country, we seem to have lost confidence in our worth as men and women. We doubt our ability to control ourselves from within and anxiously consent to being organized from without. And the imposed organization we accept is not always based on our personal values, but rather the agenda of a vocal minority.

A classic example of this selective social engineering just took effect in James City County, Virginia. Because of the aggressive anti-tobacco crusade, in this county newly hired firemen and police officers must refrain from smoking or chewing tobacco, or risk getting fired. That means no smoking at home, at work, or anywhere else. The county will grant employees three slip-ups and fire them if they are caught sneaking a smoke or using a tobacco product a fourth time. However, seasoned employees can light up a cigarette or chew a wad of tobacco in front of the new employees without any repercussions.

The action is justified because the county's worker's compensation liability will decrease with the new rule. The county does not plan to test the employees, but that may be a future rule. "It's perfectly constitutional," said a professor of constitutional law, "the county requires these employees to follow other conditions of employment, like wearing a uniform. ... If they wanted to ban steak and eggs for these employees, they could if they think it will improve the performance of these officers."

Note that these selective social engineers are not including restrictions on alcohol use by the employee—another costly habit which may wreak greater havoc on families, and which can diminish an employee's work performance. Nor are they proscribing varieties of sexual activity which court debilitating diseases, massive medical bills, and diminished performance. The point I am trying to make is not to argue the virtues or vices of tobacco, but rather to illustrate the result of our passively consenting to being organized from without.

One of the most blatant examples of organizing by a pressure group is in the drive for a uni-sex fleet in the Navy. Consider the proposal: Select hundreds of young married women and men at their sexual prime. Separate them from their spouses. Place them with other separated spouses for up to six months at a time aboard ship in intimate living arrangements. Provide no legitimate sexual outlet. In fact, forbid married couples from serving on the same ship. The implications of that policy, not only from a "hormonal" standpoint, but also from the jeopardy in which young married people are placed, are as radical as they are disruptive.

Yet, in the name of gender equity, the extinction of the managable single-sex population is what the government is imposing by fiat. Marriages are endangered, illicit pregnancies soar, Navy day care centers are swollen with the children of single parents, good order and discipline is compromised. Many young women and men come into the Navy for a refuge so that they can sort out their lives in a secure atmosphere. Social engineering makes the actual situation aboard ship mirror the chaos they came from. When this kind of social engineering is fostered on the highest of government levels, it is no wonder that people have decreasing respect for authority.

There is another side to the coin. Not only have people lost faith in authority, those in authority have lost faith in people. Out of fear of the fraying social contract evidenced by a breakdown of order from the barrios of Miami to the streets of New York, leaders presume that people must be controlled, rather than being encouraged to act in the interests of the common good.

Only the repressive societies of China, Russia, and apartheid South Africa approach our percentage of citizens behind bars. Between 1980 and 1993, the number of inmates in prison in this country tripled. We warehouse suffering offenders in bursting prisons, issuing them condoms so that when they rape or are raped (which is our expectation) they will have "safe sex." Taking into account the prison population, there are more *men* than women who are raped in the United States each year. Yet, we take no responsibility for the chaotic living situation that we have imposed upon them.

I find it unconscionable to live in a society that places a man behind bars because he has broken prescribed social limits by stealing a $200 TV set, and yet takes no responsibility for enforcing social limits in prison. The likelihood is that because of *our* action, not his, he will be attacked and probably sexual abused. We are out of balance, and I find the lack of social conscience threatening to my well being, and to the well-being of my family.

Our Addictive Society

Things are going to slide in all directions
Won't be nothing, nothing you can measure anymore.
The blizzard of the world has crossed the threshold
and it has overturned the order of the soul.

—*Democracy Is Coming to the USA*, Leonard Cohen

A widely accepted metaphor used to describe our American way of life in the 1990's is that of addiction. Dr. Patrick Carnes, the premier research scientist in the field of sexual abuse and addiction, has definitively described the behavior of our culture in a landmark study titled *Don't Call It Love*. Although Carnes' primary illustrations are in the context of sexual addiction (the fall out from sexual abuse and trespassed boundaries), the truths which he extrapolates from the sum of his patients over the years transcend the particular and apply to us all.

A recent estimate of all of the addicts in our culture, Dr. Carnes reports, places those affected by addiction at over 131 million (including 28 million children of alcoholics). "When over half of the population is involved with addiction, addictive norms become central to the cultural experience," Dr. Carnes observed. He continues, "If we were to design a society in which addiction could optimally thrive, many of the components required already exist in our own." *Don't Call It Love* discusses the key components:

- Our culture celebrates high stress with people living overextended, over-committed lives leading to chronic anxiety; where the compulsive worker is valued until his production ceases, because of the emotional toll the job has exacted.

- Our culture is one where the underclass, mired in poverty looks for a quick fix, and is preyed upon by the gambling encouraged by the lotteries of state after state across the United States.

- Our convenience-oriented culture removes obstacles to satisfaction by promising instant gratification—we can call a plumber at 3:00 AM to fix a leaky faucet, or terminate an "inconvenient" pregnancy on demand.

- Our culture believes that sophisticated technology can resolve all our problems, thereby absolving ourselves of personal responsibility for our actions—the most flagrant example being the AIDS epidemic.

- Our culture seeks entertainment and escapism rather than searching for meaning—as in the *Rambo* and *Terminator* movies, or perhaps the CNN blockbuster: *Desert Storm*.

- Our culture reels from disrupted family life and, for the first time in history asks just two people (a couple) to raise children, and settles for one working mother and an anonymous day care center.

- Our culture has lost a sense of community due to our constant moving and the isolation which result in the disintegration of community networks and the extended family.

- Our culture is exploitative of others through a capitalism devoid of social conscience, and thereby generates an environment of distrust upon which an addict feeds.

- Our culture essentially denies limitations, including even natural death, by artificially extending life through extraordinary means.

- Our culture is one where the media promotes casual sex; where credit cards are indiscriminately offered to college seniors to encourage a habit of gross debt and living on the edge; and where alcohol is urged upon a population heavily involved in substance abuse.

Whether within a person or a society, *Addiction is a response to pain and will continue unabated until the pain that the addiction generates exceeds the pain that it masks.* At its roots the pain is generated by a spiritual void, and no amount of social engineering will fill it. It takes a change of the heart. This I believe (as do the millions involved in Twelve Step programs and faith communities), and this is the cornerstone of Credo.

Our world is in such a state of flux that the natural convulsions of our personal lives find no solid point of reference. The disorientation we feel within ourselves and the world in which we interact is bound to exacerbate feelings of powerlessness, alienation, and depression. Such an environment provides fertile ground for addiction. We have drifted from familiar social and personal moorings and find ourselves at sea.

In a speech delivered in Seattle in 1992, George Carey, the Archbishop of Canterbury, put it this way:

> One can imagine, perhaps, being on a large luxury liner, crossing the Atlantic. At the outset, when the ship is moored, it and the land are merely an extension one of the other; then slowly, almost indiscernible, as the vessel sets sail, a gap appears, but one that could be bridged without too much difficulty. The passengers soon get absorbed in all the activities of life on board. The ship is a community; it has a life all its own. Meanwhile, the land has disappeared; it has no further relevance and the chasm between it and the floating, self-sufficient land is immeasurable. Suppose that a new generation was born without the ship docking. What would they know of the land they left behind? What relevance would it have to them and the life-style they inherit? The ship of new technology and self-sufficiency is denying not only our generation but the next generation's exposure to a religious heritage and spiritual values. I do not believe this leads to anti-religious feelings, but rather to no religious feelings. That is a truly tragic state of affairs, and one which can unwittingly disable the human spirit.

17

The Breaking Of The Ancient Western Code

There'll be the breaking of the ancient western code,
Your private life will suddenly explode ...

—*Democracy Is Coming to the USA*, Leonard Cohen

Our fear about being assaulted by those around us, and our anxiety about the food which nourishes us, is a symptom of an even more deep-seated fear: that of survival. How did we get where we are today, with mace in our Christmas stockings and food made fearsome? What is at the root of this spiritual malaise, this isolation and fear? Above all, I see three aspects of our culture which may contribute to our current situation: *our view of nature; our response to technology;* and *our source of hope*.

Our View Of Nature

Our relationship to nature is changing rapidly. For us Nature is not a shelter for the spirit, as it was once viewed.

In our culture Nature is a cold body of facts which we manipulate to our own ends: genetic engineering for higher milk production, organ transplants for an extended life, abortion as a means to make our lives more convenient, air conditioning so that we can build cities where they never could have been before. When we feel powerless over some natural event such as a California earthquake or a Georgia flood, our insurance companies call it "an act of God." We view nature (and perhaps God) as the enemy.

It was not always that way. Nine hundred years ago European Christians viewed life in quite a different way, one in which the supernatural had a *greater* reality than the physical. It is hard for any of us to appreciate their view because we are prejudiced by history and science books written by those who are not concerned with the transcendent.

These authors, people of good will who are heirs of the Enlightenment, refer to this earlier time as the Dark Ages. I would transpose those two titles: my understanding of the "Enlightenment" (18-20C) is that it has been a gradual progression toward a dimming of the spirit and the depersonalizing of human beings; whereas the "Dark Ages" had at their base the light of a faith which brought meaning to all people's lives.

Those in the Age of Faith of eleventh century Europe, believed the cosmos to be in Divine Harmony, (a world view which some, in their lack of knowledge, attribute exclusively to the Native Americans). In the medieval mind, God extended beyond the world, and yet God also dwelled at its center: in our hearts and souls. Every aspect of life was ordered by the Creator, and infused with His Spirit. Following the teachings of Jesus, the rank and value of all things was determined by the degree to which they bore the stamp of God.

> *Are not five sparrows sold for two farthings?*
> *And not one of them is forgotten before God.*
> *Why even the very hairs of your head are numbered.,*
> *Therefore, fear not, you are of more value than many sparrows.*
> —Luke 12:6,7

There was an overarching biblical understanding of balance: a hierarchy intended by God where every human being was equal in God's sight, from monarch to villager, and they all had a sacred responsibility. Francis of Assisi affirmed,

> Our Dominion, created by the Lord our God over the beasts of the earth, the birds that fly, the flowers that grow in the meadow, and the very trees of the forest is not tyranny, but a sacred trust.

Everything was sacred: nature, humanity, society. Within the Christian liturgy, the symbolic language shared at that time by all civilized Europeans, even the rotation of the earth was linked to a sacred rhythm. Christmas coincided with the winter solstice: as they marked the daylight becoming longer, so also they celebrated the coming of the light of the Son into the world. Easter was celebrated at the vernal equinox: Springtime was equated with the emerging new life of the Resurrected Lord.

In our current materialistic society, Nature is not viewed as given by God for us to rule and serve. As my children watched televised nature shows, they were being taught that "natural" consists of all which exists before humanity does anything to it: a Garden of Eden devoid of a partnership with the Creator. Humanity is the corrupter; and the European man is singled out as the most corrupt of all, pitted against Nature. Humans are not portrayed as a vital part of one sacred ecology.

Today, except in church, it is rare that I hear myself described as being sacred, called to serve God's creation. It is more likely that I will be told that I am the spoiler, the head of the food chain, unique for my capacity to be wanton and destructive. Nightly I witness narrators of news programs and "nature" specials rail against our ravaging of the environment. Rain forests disappear, nuclear reactors crack, and we feel out of control as a society.

In 1992, I had a balanced understanding of the voyage of Columbus to America. As I honored the individual faith and bravery of Columbus and his crew acting within their world view, I also regretted that the limited understanding of both the Spaniards and the Native Americans caused such mutual destruction.

But in school my children were presented with a more jaded view which tipped the balance toward anger and fear. They were taught that the event was an invasion by European man, driven by economic gain, the spoiler of Native American innocence. A *Nature* special on PBS went so far as to say that the gift of plows and cattle by the Spanish Jesuits to the Indians of the American Southwest was essentially wrong because it disturbed the growing pattern of the field grasses. The narrator did not acknowledge that these gifts from European men averted hunger by bringing a steady food supply to the Indians.

No wonder it is hard for any of us to place trust in the work of humanity. I am indoctrinated with examples where the capacity within the human spirit is used for deliberate destructiveness:

One million Iranian and Iraqi sons, husbands, and fathers died for nothing in the Iraq/Iran War. Millions of Kurds, Iraqis, Eritreans, Somalians are starved because of political convenience. Roman Catholic Croatians, Serbian Orthodox, and Bosnian Muslims are busy "ethnically cleansing" each other, as Rwandan Hutus and Tutsis litter their roads and rivers with bloody corpses.

If it is only a pious fiction that I am made in the image of God, and therefore sacred, then the harrowing record of the behavior of humans around me can only breed mistrust, even of myself in my capacity as a man.

Our Use Of Technology

Because we live in the late twentieth century, you and I have no choice but to be children of technology. If we uncritically embrace the faith system of technologists (and it most certainly is a faith system), then we become convinced of our power to eliminate the unacceptable. But experience tells us that without love power is dangerous.

Technology has no room for the element of love. If, as a true believer in this technological idol, we overlook this crucial omission of love, we will become desperate as we hunt for a way out of the social breakdown. We are in a bind: we cannot accept disintegration as a state of affairs and want to find a way out, but we sense that technology has no final answers, and can only render a false sense of hope.

In the winter of 1991 I watched a remarkable PBS series on the Soviet Union built around an interview with Nicholas Ryzkov, a Soviet composer of deep faith and no religion. The concepts and images of the Christian world have lost their power to bring insight to him, yet he has found nothing else. Ryzkov is very much a contemporary man as he composes at an electronic console. He finds no meaning in the thousand year old symbols of religion which formerly were the fiber of Russia. Nevertheless, the title of his masterwork was, *Holy Eucharist for Unbelievers*. What a fascinating juxtaposition of belief and unbelief: the body and blood of Christ for those who do not acknowledge his existence.

In an animated exchange with Howard K. Smith, Ryzkov recounted how the Chernobyl devastation was wrought by technology, how the reactor still spreads death throughout the very countryside that depends on it for power. He recalled the recent Armenian earthquake in which 80,000 were buried alive and 200,000 more are still living hand to mouth in tents.

With anguish, he reflected upon the death of thousands of young soldiers in the futile war in Afghanistan. Paradoxically, this man of no religion speculated that there might be some truth to the prophecies of scripture that the end times were upon us. At the brink of a collapsing Soviet Union, he cried out:

> I cannot accept this as a state of affairs. I look to the fundamentals of our society, the root causes of its malaise and I want to find a way out. We have to create, to sow eyes which will enable us to see. Yet today there are less and less of these unclouded eyes. They have been clouded by indifference. People simply do not want to see anymore. Do they fear doomsday? Or are they simply tired of their souls being mangled with hopes and failures; with hopes followed by more failures. Hopes and failures over and over again, it is becoming too much for us.

Many people in our culture view humanity in terms of a trinity of science, materialism, and economics. Solutions are proposed with no thought given to the human spirit. Operating from a faithless faith system, technocrats squeeze men and women into mechanical, biological, psychological, sociological categories where they can never fit.

The War on Poverty was to be won by cash. The War on Drugs is to be won by force. Homelessness will be banished by building houses. Addiction will be conquered through an increase in criminal prosecutions. Medical care will be available to all, with a cap put on expenditures for psychotherapy, as if our health is solely a physical matter, and spiritual wholeness a luxury.

The reality is that the foundation of poverty, homelessness, and addiction is a spiritual lack instead of a material one. A house is not a home. The failure of our response as a nation to our social ills is that we impose categories without any consideration of the human spirit. We are submitted to form without content.

The answer is not visible to the technical mind because spiritual disintegration cannot be measured in the concrete. The answer is not obvious because it is complex—drawn from that intangible, elusive and tender relationship of love, which is life itself. The solution is not material.

Twenty-seven years ago Senator Daniel Patrick Moynahan framed the decline of the inner city not in terms of economic decline, but rather in terms of missing relationships, of an absence of love:

> A community that allows large numbers of young men to grow up in broken families, dominated by women, never acquiring any stable relationship to male authority, never acquiring any set of rational expecta-

tions about the future; that community asks for and gets chaos.

People of an earlier age (who had no concept of technology), viewed the word "chaos" as a synonym for Hell. They believed they were the image of God in an ordered world. In their understanding chaos was opposition to God, whose essence was order.

Our Source of Hope

The people who embraced the faith system of the Christian Middle Ages would not comprehend our lack of a view of the sacredness of an individual. They also would not understand the way we use technology to establish fundamental truths. If they were alive today they would ask why anyone would seek the truth through gathering samples of materials and examining them. They would not understand why we arrive at the truth by taking surveys and imposing human reason.

The fundamental question they would ask is why we limit ourselves to material things, since reality is not confined to the material. To seek reality and truth, they would insist, one must meditate and reflect, since hope is based on belief, and every aspect of life is governed by God in a divine ecology.

What could be more foreign to today's way of thinking? When the Bible narratives are read through the eyes of a technologist, they seem to be a primitive, even childish, description of life. References to a God actively involved in the lives of his people seem to the materialist to be naive anthropomorphisms. But is it not a paradox that those who view everything as material, reject concrete figures of speech that make God appear tangible?

Our Convulsive Society

At the end of every era, whether it be classical, medieval, or modern, there is a time of convulsion which creates general anxiety. For some it *is* a private hell as they purchase mace for Christmas stockings. As we discard old answers, new ones are not apparent. We are spiritually homeless, neither belonging to the new nor the old. We sense the confusion in our own lives: What is it to be a man or a woman? What are families all about? What are appropriate ways to express our love sexually? What is the role of pleasure in life?

Because the voyage of Columbus was celebrated a year or so ago, the late fifteenth and early sixteenth centuries in Europe have been very much on my mind. It was a time like ours: witnessing the end of the old order and looking to an uncertain future. The holy Christian city of Constantinople was desecrated by the Muslims at the same time as Christian Spain expelled the Moors and Jews.

The discoveries of Columbus and Galileo shattered the medieval view of a cosmos centered around European Christians. Galileo overturned the limited understanding of the cosmos. Columbus's voyages challenged Europe's political mind-set. Luther raised questions which destroyed the centuries old equilibrium achieved by the Church in Western Europe. Mystics, inquisitors, and revolutionary reformers such as Luther and Calvin were remolding the Christian Church which would never be the same.

These three men, Galileo, Columbus, and Luther undermined the medieval vision of unity. They left the European world reeling for centuries. The venerable concept of the unity of creation, religion, and geography was dismembered, never to be put together again.

Out of this cataclysm, modern man emerged. The intervening years yielded constructive results in the understanding of personal freedom and dignity, but also tragic ones such as The Hundred Years War. Then, as now, there was a struggle for balance.

Many events and people in the twentieth century have brought forth a convulsiveness in our lives similar to that of the sixteenth century. I wistfully look at the remnants of the church, the close extended family, the small town society and realize that what was will never be again. Since I am in the midst of the fallout it is hard for me to have a clear perspective. I am sure people such as Darwin, Freud, Marx, Einstein, and even Hitler will figure prominently. But now, as we approach the twenty-first century, we are grappling with the concept of our status as mass man, manipulated in our anonymity by computers, and it shakes my spirit.

As I look around the political landscape I see how ill-prepared we are to take charge of our awesome inheritance of power. We are haunted by the fear that in the end only violence will be used to solve the flood of problems that threaten to engulf us. Prophetic voices remind us that human freedom cannot save us from human folly. They warn that we are engulfed by fear caused by our confusion.

A Machine Running Without Oil

We are afraid of being at the edge of chaos because the world in which we live lacks harmony. We see that we have power over things, but we fear that we do not have power over our own power. Each social "advance" ushers in further social ills. As the position of women is advanced, we apparently unleash the dark side of men. No wonder we are fearful. Far from being sacred, we view ourselves as demonic. As the contemporary Russian composer

The Breaking Of The Ancient Western Code ♦ 319

Nickolas Ryzkov remarked, "Our hearts are mangled by hope and then failure. It is becoming too much for us." Along with much of contemporary humanity, Ryzkov yearns for a vision larger than his own ever-changing material perspectives.

The contemporary Dutch theologian, Henri Nouwen, suggests in an article in *Weavings*, that there is a single simple biblical phrase, *You are my beloved, with you I am well pleased* (Luke 7:22) that might address the deep yearning of all the people for whom the concepts and images of Christian tradition have lost their power to offer them any insight. Nouwen believes that this yearning could be stilled if people genuinely felt beloved—and that this could be accomplished even within the increasingly complex world of single parenthood, "blended" families, corporate takeovers, economic uncertainty and political unrest.

At the core of my hope is a yearning to feel beloved, to experience harmony, the peace which passes all understanding. I experience a glimpse of this on each Credo Weekend. For that brief window in time I understand the unity of nature, the irrelevance of technology, and the hope wrought through my intimate connection with my brothers and sisters, one by one. Once more I am able to affirm that closeness and intimacy, when experienced in harmony, are the bedrock of my spiritual life. They are the source of grace.

Once again I would like to turn to the book, *The Art of Intimacy*, and draw on the reflection of Dr. Thomas Patrick Malone, and his son Pat who was my colleague and friend in the psychiatric wards of the Naval Hospital:

> We are convinced that crucial problems like the threat of nuclear destruction, world hunger, terrorism, and nationalistic megalomania will not be dealt with simply politically. They must be dealt with personally.

> They will be dealt with when we are neither willing to destroy our selves nor need to destroy the other... We have to begin in the simple, one-to-one, human relationship. You and me. We are far more alike than we are different. Can we reclaim some natural balance?

This is what we are dealing with both in the world within which we live, and the world within ourselves. As we begin to comprehend the tragic elements of our human attempts to live without nurturing the spirit, we will understand the depth of our calling to bring to others the intimacy and friendship which is the medicine of life.

In spite of the many traits we share with animals, we are distinguished from them all. We are stamped with that which is our own: our spirit which Jews, Muslims, Christians, Buddhists, or Hindus would define in their own way as the image of God. The answer to what makes a human a human cannot come from any material source. It is our loving relationships which make us unique. Without relationships of love and mutual responsibility, life becomes a machine without oil. Even if it functions, some part is always burning out.

Love in all its interpersonal manifestations is the basis of our life. The bonds of love are understood by religious people as being inspired by a loving God. My humanist friends would see love's inspiration coming from what used to be called the Brotherhood of Man. The scripture held in common by Christian and Jew views love as an imperative: "You should love the Lord your God with all your heart, mind, and spirit. and you should love your neighbor as yourself."

Our human spirit is unique and cannot be categorized, for it is something we all posses. We are a microcosm of the world. As members of that society, we are inextricably bound within that alienation. I was interested in seeing the comments of Lee Atwater, a master in generating fear in political campaigns, when he observed on his death bed that:

> I used to say that the President might be kinder and gentler, but I wasn't going to be. How wrong I was. There is nothing more important in life than human beings, nothing sweeter than the human touch.

I hope that in an atmosphere of safety experienced by life within communities such as Credo, *Cursillo*, AA, or the local parish, we can face squarely the tragic elements of our life together. Once acknowledging these realities, we can learn to be accepting and compassionate: kinder, gentler, as Mr. Atwater would say, nurturing hope among each other.

Yet, for us to discover that common ground of hope is not easy in a society with so few boundaries. Credo hopes to cut through to the core to help clarify the changing systems of thought that confuse us as individuals and members of society. Credo gets to the basic mooring which is unchangeable: the human spirit nourished by the grace of love and friendship.

The Fearful Fall

I opened this book explaining my understanding of a central parable in Western culture which is the conflict between love and fear and how it plays out in the life of Jesus. I close with my understanding of the conflict between love and fear as it plays out in the story of the Temptation of Adam and Eve, a story basic to the three great monotheistic religions of the world.

The Temptation is an archetypal story. It is the story of how our sin originated—our original sin. God gave us everything we needed: the Garden of Eden. He asked but one thing: that we trust him in his Providence. But we wondered what we were missing. We became obsessed with what we could not have, and did not trust God's care and judgment. So we went beyond our boundaries and wanted to be like God.

Like Him, we wanted to know good and evil. God permitted that too; He gave us the choice to trust Him, or to want more—even though he knew the sorrow which would come from our knowledge of evil. When our eyes were opened, when we saw good and evil, we were *afraid*.

Fear is the antithesis of love. Just as perfect love banishes fear, so fear banishes the bliss of love. Our fallen state as humans, then, is fear. And we pass this on from generation to generation. Our original sin is fear. It is not that babies are born evil, or that by sexual intercourse sin is transmitted, it is because from our very beginning we do not want to accept our God-given boundaries, our limits. We do not trust, we are not satisfied. We become acquainted with the reality of evil and we live our lives in fear of it, rather than in trust of God's love. This is what we pass on to each subsequent generation.

We need a radical emphasis on individual responsibility as a companion piece to our exaggerated emphasis on individual freedom. We constantly make excuses—the symptom of our fallen nature. After disobeying God, Adam and Eve first hid themselves. Then, when confronted with their sin they immediately excused themselves by blaming others. Adam blamed Eve. Eve blamed the serpent. Later, as the story unfolds Adam tried to blame God, "The woman you gave me for a companion, she gave me fruit from the tree, and I ate it."

God asks us to take responsibility for our actions and not make excuses that we are victims. We want to be as gods; we want to defy natural boundaries and we don't want to take responsibility for our choices. We talk of the fight against cancer and heart disease, and act as gods transplanting organs to minimize the fallout of our actions. But we take no responsibility for the lives of stress which we impose upon ourselves and which contribute to our conditions of cancer and heart attacks.

In substance abuse we talk about the war against drugs, yet in the first correspondence with incoming freshmen one college asks the new student about room placement. "Do you mind a roommate who drinks?" (all are under age) "What about drugs?" (illegal for all). "What about staying up into the night?" (abusing the body)?

Probably the justification given for asking these questions is that it is unrealistic to expect the students to assume responsibility—they will do it anyhow. Then the school launches substance abuse education programs so as to control the academic, emotional, and sexual fallout of irresponsible decisions. The administration wonders how to impose the boundaries the students violate. It does not seems to occur to them that by accepting this behavior in their first correspondence to incoming students, they are condoning irresponsibility.

We want to be as gods and eliminate AIDS in the United States through some wonder vaccine. We know that if blood supplies were properly screened there would be few innocent victims. If people lived responsible lives within natural boundaries there would be no epidemic. People need to be shown that their sexual behavior may be as much an addiction as their substance abuse, and we need to provide help to them by responding to their spiritual void. Put another way, if we were to offer help rather than tolerance and if a person's spiritual pain was acknowledged, there would be less need to worry about dirty needles and rampant venereal diseases.

If we as a society chose to live within boundaries, rather than being over-committed and over-stressed, there would be far less disease and pain to mask. Transplanted hearts, clean needles, free condoms, abortion on demand, relaxation exercises—all of these address the *symptoms*, and therefore are effective only in a limited way. But if we chose to take responsibility, as Adam and Eve did not, we would address the cause. Original sin is living in fear. It is exceeding boundaries and distrusting God's care. It is avoiding responsibility for our own choices. This is our plight.

But even in this archetypal story of the Fall, even in this account of the sad result of our actions, God is shown as caring. He sees Adam and Eve's shame. He knows its genesis. He understands our nakedness, our shame, and even though we are fully responsible, he clothes us, and cares for us.

The Lord God made tunics of skin for Adam and his wife and clothed them.
—Genesis

That is what God is doing for us today. When we acknowledge our sins, and when we acknowledge that we are powerless over our actions, God clothes us. He protects us from ourselves and nourishes us with his Spirit. Original sin is not some ugly early church concept, it is a metaphor acknowledging that from the beginning we are in need of help, because of the fear we generate within ourselves. And God's reply is: "I will cover your shame. I will nourish and protect you, you have nothing to fear. I will be with you always, even unto the end of time.

There's A Crack In Everything

Every heart to love will come
But like a refugee

So I come full circle. Mine has been a long and tortuous pilgrimage, but it has also been one bathed in grace. I have participated in the tears of many of my brothers and sisters, hoping that by caring for them, I would receive the comfort I missed as a child. I have now learned, after following fifty years of this path, that I first need to accept my self, to honor my self, so that as friendship, the medicine of life, is offered to me, I can accept it and participate in its healing grace.

Forget your perfect offering.
There is a crack in everything.
That's how the light get in.

Works Cited

Publications

Aelred of Rievaulx. *Spiritual Friendship.* Translated by Mary Eugeneia Laker SSND. Kalamazoo: Cistercian Press, 1977

Anker, Charles C. *The Waysign,* Vol. XLIII, No. 19. 8 May 1994.

Atwater, Lee. "Atwater's Last Campaign.' *Life.* Vol. 14, Issue 2, February 1991.

Barr, Martha. "Sharing Bread, Sharing Tears." *The Other Side,* March-April 1993.

Buechner, Frederick. *Telling Secrets.* San Francisco: HarperCollins, 1991

Carnes, Patrick J. *Don't Call It Love.* New York: Bantam Books, 1991.

Chaplain Resource Board, *Currents,* "Waysigns" Vol.3, No.7.

Daniel, Walter. *The Life of Ailred, Abbot of Rievaulx.* ed. F. M. Powicki. London: Nelson, 1950.

Forbes, James A. *Release Your Song* New York 1988 unpublished, used with permission of the author.

Girzone, Joseph. *Joshua.* New York: Macmillan, 1983.

Gould, William Blair. *Frankl: Life With Meaning.* Florence KY: Wadsworth Press, 1993.

John of the Cross. *Collected Works.* Translated by Kieren Kavenaugh O.C.D. and Otilio Rodriguez O.C.D. Washington: Institute of Carmelite Studies, 1979.

Malone, Thomas Patrick and Patrick Thomas. *The Art of Intimacy.* New York: Prentis Hall, 1987.

Gonzalez, Don Juan Cardinal Marcelo, Archbishop of Toledo, as quoted in *ABC* June 11, 1988. Translation by author.

McPhatter, Thomas H. *Caught in the Middle, A Dichotemy of an African American Man (They Called Him Troublemaker).* San Diego: Audacity Books, 1993.

Merton, Thomas. *Seeds of Contemplation.* New York: New Directions Books, 1949.

Milton, John. "Lycidas" *The Poems of John Milton.* Edited by James H. Hanford. New York: The Ronald Press Company, 1953.

Nouwen, Henri J. M. *Reaching Out.* New York: Doubleday & Company, 1975.

———. *Out of Solitude.*, Notre Dame IN: Ave Maria Press, 1974.

Ryzkov, Nikolas, *The Soviets.* Interview by Howard K. Smith. PBS March 1991.

Santana, Carlos. "Heart" *The Other Side.* Vol 30, No.#3, May-June 1994.

Squire, Aelred. *Aelred of Rievaulx: A Study.* Kalamazoo: Cistercian Press. 1981.

Willemon, William. "Reaching and Teaching the Abandoned Generation." *Christian Century,* 20 October 1993.

Songs

"All You Need Is Love"
    The Beatles: *Yellow Submarine*
    © John Lennon

"Amazing Grace"
    Judy Collins: *Colors of the Day*   Elektra 75030-2
    © arr. adapted Judy Collins Rocky Mountain National Park Music (ASCAP)

"Anthem"
    Leonard Cohen: *The Future*   Columbia CK53226
    © 1992 Leonard Cohen, Stranger Music (BMI)

"Attics of My Life"
    Grateful Dead: *American Beauty*   Warner Bros 1893-2
    © 1970 Robert Hunter and Jerry Garcia. Ice Nine Publishing Company (ASCAP)

"Ball and Chain"
    Janis Joplin: *Greatest Hits*   Columbia CK 32168
    (monologue from)
    © 1973 Willie Mae Thornton, (BMI)

"Ballad of the Sad Young Men"
    Roberta Flack: *First Take*   Atlantic 8 230-2
    © Francis Landesman and Thomas J Wolfe Jr. Empress (ASCAP)

"The Beast In Me"
    Johnny Cash: *American Recordings*   American 9-45520-2
    @ Nick Lowe, Plangent Visions Music Inc. (ASCAP)

"Behind the Wall"
    Tracey Chapman: *Tracey Chapman*   Elektra 9 6077-2
    © 1983 Tracey Chapman, SBK April Music Inc Purple Rabbit Music (ASCAP)

"Bird On A Wire"
    Johnny Cash: *American Recordings*   American 9 45520-2
    © 1968 Leonard Cohen, Stranger Music (BMI)

"Bird On The Wire"
   Leonard Cohen: *Songs From The Room*   Columbia CK 9767
   © 1968 Leonard Cohen, Stranger Music (BMI)

"Cats In the Cradle"
   Harry Chapin: *Greatest Stories Live*   Electra 6003-2
   © 1976 Sandy and Harry Chapin, Story Songs Ltd (ASCAP)

"Cheap Is How I Feel"
   Cowboy Junkies: *The Caution Horses*   BMG 2058-1-R
   © Cowboy Junkies, Paz Junk Music/ BMG Songs Inc.(ASCAP)

"Democracy Is Coming"
   Leonard Cohen: *The Future*   Columbia CK53266
   © 1992 Leonard Cohen, Stranger Music (BMI)

"For A Dancer"
   Jackson Browne: *Late for the Sky*   Asylum 7E 1017-2
   © 1974 Jackson Browne (BMI)

"Get Together"
   The Youngbloods: *The Best of*   BMG 3280-2-R
   © 1975 Chet Powers. Irving Music (BMI)

"Good Shepherd"
   Jefferson Airplane: *Volunteers of America*   RCA 4238-2R
   © 1969 Jorma Kaukorian

"Here Comes the Sun"
   The Beatles: *Abbey Road*   Capitol C21Z46446
   © 1971 George Harrison

"How?"
   John Lennon: *Imagine*   Capitol CDP 7 46641-2
   © 1971 John Lennon

"I'm Scared"
   John Lennon: *Menlove Avenue*   Capitol CDP7 46576-2
   © 1971 John Lennon

"Isn't it A Pity?"
   George Harrison: *All Things Must Pass*   Capitol CDP 7 46689-2
   © 1970 Harrison, George. Harrisongs Ltd (EMI)

"Like A Soldier"
    Johnny Cash: *American Recordings*   American 9-45520-2
    © Johnny Cash (ASCAP) Jalma Mucis (ASCAP)

"Men"
    Louden Wainwright III: *History*   Charisma V2 86416
    © Louden Wainwright III. Snowden Music Inc (ASCAP)

"Only Love"
    John Prine: *German Afternoons*   Oh Boy Records OBR 003CD
    © John Prine

"The Only Child"
    Jackson Browne: *The Pretender*   Asylum 6E 107-2
    © 1976 Jackson Browne

"Please Don't Pass Me By"
    Leonard Cohen: *New Skin*   Columbia C33167
    © 1971 Leonard Cohen, Stranger Music (BMI)

"Pretty As You Feel."
    Jefferson Airplane: *Surrealistic Pillow*   RCA PCD 1-3766
    © 1971 Jack Casady, Joey Covington, Jorma Kaukorian

"Reach Out and Touch"
    Aretha Franklin: *Live at the Fillmore*   Atlantic SD 7205
    © 1970 Nickolas Ashford and Valarie Simpson (BMI)

"Somebody to Love"
    Jefferson Airplane: *Surrealistic Pillow*   RCA PCD 1-3766
    © 1971 Grace Slick

"Sunday Morning Coming Down"
    Kris Kristofferson: *Kris Kristofferson*   Monument Z 30817
    © Kris Kristofferson

"Suzanne"
    Leonard Cohen: *Songs From The Room*   Columbia CK 9767
    © 1967 Leonard Cohen, Project Seven Music (BMI)

"Tainted Love"
    Coil: *Coil*   Wax Trax Records, Wax 013
    © 1982 Ed Cobb

"Tower Of Song"
    Leonard Cohen: *I'm Your Man*   Columbia CK 44191
    © 1989 Leonard Cohen, Stranger Music (BMI)

"Vienna"
    Billy Joel: *The Stranger*   CBS CK 34987
    © 1970 Billy Joel. Joelsongs (BMI)

"Voices of Old People"
    Simon & Garfunkle: *Bookends*   Columbia CK 9529